The
Fast Forward MBA
in Negotiating
and Deal Making

THE FAST FORWARD MBA SERIES

The Fast Forward MBA Series provides time-pressed business professionals and students with concise, one-stop information to help them solve business problems and make smart, informed business decisions. All of the volumes, written by industry leaders, contain "tough ideas made easy." The published books in this series are:

The Fast Forward MBA in Business
(0-471-14660-9)
by Virginia O'Brien

The Fast Forward MBA in Finance
(0-471-10930-4)
by John Tracy

The Fast Forward MBA Pocket Reference
(0-471-14595-5)
by Paul A. Argenti

The Fast Forward MBA in Marketing
(0-471-16616-2)
by Dallas Murphy

The Fast Forward MBA in Hiring
(0-471-24212-8)
by Max Messmer

The Fast Forward MBA in Technology Management
(0-471-23980-1)
by Daniel P. Petrozzo

The
Fast Forward MBA
in Negotiating
and Deal Making

Roy J. Lewicki
Alexander Hiam

John Wiley & Sons, Inc.

New York • Chichester • Weinheim • Brisbane • Singapore • Toronto

All materials taken from *Flex Style Negotiating* by Alexander
Hiam, copyright © 1997, are reprinted by permission of the
publisher, HRD Press, Amherst, Massachusetts.

This book is based on *Think Before You Speak: A Complete Guide
to Strategic Negotiation* by Roy J. Lewicki, Alexander Hiam, and
Karen Wise Olander (New York: Wiley, 1996).

This book is printed on acid-free paper.∞

Published by John Wiley & Sons, Inc.
Published simultaneously in Canada.

This publication is designed to provide accurate and authoritative
information in regard to the subject matter covered. It is sold
with the understanding that the publisher is not engaged in
rendering professional services. If professional advice or other
expert assistance is required, the services of a competent
professional person should be sought.

Library of Congress Cataloging-in-Publication Data:
Lewicki, Roy J.
    The fast forward MBA in negotiating and deal making / Roy
Lewicki, Alexander Hiam.
        p.   cm. — (The fast forward MBA series)
    Includes bibliographical references and index.
    ISBN 0-471-25698-6 (pbk. : alk. paper)
    1. Negotiation in business.   I. Hiam, Alexander.   II. Title.
III. Series.
    HD58.6.L488   1998
    658.4'052—dc21   98-24242
                                                              CIP

Printed in the United States of America.

10 9 8 7 6 5 4 3 2

ABOUT THE AUTHORS

Roy J. Lewicki is the Dean's Distinguished Teaching
Professor and Professor of Management and Human
Resources at the Max M. Fisher College of Business,
The Ohio State University. He teaches and writes in the
fields of negotiation, conflict management, trust, leadership, and ethics. He is the author or editor of 19
books, including *Think Before You Speak: A Complete
Guide to Strategic Negotiation* (with Alexander Hiam
and Karen Wise Olander) and *Negotiation* (with David
Saunders and John Minton). In addition to his university responsibilities, Professor Lewicki provides a range
of education and consulting services to Fortune 500
companies and university-based executive programs.
Roy Lewicki can be contacted at: Fisher College of Business, The Ohio State University, Columbus, OH 43210,
(614) 292-0258; e-mail: Lewicki.1@osu.edu.

Alexander Hiam is the author of the *Flex Style Negotiating* line of training and assessment products and the
coauthor of *Think Before You Speak*. He has written numerous other business titles including *Marketing for
Dummies, The Portable MBA in Marketing, Second Edi-
tion, The Vest-Pocket CEO, The Vest-Pocket Marketer,
Closing the Quality Gap, The Entrepreneur's Complete
Source Book,* and *The Manager's Pocket Guide to Creativity.* He is a frequent speaker and trainer on negotiation, leadership, and creativity. Currently, Mr. Hiam
runs a consulting firm based in Amherst, Massachu-
setts, and his clients include GM, Coca-Cola, Kellogg's,
The Conference Board, and Mass Mutual. He has an
MBA from U.C. Berkeley's Haas School of Business.
Alex Hiam can be contacted at: 69 S. Pleasant Street,
Amherst, MA 01002, (413) 253-3658; e-mail:
Hiam@javanet.com.

We would like to thank:

- Karen Wise Olander for her extensive contribution to *Think Before You Speak: A Complete Guide to Strategic Negotiation,* the predecessor to this volume.

- Robert Carkhuff of HRD Press for his support and cooperation.

- The students in Roy Lewicki's Managerial Negotiation classes at the Fisher College of Business, The Ohio State University, during the Winter Quarter, 1998, for their extensive contributions to the checklists in Chapter 12.

- Finally, we wish to thank our editors at Wiley for all their good work and our families for allowing us the time to complete this project.

This is the second time we have been asked to collaborate on a book for John Wiley & Sons. The first, written with Karen Wise Olander, is called *Think Before You Speak: A Complete Guide to Strategic Negotiation,* and it is often used in courses on negotiation and conflict management. We were thrilled to be asked to update and adapt that book for Wiley's *Fast Forward* series, as it gave us a chance to present the theory and practice of negotiation in a more hands-on, succinct format.

Here, after extensive rework, is our latest and (we trust) best effort to help you acquit yourself successfully in conflicts, deals, and negotiations—whether in private or professional life. We've included lots of tips, warnings, examples, tactics, and strategies to help you win (or, better yet, *win–win*) in every negotiating session.

We are also pleased to be able to include activities and self-assessment tools from the *Flex Style Negotiating* training products Alex distributes through HRD Press, as well as lots of tips and insights gleaned from the authors' workshops and training sessions on the subject of negotiation. All in all, you should find this book to be a great source of *real-world* advice and methods, grounded in the careful research that makes up the academic field of negotiation. It has been our pleasure to translate from the world of theory to the world of practice, and we hope you will find as many exciting insights for your own negotiations as we did. There is always more to learn about this fascinating subject, and its importance in all our lives makes the learning especially worthwhile.

ROY J. LEWICKI
ALEXANDER HIAM
September 1998

The Fast Forward MBA in Negotiating and Deal Making

Conflict

Conflict is so much a part of our daily routines that we barely notice it in the majority of cases. We have conflicts of interest with dozens, sometimes hundreds of people in a day. From when to set the alarm and who uses the bathroom first, to who will be responsible for what, when, at the office, each of us navigates through a maze of minor conflict situations every hour. It is part and parcel of living and working with other people—so much a part of our social behavior that we deal with most conflict quite unconsciously.

Except when the stakes seem high or the problem is more puzzling or emotionally arousing than usual. Then we become aware of a conflict of interest and struggle consciously with how to handle it. At such times in your life, you are no doubt open to learning and applying conflict-management techniques from the field of negotiation. However, we want you to think about using improved conflict-resolution methods in *all* the many conflicts of interest you encounter, not just in the few that shout for your attention.

CONFLICTS ARE EVERYWHERE IF YOU KNOW WHERE TO LOOK

Think about the many requests and instructions you receive from those above you in the hierarchy of your workplace. The majority of such instructions are treated as routine. Although you and your employers have a fundamental conflict of interest (they want you to do more for less pay and you would prefer to be paid more for doing less!), you are able to come to easy terms in most cases. But sometimes a situation troubles you, a request or instruction seems unjust or ill informed. Then the conflict of interest surfaces and occupies your conscious mind.

Either way, however—whether it is a routine, trivial conflict of interest or an important one—your handling of it has a big impact on your work and life. If you choose, you can turn each conflict situation into an opportunity to maximize what you get out of it— whether what you seek is a bigger piece of the pie for yourself or a collaboration that grows the pie for all. This book will show you when and how to do both.

THE HIDDEN INFLUENCE OF CONFLICTS AT WORK[1]

If you ask most people whether there is conflict in their workplace, they immediately say "no." Yet if you carefully observe any employee for an hour or two, you will probably unearth a variety of conflicts. Here are some of the ordinary, everyday conflicts in the life of a typical white-collar worker:

- Competition for the use of office equipment, such as copiers and printers
- Disagreements with coworkers about how or when to do a task
- Disputes with someone about who's responsible for problems
- Resentment toward bosses for criticism over problems
- Debates with others in meetings about how to plan projects
- Requests to bosses re working conditions or performance measures
- Requests from customers for more rapid delivery than is feasible
- Price increases by suppliers on materials that already seem overpriced
- Complaints from customers about the quality of customer service

 All of these, and many others, are conflicts because there are *two or more parties with differing goals or needs* involved. Usually the differences in workplace conflicts are swept under the rug because it's inappropriate to engage in heated arguments at work. A superior may pull rank, or an employee may hide dissatisfaction, in order to avoid conflict. And sometimes negotiating techniques are used to resolve conflicts in a *polite* manner. The etiquette of negotiating makes it possible to turn potentially messy or unpleasant conflicts of interest into profitable games. There are a variety of games you can choose to play, each appropriate in specific situations. The key to mastering conflict situations is to learn how to play each of these negotiating games, and when to play which one. This book will teach you both of these skills.

People think, mistakenly, that etiquette means you have to suppress your differences. On the contrary, etiquette is what enables you to deal with them; it gives you a set of rules. On the floor of the Congress, you don't say, "You're a jerk and a crook"; you say, "I'm afraid the distinguished gentleman is mistaken about so and so." Those are the things that enable you to settle your differences, to bring them out in the open. Everything else just starts battles.

—Miss Manners[2]

The reason it pays to reconsider how you handle conflicts in your work is that these conflicts present opportunities to innovate and create *win–win* solutions. By avoiding conflicts, you fail to take advantage of cooperative negotiation to push the limits of your business. *The daily conflicts represent your business's current limits,* and if you can apply genuine creativity and problem solving to these conflicts, you can find ways to boost performance and productivity.

Negotiation training, especially training that focuses on trust building and cooperative conflict resolution, helps people learn to take advantage of conflict. It leads to a more innovative workforce. It turns an overlooked problem into a business opportunity. The following training activities come from the *Flex Style Negotiating* training materials by Alex Hiam, published by HRD Press in Amherst, Massachusetts. Use them on your own to help you think about the types of conflicts you have encountered recently, and to give some thought to how well you resolved these conflicts, from both your own and the other party's perspective.

WHO WON? YOU, THEM—OR BOTH?

Let's say that you and another person both want the same thing. If you get it, they'll be dissatisfied. If they

Activity: Personal Conflict Experiences

Directions: Take a few minutes to think back over the last two weeks. What conflict situations did you encounter? List at least three conflict situations you can recall. Describe each conflict situation using the following table. you may use the other party's name or a generic description, such as *coworker* or *family member.*

Who Was Conflict With?	What Was Conflict About?
a. _____	_____
Ranking _____	_____
b. _____	_____
Ranking _____	_____
c. _____	_____
Ranking _____	_____
d. _____	_____
Ranking _____	_____
e. _____	_____
Ranking _____	_____

Now that you have listed some conflict situations, read back over the list and rank them according to how important they were to you. Give the most important situation a number-1 ranking, and so on. (No ties please!)

Next, reexamine your highest-ranked conflict situation. Decide how satisfied you were with the outcome, using the following rating scale:

1 = very unhappy

2 = moderately unhappy

3 = indifferent

4 = moderately happy

5 = very happy with the outcome

Enter your satisfaction rating here _____.

Finally, consider the outcome from the other side's point of view. How satisfied do you think the other party was? If they were to use the same scale, enter the score you think they would give here _____.

Now have a quick look at Figure 1.1, a graph on which you can plot your satisfaction score and the other person's score. All conflict situations, and therefore all negotiations, fall somewhere on this graph. But the question is *where*, because much of the area of this graph is undesirable from your perspective. For instance, any outcome below the middle of your satisfaction range—in other words, to the left of center—will not be a good one for you. In fact, you'd prefer to have all outcomes land on the right-hand side of the graph, and as you gain skill in negotiating, more and more of them will.

SOURCE: *Alex Hiam,* Flex Style Negotiating Participant Workbook *(Amherst, Mass.: HRD Press, 1997).*

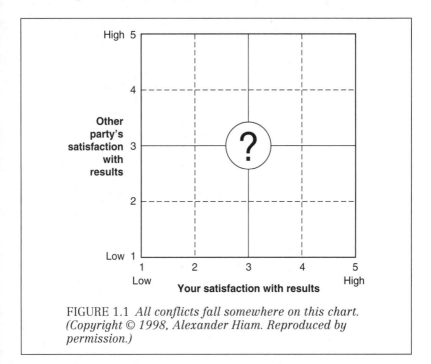

FIGURE 1.1 *All conflicts fall somewhere on this chart. (Copyright © 1998, Alexander Hiam. Reproduced by permission.)*

get it, you'll be unhappy. Even if we divide it in half, and you get half of it, you won't be completely happy. That's because your gain is their loss, and vice versa.

 When your gain is their loss, you are playing a win–lose game. If your satisfaction score is high, it will be at the *expense* of the other party's score. Assuming satisfaction varies directly with outcome, a 5 for you means a 0 for them. If you compromise by giving in partially to them and rate your satisfaction at 4, then theirs can rise to 1. Or it could be 3 and 2. But as long as the outcome is a trade-off, you can't get off the win–lose line in Figure 1.2.

And many conflicts do result in scores that are on or near the win–lose line. That's where competitive or conflict-oriented resolutions always fall. So if you are in one of these types of conflicts of interest, you need to compete hard in order to make sure the trade-offs go in your direction, not the other way!

 Many conflict situations also fall *below* the win–lose line. As Figure 1.2 shows, this is where lose–lose outcomes show up on the graph. When the conflict leaves neither party satisfied, then both lose. Unfortunately, that's the case far too often. By gaining mastery of negotiation methods, you will learn to avoid lose–lose outcomes.

Finally, there are the win–win outcomes in which both parties end up being highly satisfied. These are

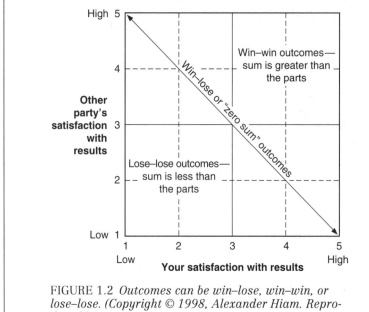

FIGURE 1.2 *Outcomes can be win–lose, win–win, or lose–lose. (Copyright © 1998, Alexander Hiam. Reproduced by permission.)*

above-the-line solutions to a conflict of interest, as shown in Figure 1.2. They require trusting collaboration and creative problem solving. You need to work with the other party, instead of against them, in order to find a way out of the trade-off that reframes the problem and allows you both to win.

 And when you both win, your negotiation game is beneficial to your employer or business, or to your personal relationship. You are turning conflict problems into opportunities for innovation and change. Instead of dividing the pie you are growing it, and growth is a very healthy thing.

 But—and this is a very important but—you cannot hope to achieve the benefits of win–win negotiations if you take a competitive approach. As Figure 1.3 illustrates, competition keeps you on or near that trade-off line and puts the entire win–win region of the outcome graph *out of bounds.*

CLASSIC NEGOTIATING GAMES MAY BE UNHEALTHY

Because competitive approaches put the best half of the outcome chart out of bounds, you need to be suspicious of traditional approaches to negotiation. They are generally highly competitive. Tough, poker-faced tactics lead only to trade-offs, never to win–wins.

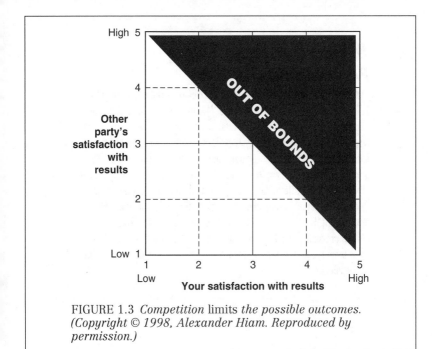

FIGURE 1.3 *Competition* limits *the possible outcomes.*
(Copyright © 1998, Alexander Hiam. Reproduced by
permission.)

Sometimes a competitive approach is appropriate.
Sometimes it's not. In this book we will help you master
five different negotiating games, including competition
and collaboration. And we will show you when to use
each so that you do not limit the possible outcomes
needlessly by competing when it is inappropriate. That
is probably the most common and most costly
negotiating error, and so we want to alert you early on
to the importance of selecting the right game before
you start to play. *Don't* let others who think they are
hotshot negotiators pull you into competitive games
when the situation does not call for them.

 TAMING YOUR EMOTIONS

One common way to find yourself pursuing
win–lose or lose–lose outcomes by accident is to lose
your temper. Conflict situations generally stimulate
emotional as well as rational reactions (we'll show you
more about how to handle them in the next chapter). It
is important to keep some perspective—and, if necessary, to create processes and rules that prevent anger
from taking control.

Negotiation is all about conflict and conflict management. As a result, conflict sometimes gets out of hand,
and the negotiation process breaks down. When perceptions become distorted because of poor communication, frustration and resentment arise. Angry emotions
begin to creep into the conversation. Biases surface and

strengthen, becoming self-fulfilling prophecies. As communication decreases, the sides become entrenched in their positions. Each party blames the other for the difficulty. Negotiation may come to a halt. Why does this happen?

KEY CONCEPT THE IMPORTANCE OF GOOD COMMUNICATION

Conflict arises when information is not flowing freely between the two parties. If the channels of communication are blocked, the parties look for reasons, and it is easy to blame the other party: "You did not tell us that," "that's not what you said before," and so forth. When the focus moves away from the issues and becomes a contest of wills, the original issues may be forgotten or blurred, and new issues may be introduced.

Temper, Temper

But why do I need a gun license? It's only for use around the house.

—Charles Addams

As the sides lose their ability to focus on issues, they may begin to focus on personalities. Negotiation becomes a we-against-them, win–lose contest where differences are emphasized and similarities begin to be overlooked. When this happens, emotional responses dominate rational ones. Plans and strategies are forgotten or never are developed in the first place. Anger often dominates conflict-oriented negotiating situations.

ASSESSING YOUR REACTIONS TO CONFLICT

When we become angry or otherwise emotionally drawn into the conflict, then our natural instincts tend to take control and it is very hard to use our communications and problem-solving skills effectively. Therefore, a better understanding of your emotional reactions to conflict will help you achieve the objectivity to master your reactions. With greater self-awareness, you are more likely to be able to *use* the good advice offered to you in this book.

 Interestingly, different people react *differently* to conflict situations. Some of us step right in and defend ourselves vigorously in a classic *fight* response. Others run away as quickly as possible in a classic *flight* response. Still others *compromise* in a balance between fight and flight. And then there are those who *cave in* quickly to make the other person happy. And finally, there are some whose natural instinct is to seek *creative collaboration,* and so they generally try to turn conflicts into cooperative problem-solving sessions.

 If you know what someone's natural instincts are, you can predict reasonably well how they will negotiate—at least until they become skilled enough to flex their style as the situation demands.

We are curious about *your* instinctive reactions to conflict situations. What is your tendency—which negotiating style do you tend to favor?

This curiosity arises from our experience in training sessions, where we find that it is easiest for people to learn new negotiating styles if they first understand their *current* approach to negotiations. And so we want you to take a few minutes to fill out a personal assessment of the type we use in corporate trainings in order for you to diagnose your style. You will find that this small investment in self-study will help you put the rest of the book into context and will make it far more relevant and useful to you.

Descriptive Style Assessment/ Self Instructions

This assessment tool is designed to help you diagnose the negotiating style you typically use in negotiating situations. (A negotiating situation is any situation in which you have a current or potential conflict of interest with one or more other people or groups.) By completing the following questions, you will describe your current tendencies in such situations, and from this description you can learn which negotiating style you tend to rely upon.

Concentrate on your behavior as best you can recall it *in the various negotiating situations you have experienced* in recent months. Decide how well or poorly each of the statements in Table 1.1 applies to your behavior in those situations. Circle a number between 1 (very poor description of me) to 5 (very good description of me) to indicate how well each statement describes your behavior in negotiating situations.

TABLE 1.1 DESCRIPTIVE STYLE ASSESSMENT/SELF

Meaning of Numbers: 1—No (Very Poor Description of Me) to 5—Yes (Very Good Description of Me).

Description Assessment

1. I fight hard for what I want.	1 2 3 4 5
2. I like to find shared needs and make them the focus of negotiations.	1 2 3 4 5
3. I like to avoid lengthy negotiations by splitting the difference.	1 2 3 4 5
4. I prefer a friendly encounter to an unpleasant conflict.	1 2 3 4 5
5. If I can stay out of a negotiation, I do.	1 2 3 4 5
6. When I have the power, I use it to insure that my needs are met first.	1 2 3 4 5
7. I like to turn a conflict into a cooperative effort at problem-solving.	1 2 3 4 5
8. I often propose a middle ground that is obviously fair to both sides.	1 2 3 4 5
9. My priority is to maintain a good long-term relationship.	1 2 3 4 5
10. I don't like to confront others with my complaints and concerns.	1 2 3 4 5
11. I don't mind a good argument if it may get me what I want.	1 2 3 4 5
12. I prefer to put my cards on the table to encourage the other party to share their information, too.	1 2 3 4 5
13. I'm happy to go half way as long as the other party does too.	1 2 3 4 5

(Continued)

14. I am strongly influenced by what the other party expects of me. 1 2 3 4 5

15. I don't feel confident that I can get what I want by negotiating. 1 2 3 4 5

16. I try not to let the other party know too much about my needs and position. 1 2 3 4 5

17. I try to find new ways to see the problem in order to find better solutions. 1 2 3 4 5

18. I don't like to waste time playing games when a simple compromise is possible. 1 2 3 4 5

19. I may not stick up for myself as much as I should. 1 2 3 4 5

20. When I think someone has an issue with me I try to stay out of their way. 1 2 3 4 5

21. I find a good bluff or threat can work wonders in negotiations. 1 2 3 4 5

22. I expect honesty and trust from others in a negotiation and they find me very trustworthy. 1 2 3 4 5

23. The fairest thing in my view is to split the difference in a reasonable way. 1 2 3 4 5

24. Some people might say I give in easily. 1 2 3 4 5

25. In many cases there is little to be gained by negotiating, so you might as well try to avoid it. 1 2 3 4 5

Scoring

To find out what your most commonly used style is, enter the number you circled for each question in the blanks. (For example, if you circled *3* for question number 1, enter a *3* in the first blank, for question 1.)
After you have entered all your scores, add each column and enter the totals in the following blanks.

1 _____	2 _____	3 _____	4 _____	5 _____
6 _____	7 _____	8 _____	9 _____	10 _____
11 _____	12 _____	13 _____	14 _____	15 _____
16 _____	17 _____	18 _____	19 _____	20 _____
21 _____	22 _____	23 _____	24 _____	25 _____

Column Totals:

T _____   T _____   T _____   T _____   T _____

Preferred Negotiating Style:*

Compete or Defeat	Collaborate or Cooperate	Compromise	Accommodate	Avoid or Withdraw

* The column with the highest total represents your preferred negotiating style. The one with the next highest total is your second-choice style. And the one with the smallest total is your least-preferred style.

WHAT DID YOU LEARN
ABOUT YOURSELF?

The Descriptive Style Assessment/Self gives you a good idea of how you are most likely to react to conflict. Do you Avoid? Concede? Compete? Compromise? Collaborate? You are most likely to take one of these approaches under pressure. And the approach that you tend to take is probably different from the approach favored by others around you—thus creating the possibility of conflicting styles.

In this book you will learn to use each one of these approaches to conflict in order to be able to negotiate in the best style for each possible situation. With training, everyone can learn to use all five styles quite comfortably.

 But that's the rational side of conflict management—learning to master conflict by reasoning out the best style, then implementing a good tactical negotiation game. The question is, can you and the other players keep it rational enough that you are able to use your knowledge of negotiation instead of reacting to the conflict situation entirely on an emotional level?

If you allow yourself or the other players to be swept up by the conflict, then you won't be able to profit from your growing knowledge. Your negotiating skills only work to your benefit if you are able to *use* them. In the remainder of the chapter, you'll learn some conflict management skills to help you overcome the most common roadblocks to effective use of negotiating techniques. You'll learn how to handle the following situations:

- The other party is unwilling to play the negotiation game.
- The other party negotiates, but *only* on price.
- The other party doesn't play fair.
- The other party engages in difficult behaviors.

In any of these situations, it is especially hard to take control of the conflict and turn it into the right sort of negotiating game. Here's how to handle these four difficult situations.

ROADBLOCK #1: THEY REFUSE TO NEGOTIATE

There are three basic options for you to follow if the other party will not negotiate. The first, which you should try before going to the second, is to try to "get behind the lines." The second is to recast the issues. And the third is to take the dispute to a third party.

By *getting behind the lines,* we mean that you need to get underneath what is happening and try to understand the situation from the other party's point of view. Try to identify their interests.

To get behind the lines, you need to ask open-ended questions and also restate what you think you hear them saying. "Why?" "Can you explain this to me?" "Help me understand. . . . ?" That way you get a reality check on your interpretation. If you are still confused by their position, try role reversal—imagine you are in their position and figure out how you'd feel and why. These methods—termed *active listening* and *role reversal*—can help you gain perspective on the other party's strategy and the reasoning behind it.

A second approach, one that often flows naturally from the first, is to try to find ways to *recast the issues:*

- Can you make the issues broader, so that they encompass the other party's concerns and underlying interests?

- Can you create other options?

When you open up the negotiations in this way, you may be able to find commonalties between the parties that will make it easier for everyone to pursue a successful negotiation.

But sometimes your best efforts at listening and redefining the issues don't work. You just can't break through, and your efforts to resolve conflict through negotiation fail. Then you may need to bring in a *third party,* someone who can act as an objective facilitator or peacemaker. In the workplace, a manager with good interpersonal skills and no obvious bias is a good choice. In the "real world," a trained mediator is often the best alternative (the American Arbitration Association certifies people to perform this task and local phone directories list mediators in your area).

ROADBLOCK #2: THEY ONLY CARE ABOUT PRICE

If you are the seller and the other party seems intent on getting the best price to the exclusion of all other considerations, you are most likely dealing with a Competitive negotiator. And their insistence on a single-issue focus throws your negotiation into a classic win–lose situation, one that you may feel it is difficult to resolve to your benefit.

There are a number of things you can do to deflect this lowest-price strategy. While you may not end up with a totally collaborative win–win situation, the outcome has potential for being better than if you let the "price grinder" run the negotiations:[4]

- Ask for something in return—"If I concede on price, what can you do for me?"

- Look for interests other than money, such as esteem, winning, or saving face. You may be able to package these with your product to make it more attractive.

- If they say they can get it elsewhere for less (one type of alternative), point out the value or unique-ness of what you are offering.

- Offer a value-added package. There may be some things that go naturally with the product or service, such as wheel balancing with new tires, or installa-tion with an appliance.

- Emphasize the personal relationship. If you have an ongoing relationship, you may be able to move the focus from prices per se (Competitive) to the idea of a good deal for everyone (Collaborative).

- Compare the situation to the other party's own business. Ask whether they could cut their own prices as they are asking you to do and still stay in business.

- Challenge them to adjust as you adjust (Compro-mise)—"I will if you will."

- Take a reality check. If all they want is a low price, is this really a party you want to be doing business with over the long term? Is bargaining worth it?

- Continue to sell value. If the product is always reli-able, then they will return. If the negotiation is only about price and nothing else, you will likely always have a difficult negotiation with this party.

 ROADBLOCK #3: THEY PLAY DIRTY

 Often our efforts to pursue win–win resolutions are blocked by what we see as unethical and underhanded behavior by the other players. It's hard to negotiate when you feel like they are constantly trying to trick or trap you or lie to you.

To turn the situation around, try to be as pleasant as you can. Put your private feelings about the people on hold while you work to find common ground. One approach is to reinforce the positive and ignore the negative. Acknowledge their good points, support them, compliment their sensitivity to your needs, and applaud their concessions.

However, if you feel that the other side is supplying false information, attempting to deceive or intimidate you, or applying inappropriate pressure, there are also some more proactive tactics you can pursue to try to turn the situation around:

Ignore the tricks. By this, we do not mean you should ignore the other party—just overlook the dirty behavior. This may be easy to say and hard to do, but sometimes if you ignore the behavior, it will subside. On the other hand, the other party may not get your subtle message, and may continue to engage in dirty tricks. In that case, step up your response tactics.

Identify the behavior. The next step is to point out the bothersome behavior. Do not personally attack the people doing it. Simply tell them when you have a problem with their behavior. This lets them know that you are aware of what is going on. Tactfully tell them that you know what they are doing, and be firm in making it clear that their behavior is unacceptable. When you confront inappropriate behavior, try to be as nonthreatening as possible. Define the objectionable behavior in nonevaluative terms. List the tangible effects their actions are having on you and tell them how you feel about it.[5]

Negotiate how to negotiate. A third approach is to take time out to talk about how the negotiation is progressing, and to set ground rules. (Actually, this should be done before the start of negotiations, depending on how familiar you are with the other party.) Even if ground rules were set up at the outset, you may need to review them or augment them at this point.

Issue a warning. If the behavior continues, warn the other party that they are endangering the negotiation with this behavior. They need to understand that you will not put up with their behavior, and that everyone may lose a lot if the behavior continues and the negotiations break off.

 We strongly recommend that you resist the urge to retaliate. Although it may be tempting to give them back some of their own medicine, this is not a good idea. It usually only escalates the tactics, resulting in an increasingly competitive response. You will have lost the opportunity for a collaborative negotiation with positive outcomes and relationships for both sides.

 And also remember that some negotiations are not worth the trouble. You can always walk away if you feel that the costs of negotiating are going to be too high to justify the likely returns.

ROADBLOCK #4: THEY ENGAGE IN DIFFICULT BEHAVIOR

KEY CONCEPT — None of us has any trouble recognizing difficult behavior. We have all seen or experienced it at one time or another. Everyone has a bad day occasionally. But if you have to deal with someone whose behavior is consistently difficult, you need to find ways to cope with that person's behavior. For some, it is largely a matter of ignoring the behavior. For others, it is a bit more work.

There are many books and articles on the topic of dealing with difficult people.[7] The basic advice is to understand why the difficult behavior exists and why it persists. Most likely, the difficult person has used this behavior before and achieved the desired results, and so continues to use the same behavior. If we give in to someone's temper tantrums, that person will tend to behave the same way in the future. If we bribe someone to go along with our wishes, that person will come to expect a bribe any time he or she is asked to do something. Although coping with difficult behavior may be a challenge, once you understand the origin of the behavior, it may be somewhat easier.

If you encounter difficult behavior during negotiation, you may not know whether the person behaves in this manner all the time or not. And you may not have the time to fully assess the underpinnings of the behavior. Nevertheless, you can take steps to defuse the behavior. We will first discuss handling a difficult person in formal negotiation, then we will explain how to deal with a difficult person on an interpersonal basis.

The Five Steps

There are five basic steps in breaking through difficult behavior and creating a favorable environment for negotiation:[8]

1. Regain your own balance and control your own behavior.

2. Help the other party control their behavior.

3. Change the tone of the negotiation from Competitive to Collaborative (see specific techniques for this step in Chapter 9).

4. Help the other party overcome their skepticism so you can find a mutually agreeable solution.

5. Achieve closure, which is the ultimate objective in any negotiation.

KEY CONCEPT — **Managing Conflict with a Difficult Person**

The main points in dealing with a difficult person are to recognize or identify the behavior, to understand it, and to find a way to cope with it, whether that involves confronting the behavior directly or learning to live with it in some way.[9] In interpersonal conflict, as in negotiation, cultural and ethnic differences and resulting underlying values and biases may be operative.

If you find yourself in a conflict situation, once you cool off but before you do anything else, you will need to decide whether it is worth trying to change the other person's behavior. Ask yourself how much work it will take, and whether a positive result is likely. Consider whether there are risks involved. You may have to accept that some people are unwilling to change. If that is the case in your situation, you will need to concentrate on the changes you can make, and the steps to take for coping with the behavior.

If you decide to try for changes, remember that successful conflict resolution depends on effective communication. This, in turn, depends on two factors: (1) acknowledging, appreciating, and productively using the differences in people, and (2) developing a personal strategy for dealing effectively with difficult people.[10] The following steps are suggested for conflict resolution:[11]

1. *Identify exactly the behavior that bothers you,* not the values that lie behind the behavior (people will throw up all kinds of resistance to changes in their values). Concentrate on the behavior, not the person.

2. *Confront the behavior* in as nonthreatening a way as possible. Stay focused on the behavior and try to avoid attacking the person. Phrase your statement

in the following way: "When you do _____, I feel _____." For example, you might say, "When you shout at me, I feel that you think I am incompetent" or "I feel embarrassed when you tell an off-color story in my presence."

3. *Be willing to hear what the other person has to say.* Use your listening skills (Chapter 4) to identify facts and feelings from the other person. Keep the discussion as impersonal as possible. Let the other person ventilate.

4. Resolve conflict by trying to *meet the needs of each party.* This is a mininegotiation and should be collaborative.

5. *Implement the resolution.*

The keys to the process of successful conflict resolution are the following:

- Separate people from the problems; remember that the problem is the *relationship,* not the people themselves.
- Acknowledge and appreciate differences.
- Be flexible about the other person's viewpoint or work style.
- Accept that a different opinion or approach is simply different, not wrong; remember that there are differences in thinking styles.
- Avoid negative labels.
- Be flexible.
- Stay focused on outputs rather than positions.

Four Benefits of Successful Conflict Resolution[12]

With all we have said about the benefits of Collaborative negotiation, the reasons for managing conflict well should be fairly clear:

1. Behavior that is perceived as negative is confronted and resolved. This helps the parties move away from stereotyping or assigning negative attributes based on differences.

2. Parties can learn about other people's needs and viewpoints and thereby can better understand the reasons for their behavior.

3. Problem-solving skills can be improved and people can learn to find creative solutions.

4. All parties can benefit from improving their understanding of and friendship with others. This builds trust that will help in future encounters.

You Can Fool Some of the People Some of the Time . . .

Is negotiation about tricking other people, or about finding better ways to work with them? If you hope to become a clever con artist through your study of negotiation, perhaps the following anecdote from comedian Soupy Sales will serve as a caution:

A famous art collector is walking through Greenwich Village when he notices a mangy old cat lapping milk from a saucer in front of a store. And the collector does a double take when he sees the saucer. He knows it's very old and very valuable. So he saunters casually into the store and offers to buy the cat for two dollars.

But the store owner says to him, "I'm sorry, but the cat isn't for sale."

And the collector says, "Please. I need a hungry old tomcat around the house to catch mice. I'll give you ten dollars for him."

And the owner says, "Sold," and takes the ten dollars. Then the collector says, "Listen, I was wondering if, for the ten dollars, you might include that old saucer. The cat seems to be used to it. It'll save me a dish."

And the owner says, "Sorry, buddy. That's my lucky saucer. So far this week, I've sold sixty-eight cats!"

END POINT

There are a great many conflicts of interest between people daily, both in private and in professional life. You have had a chance to surface some of the conflicts affecting you in recent days, and to analyze the outcome of the most important one. Whether you and the other party were fully satisfied or not, we are certain that you can gain skills allowing you to achieve high satisfaction scores in the majority of conflict situations. And this book will share our knowledge of five important negotiating strategies in order to help you master all the conflict situations you'll encounter in the future.

You, like all of us, have a specific, natural response to conflict. The assessment in this chapter can help you clarify your understanding of your own conflict response. Whatever your preferred approach, we want to make sure you expand your range of conflict responses significantly. We expect that you will be comfortable with any one of the five negotiating strategies by the time you finish this book.

However, we also know you will encounter many people who make it hard to use your newfound mastery of negotiation—people who take a less educated and, at times, infuriating approach to conflicts of interest. That is why the last half of this opening chapter is devoted to a variety of tactics for overcoming roadblocks that might keep you from using your growing negotiation skills.

In the next chapter, we assume you have managed to initiate a healthy negotiation process, and we will show you how the game is played. There is a predictable sequence of stages, and there are some important general rules you need to know in order to be prepared for any type or style of negotiation.

The Negotiation Game

In the previous chapter, we discussed the nature of conflict. We made the following points:

- Conflict is pervasive in all of our lives—we cannot have a life (or even an average week) without some conflict.

- Some conflicts are win–win, some are win–lose, and some are lose–lose.

- We have choices about the way we manage conflict, and there are different strategies we can use to handle a conflict.

- There are strategies we can use with people who are relatively easy to deal with, and other strategies for people who are difficult to deal with.

 In this chapter, we want to focus on the essential nature of negotiation. We will try to show that negotiation is not a random process, but that it actually has a predictable sequence of steps or stages. We will also show that we negotiate with all different kinds of people, and that *who* we negotiate with determines a lot about how the negotiation process will proceed.

NEGOTIATION IS EVERYWHERE

Do you negotiate frequently? If you think not, you are like most readers—and you are wrong! When dealing with other people, many of us negotiate *more than once in every waking hour,* but we do not recognize the majority of these negotiations as being such. We may not take seriously even the fewer, more major negotiations of our day or week. But by overlooking opportunities to negotiate strategically, we settle for suboptimal results. We either get less than we could have, or we end up wasting time and energy on conflicts and problems that we create through poor negotiation.

Even those of us who have already studied negotiation may suffer from both problems—overlooking opportunities for negotiation, and negotiating poorly. Why? Because we are generally trained in only one of many negotiating styles and we try to apply it in every situation. We lack the breadth of knowledge to negotiate strategically.

Think back on the events of a recent day. Did you negotiate? Did you win? Following a fictional character through her daily events may help you answer those questions. Helen awoke to the alarm clock at 6:45 A.M. She waited a moment, but Jim did not stir, so she climbed over him to turn the alarm off. Irritating, especially with her bad back. Jim's son Noel, from his prior marriage, was staying with them for the week while his mom traveled, so Helen went to his door and called to him, then headed for the kitchen to pack his lunch for school. Then she went upstairs to get ready for work. But the bathroom door was closed and the shower water was running. Noel? No, Jim was no longer in bed, so it had to be him. But that meant no time for her to shower before work, since it was her turn to drive the car pool to work and she had to leave home early to get everyone else. She wished she had remembered that Noel was coming when they discussed the car pool schedule at work—it would have been more convenient to drive next week. As she stood in front of her closet, she debated whether to wear the new red skirt that she had just bought, or the older gray one. After looking to see what blouses were clean, she decided that the red skirt would have to wait until she had time to do some ironing.

Helen has not gotten very far in her day, and already she has ended up on the wrong side of *five* negotiations. Did you take note of them? She accommodated Jim's irritating habit of sleeping through the alarm. She generously packed a lunch for his son, and by so doing she lost her opportunity to take a shower before rushing to her car pool. To Helen, all three interactions with her family are probably losses, and there's no point losing in any situation unless you gain something in the future from it. These sacrifices were not likely to be noticed and reciprocated. And her fourth loss—agreeing to drive during an inconvenient week—also accomplishes nothing in the long term. It is an example of suboptimal results due to incomplete information—a remarkably common problem for most negotiators.

Finally, her "negotiation" with herself over which skirt to wear led to a decision to wear the older skirt because she had nothing ironed to go with the new red one. But let's not dwell on Helen's morning, as her working day is likely to hold many more negotiation situations for her.

Helen left the house a little late—and a little mad at Jim, who had driven off without offering an apology. Perhaps that was why she drove faster than usual on the freeway, and why she was pulled over by a state trooper. Even worse, she forgot how outspoken Fred, who was riding in the front seat, can be—or she certainly would have told him to keep his mouth shut! The police officer had clocked her at only five miles over the speed limit and seemed ready to let her off with a warning, when Fred started arguing with him.

Fred is a senior manager at her company, and he often loses his temper at subordinates. He was angry this morning because he had an early staff meeting, and he told the officer in no uncertain terms how inconvenient the situation was for him. Now Helen had a speeding ticket to pay and Fred was going to be even later for that meeting.

What mistake did Helen make this time? Another common one: She failed to *plan and control communication* in her negotiation with the police officer. Many negotiations turn sour when the wrong person gets involved or the wrong message is communicated. This point was brought home to Helen later that morning when her project team met.

The team was charged with cutting costs in the assembly of one of her company's products. They had begun to work with suppliers to reduce prices, and one of the suppliers was resisting the changes they proposed. Then Helen had called an old friend at the supplier company, who was able to get his firm to agree to a concession. Just as a solution was in sight, however, her friend took a new job and left the company. Now the supplier was refusing to sign the new contract. Her boss was impatient and wanted her to disband the current team and start all over again. But Helen knew this would hurt her relationships with the team members— all of them key personnel from the main functional areas of her firm. She suspected that these business relationships with the team members were more important than the small price cut her boss wanted her to obtain from the supplier. But how could she get her boss to see it that way? She was not sure what to do, but she knew she had some difficult negotiations ahead of her.

Before even taking her lunch break, Helen has had to cope with many negotiations. Some seem trivial, some are minor but irritating, and others are vital to her career or personal success. These situations and similar ones we all face daily are important for four reasons.

First, we care about the results. We care because we have one or more *goals* that we hope to accomplish, and our goals often conflict with other people's goals. The traffic cop wants to meet his quota for tickets, but we want to minimize travel time and cost. Our boss wants a quick, forced solution to a problem, but we have to live with our associates afterward, so preserving our relationships is more important. If people shared all their goals, they would not have a problem, or at least the problem would be one they could solve together easily. In fact, as we will soon see, aligning our goals is a useful negotiating strategy in contexts where collaboration is feasible and important, but it can be a wasteful, even damaging, strategy in other situations.

Second, we have *emotional* as well as rational goals and responses to negotiating situations. This is perfectly natural because negotiation is a human activity, and humans are both rational and emotional. And when we blunder through negotiating situations without recognizing or planning them, then we operate less out of rational action and more out of our emotions, almost by default. But emotional responses get in the way of good negotiating, and it takes a careful strategy to prevent passions or gut instincts from spoiling the outcome.

Third, our rational and emotional goals lead us to work with the other party to pursue specific *outcomes* in the negotiation. The outcome is a product of the way that the parties resolve conflicts in their goals, and what they agree to do as a result of their discussions. The outcome may be close to one of our goals, or it may favor the other and be very disappointing to us. And it may be critical for us, or it may not have a big impact. The outcome is the traditional focus of negotiators, and it is, therefore, helpful to keep it in context, but only as *one* of the four main concerns of strategic negotiation.

Fourth, we have *relationships* with the other people involved in the negotiation. All negotiations affect relationships, and the importance of a relationship must therefore be considered carefully in the development of any negotiating strategy. Outcome and relationship issues often conflict. Helen accepted a negative outcome in some of her negotiations because she wished to maintain a good relationship with that person; for example, she didn't shake Jim and tell *him* to turn off the alarm clock.

Many people plan and execute negotiation strategies without considering the impact on the relationships involved. If your relationship with the other party is one you value and want to keep strong—maintain trust, good communication, and positive feelings—*be careful what you do!*

These four concerns are the cornerstones of a strategic approach to negotiation (see Figure 2.1). In the discipline of strategic planning, they would be termed *strategic issues,* defined as the elements that have a major impact on your strategy and that do not have obvious answers. It is important for any strategist to identify and think about strategic issues before planning or acting. But most negotiators omit this critical step, and as a result often adopt flawed strategies.

In this book, you will learn how to take a strategic approach to negotiations—both the occasional formal ones and the far more frequent informal negotiations that fill our days and affect the quality of our lives and work. This means, first, clarifying your goals and the goals of those with whom you must negotiate. Second, it means substituting a careful, rational plan for the impulsive, emotion-based approach we naturally tend to take to such situations. And third, it means optimizing outcomes or relationships, or—if you are really good—both.

 NEGOTIATION IS A GAME

One way to think about negotiation is that it is a *game*. Thinking about negotiation as a game has lots of advantages:

- First, we can *understand* the game. It is not a completely random process. Most negotiations can be analyzed after they are over, and with increasing understanding comes the ability to *predict* and *control* what happens.

- Second, the game has a *predictable sequence of activities.* Many people who do not understand negotiation see it as a chaotic, almost random series of

Tangible goals

Intangible, emotional goals

Specific desired outcomes

Relationship with the other party

FIGURE 2.1 *The Four Major Concerns of Negotiation*

events. While it is true that it may be difficult to accurately predict exactly what a party will do next at any given point, the entire negotiation sequence generally follows a clear, understandable pattern. Our extensive discussion of strategies in this book assumes that you can increasingly predict and control how parties move from disagreement toward agreement.

- Third, there are *players* in the game. As we can see from the earlier example, there can be only one player (when Helen negotiates with herself about which skirt to wear), or there can be two players (her negotiations with Fred and Jim), or there can be multiple players (her negotiations with her team). Who the other players are, and what they do, has a great deal of impact on how you should plan and execute your strategy.

- Finally, the game has *rules*. There are *do*s and *don't*s for what can be done in negotiation. In some negotiations, these rules are clear, written, and quite explicit. (For example, in your negotiations with the tax bureau every April 15, the rules state that you have to report accurately how much income you earned and what you owe them. You can't simply make them an opening offer and hope they accept it!) In other negotiations, the rules are less clear and not written. This book will identify some of the most important informal rules—the *do*s and *don't*s—that will help you plan your game strategy. We also encourage you to consult Chapter 11, on legal and ethical issues, to define the boundaries.

THE NEGOTIATION GAME HAS STAGES AND PHASES

Many inexperienced negotiators think of the negotiation process as being akin to entering a long, dark tunnel. They are moving into a process that they don't understand, and they have no idea what is going to happen. Feeling out of control, these people do a number of foolish things:

- They formulate a desired outcome or objective and cling to it desperately, refusing to compromise or modify their objective based on what the other party also wants. This plan usually winds up with angry parties and in a standoff with no satisfactory resolution.

- They formulate a desired outcome or objective but then immediately surrender it in order to get a quick outcome based on what the other side has offered. This plan usually leaves the negotiator with a deal, but not a very good one; most negotiators who do this have a lot of regrets that they could have done better.

- They change their desired outcome or objective midway through the discussion, leading the other side to believe that they may not have a strategy, don't understand what is going on, or don't know what they want. These negotiators often anger their opponents, leading either to the breakdown of talks or to settlements that make little sense down the road.

There are a number of ways to represent the different stages or phases of a negotiation.[1] One way is shown in Figure 2.2.

 One way to think about a negotiation is to see it as the four stages in Figure 2.2. The four stages, and the key steps within each one, follow.

Stage 1: Preparation

The first stage of negotiation is the preparation stage. There are a number of things that go on during this stage.

1. *Collect information.* The first step of negotiation is the process of gathering information. You need to decide what kind of information you need, but it should be of two forms:

   - Information that will help you define your own objectives and argue for what you want to achieve in the negotaition.

   - Information about the other side, their goals and objectives, how they are likely to view you, and what they may want to achieve in the negotiation.

   The type of information you need will vary from negotiation to negotiation, but might involve knowing specific things about the issues to be discussed, gathering financial information, examining the history of this issue between the parties, understanding market conditions, understanding the structure and politics of the organizations in which the negotiation is taking place, understanding the culture in which the negotiation is taking place, and so forth. Chapter 4 specifically focuses on how you can gather information about the other side.

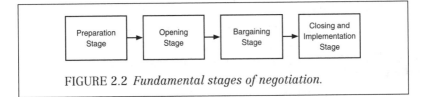

FIGURE 2.2 *Fundamental stages of negotiation.*

There are two essential skills to great information gathering: the ability to ask probing questions and the ability to listen intently. Asking informative, probing questions usually requires being able to ask *open* questions.[2] An open question is one that gets the other to talk extensively, and uses such phrases as *why, how, tell me about . . .* , or *explain to me.* Great listening skills require being able to accurately understand what the other is saying, read the emotion in their voice as well as the words, and understand their underlying interests.[3]

Susan Pravda, the co-managing partner of a Boston law firm, has learned that schmoozing is an important part of preparation. "Don't walk in and start going through your list. If they have a baby picture on the desk, it doesn't hurt to say, 'Oh, is that a new grandchild?' People like to talk about themselves. It can segue into what you are trying to achieve." She tries to find out everything she can about the other side.

The toughest part of negotiating, she says, is listening—really listening—to the other side. People who negotiate generally like to talk. The better you can listen and understand the problem, the greater chance you have to craft a creative solution.[4]

---

2. *Do planning and goal setting.* Planning and goal setting are also a key part of the preparation stage. We need to try to map out the way we want the negotiation to proceed, and we need to spend time determining what we want to achieve.

Important parts of planning and goal setting include:

- Defining what you want to achieve
- Defining your limits, or how far you will go
- Deciding on your opening bid
- Determining what alternatives you have if you cannot successfully negotiate this deal
- Assembling the information you gathered to understand how the other party will approach the negotiation
- Assembling the information you gathered to decide how to present it in order to achieve your objectives.
- Developing a proposed discussion agenda

As will be pointed out constantly through this book, planning is probably the *most* important stage of negotiations. Yet it is also the stage that many negotiators neglect, because they want to get into the action. Great planning is the key to successful negotiations. Chapters 3 and 4 discuss the planning process and the critical steps you need to take in the planning phase, such as identifying interests; specifying targets, walkaways, and opening bids; identifying alternatives, and planning the agenda for the upcoming discussions.

You should plan to cycle back from planning and goal setting to information gathering. As you get to know the other party better and get more information about what they want, what you want and the situation you are in, this will give you the opportunity to continually update your plan.

 Don't proceed on to the opening stage until your planning process is complete!

Stage 2: Opening

In the opening stage, you lay out your arguments. You use the information you have gathered to construct the most persuasive argument you can for what you want, why you want it, and why the other side should give it to you. Here is where it is important to be clear about your goals, to be able to argue well for what you want, and to be able to listen to what the other party wants so that you can present counterarguments.

In the opening stage, you also listen to the other side's presentation. You should try to take notes on what they say, and listen clearly for what you think is most important to them. Here is also a critical place to ask questions and learn as much as you can about what they want.

Stage 3: Bargaining

In this stage, you play the classic negotiation game of give and take. Parties in negotiation normally expect that opening demands are exaggerated, and that one or both parties will have to make concessions to reach some agreement. The bidding process is the process of moving from your opening bid toward your target, and getting the other side to do the same thing. Depending on whether the game is more competitive or more cooperative, you will want them to do more of the moving than you, or you will want to move at approximately the same distance and pace. More is said about the information use and bidding processes in Chapters 6 to 10, which lay out the basic game plans for each of the five major approaches to negotiation.

Stage 4: Closing and Implementation

In this stage, you wrap up the final agreement. You review what you have agreed to. You may write out a contract or written agreement. You clarify anything that was left ambiguous or incomplete in the previous discussion. You shake hands. You may exchange money or resources as specified in the deal. Finally, you may celebrate your accomplishment with a meal or drink.

 Closing rituals are very important in negotiations. Even in very short or very competitive negotiations, it is important to use the closing stage to formalize what you have agreed to, write it down in a *memorandum of understanding,* and work to smooth over any anger or animosity that may have been built up in the bidding stage.

 Watch out for *nibbling* during the closing stage. In a competitive negotiation, the other party may try to get a bit more on their plate by raising new issues. If the other party wants to raise a new issue that they "forgot," you have the right to reopen the entire negotiation package and discuss other issues as well.

Implementation is also a critical stage of the negotiation. Once you have formulated an agreement, you need to put it into action. At this point, parties often discover that the agreement was incomplete or flawed. New issues come up. Problems arise that you didn't anticipate. The other party didn't do things they said they would do. So this is a critical phase for being able to go back to the other party and fix the agreement you arrived at earlier. Every good agreement should create the opportunity for the parties to reopen discussions if there are problems in implementation.

 Almost every negotiation goes through all of these stages. The amount of time spent in each stage may vary, depending on the following factors:

- Who the other party is and how well you know them or want to know them (the less you want or need to know them, the shorter the stage).

- How well prepared you are already, versus how much information you need from the other side to formulate your own interests and goals.

- The culture you are negotiating in. In the United States, negotiators are known for spending very little time in relationship building (even in situations where having a strong relationship would enhance that negotiation). In contrast, Japanese and Chinese negotiators will spend a very long time in relation-

The Formula-Detail Dynamic

A great way to think about what happens in the bidding and closing process is called "formula-detail." When using formula-detail, negotiators should first start with the diagnosis and preparation process we described in the earlier steps. Then both parties should try to create a common statement of what the problem is (the "formula" stage), such that both sides have a common view of the problem, what caused the problem, why the problem exists, and what will be necessary to resolve it. The parties should then move to the "detail" phase, in which they use the common formula to work out details that will be beneficial to each side. Parties cycle back between formula and detail until they achieve an agreement which is satisfactory to both sides.[5]

ship building and information gathering, and a much shorter time in the bidding and closing processes.

THE PLAYERS IN THE GAME

Earlier, we said that knowing the players in the game is critical to understanding the negotiation. Knowing who they are, what they want, how they are likely to behave, what kind of a reputation they have, and what kind of a *role* they will take is essential to understanding and playing the game.

Let's take a look at the roles played by different players, and the consequences when we bring additional negotiators into the game.

Negotiating with Yourself

Most of what is written about negotiations assumes it is a process involving *at least* two parties.[6] But in fact, we negotiate with ourselves all the time.

 Negotiations inside ourselves are usually conversations between our conscious (rational) and our subconscious (intuitive) selves. Our consciousness tells us what we want to do, what we need, what we should do. Our subconscious is telling us what we should do, ought to do, *really* need to do.

These are the "should I or shouldn't I" discussions in our heads. These are the "on the one hand" versus "on the other hand" debates. These are the "I really don't want to . . ." versus "I really ought to . . ." dialogues that we carry on constantly.

What does it mean to "negotiate with yourself"? One way to represent this is to think of it as two ways of processing information and making decisions. One way is largely based on facts, figures, and information that leads to a rational conclusion. The other tends to be more emotional, intuitive, and based on our personal values. Table 2.1 represents these two sides of ourselves.

Each person tends toward one end or the other of this range—makes decisions more rationally or emotionally. And so, while the discussions go on within us, our personality will lead us to favor one or the other in the way we process information and make decisions.

 There are many personality tests that can tell you whether you tend to be more rational or emotional.[7] This is important for you to understand, because it says a lot about how you will approach negotiation and make decisions.

 The most important thing to understand in negotiating with yourself is to *continue to pay attention to both sides of your brain*. The little voice of your intuition will often try to talk to you when something doesn't feel right, doesn't add up, or doesn't make sense. Particularly those of us whose preferences tend to lean toward the left side of Table 2.1 may tend to let the rational side drive out the emotional. Learning to listen to your inner voice may be the best thing you can do to avoid a negotiation disaster.[8]

Negotiating with an Opponent

Because the rest of this book is primarily directed toward negotiating with a single opponent, we will say very little about it here. But there are some important aspects of that other person that you need to remember:

- *How well do you know the other person?* The better you know the other party, the more information

TABLE 2.1 TWO STYLES OF THINKING

Rational	Emotional
Logical	Intuitive
Hard	Soft
Words	Images
Fact-based	Value-based
Rule-following	Ethics-following

SOURCE: Alex Hiam, *Marketing for Dummies* (Foster City, Calif.: IDG Press, 1997).

Emotional Intelligence and Negotiation

In recent years, scientists who have studied emotions have determined that some people differ in their level of "emotional intelligence." Emotional intelligence is "the intelligent use of emotions: you intentionally make your emotions work for you by using them to help guide your behavior and thinking in ways that enhance your results."[9] Just like people can vary in their intellectual or cognitive intelligence, people differ in their emotional intelligence. Researchers who have studied emotional intelligence have determined that there are four key components:

- The ability to accurately perceive, appraise and express emotion;

- The ability to generate feelings on demand when they can help understanding yourself or someone else;

- The ability to understand emotions and the knowledge that derives from them;

- The ability to regulate emotions to promote intellectual and emotional growth.

Clearly, emotions play a large role in negotiations. The more effective a negotiator is in expressing appropriate emotions (or perhaps even manipulating them), and the more effective he/she is in "reading" the emotions of others, the more that emotional messages and communications can be an effective leverage tool. Expressing appropriate emotions involves developing high self-awareness of emotional states, managing one's own emotions, and motivating oneself. Using emotional intelligence in negotiation requires us to develop effective communication skills, learning how to skillfully relate to others, and being able to help others understand themselves.[10]

you have about them. You know what they are like, how they speak, what they are likely to ask for, and how they play the game. Players in all types of games study their opponents carefully. The more often they have interacted, the more they know about each other.

- *What kind of a relationship have you had with the other person in the past, and what kind do you want to have in the future?* If you have a good relationship and want to maintain it, you are probably going to negotiate very differently than if you have had a bad relationship and don't care to improve it. The more you care about the relationship with the other party, the more cooperative you want to be.

  If you have had a bad relationship and want to improve it, you should probably plan to be accommodating, and help the other party achieve their objective.

  If you have had no relationship and don't care about starting one, you should use a strategy that maximizes your negotiating goals, such as a competitive one.

- *Does the other person have a reputation that should cause you to be cautious?* Chapter 1 extensively discusses how to deal with people who don't negotiate well or who behave dangerously and unpredictably. Follow this advice!

Negotiating through Agents

Agents or representatives are often used in certain kinds of negotiations. You may employ an agent to negotiate on your behalf for several reasons:

- The agent may have some expertise in the subject matter that you do not possess. You contract with a real estate agent to negotiate selling a house because the agent has more expertise in the house-selling process (and a better network of contacts) than you do. You hire an attorney to negotiate in a bankruptcy because the attorney knows the law better than you do and can protect your rights better than you can on your own.

- The agent has more negotiating expertise. For example, in many cities you can now find a professional buyer who will buy an automobile for you; companies often hire such experts to conduct major financial transactions.

- You are too emotionally involved in the issue to negotiate effectively. Agents can be helpful as somewhat detached, impartial representatives of a party.

CONCEPT

Because agents can represent you in a dispassionate way, they may help to get you a better agreement than if you tried on your own. It is particularly useful to have agents do the bargaining if the principal parties are adversarial.[11] Finally, agents are commonly used when there is a group of people on each side in a negotiation. Because negotiation can become chaotic when many people are trying to speak at once, agents can focus the discussion and maintain order in the process.

There are also disadvantages to using an agent:

- When you add agents to the negotiation equation, you are adding more people. The more people, the more complex the mix because there are more conversations going on.

- Agents may not do exactly what you want them to do. While the parties often give their agents clear instructions (what to do, what can be agreed to, etc.), agents often decide that they cannot follow these instructions directly. So while you may gain something by using an agent, it is possible that the agent may not come back with the deal you really wanted.

- Agents seldom perform their services for free; therefore, adding an agent increases the costs of negotiation, sometimes to the point that you need to get a better deal than if you had negotiated yourself.

- Communication can be more complicated as agents are added because the information passes through an additional filter, increasing the potential for distorted messages. A prime example of this is a divorce case, where the two parties may have to have some sort of relationship after the divorce is over (e.g., joint custody of children) but have relied on their attorneys to do the negotiating. While the attorneys may have negotiated a good deal "in principle," the details of day-to-day coordination are probably best worked out by the parents themselves.

- Agents can sometimes make the deal *more* difficult. They may become adversarial with each other and lose their ability to represent their constituents well. On the other hand, the agents of two or more parties may form an alliance that affects the outcome. In this situation, the agents may collude to work out a deal that is good for them, but is not necessarily good for their clients.

- Finally, the client and the agent may simply have different aims. For example, the agent might be inclined to behave in a Collaborative or Compromising manner, while the client prefers a Competitive approach. Or vice versa. There may also be differences in their ethical values or their definitions of appropriate behavior.

As noted earlier, agents are frequently used because they are experts. They may be authorities in a *subject* area that is of concern in the negotiation, such as labor in the airline industry. Or they may be *process* experts, who are highly skilled in negotiation itself. Or they may have a sphere of *influence* important to the negotiation, such as a political connection or a circle of influential friends whom they can call on (lobbyists are good examples of this type of agent). If a party is composed of a large group, then an agent is helpful in managing the group and serving as a spokesperson.

Rules for Negotiating through an Agent

Here are some key points to keep in mind if you are going to be negotiating through an agent or are hiring an agent to negotiate for you:

- If you have the option of picking an agent, find a person you feel comfortable with. Since you are asking this individual to negotiate on your behalf, you need to feel trust and a sense of compatibility with him or her.

- Make sure the agent knows your objectives and interests. You need to spend enough time to help the agent understand what you are trying to achieve, your goals, target, and walkaway. You may need the agent's expertise to help you set these points, and if the person is a professional, he or she will interview you about these issues anyway.

- Discuss whether you wish to be present for some or all of the negotiations, or whether the agent will conduct all the negotiations independently. If you are to be present, also be clear about the conditions under which you will be able to speak and participate, as opposed to letting the agent do all the talking. Make sure you and the agent talk about whether you can conduct any separate and independent discussions with the other party without agents present. Negotiations can get very confused if agents are discussing things at one level while the parties are dealing with each other directly without the agents being aware of it.

- Be very clear about how much authority the agent has to make a deal on your behalf. Does the agent need to approve the deal with you before settlement? Can the agent make a tentative settlement? Does he or she understand the *limits* of a possible settlement?

- Make sure you have discussed a schedule for receiving progress reports.
- Finally, make sure you and the agent understand the terms of the agent's compensation for time and services. Again, agents will usually raise this issue and explain their fee structure—whether a percentage of the sale, by the hour, or some other scale. *Remember that these rates are also negotiable.* Particularly if many agents are available, it is often possible to negotiate rates. You should do this if the agent is providing limited services but is trying to charge you the "standard rate."

Negotiating in Groups and Teams

Team negotiation occurs when there are two or more people on a side. The members of a negotiating team work together and basically have the same responses and interests, but as the group expands, the process tends to become less manageable. Team members may include the spokesperson or agent, experts who serve as resources, advocates for smaller groups within the group, legal or financial counselors, a recorder, an observer, a statistical analyst, and so forth.

Team negotiation is most common in labor–management negotiations, diplomatic situations, and business deals. In such cases, though there are a number of people in the party, there may be only one spokesperson or agent who represents the group. Most of the formal communication between the parties occurs through the spokesperson, and this cuts down on any inadvertent revealing of information. Spokespersons usually insist on strict discipline within the team—particularly when they are at the table with the other team—so that individuals do not speak out of turn, give away confidential information, or make unauthorized agreements.[12]

Negotiating in groups and teams is far more challenging than negotiating with one other person, or through an agent, for a number of reasons:

- There are more people, and so there are a lot more conversations going on.
- The number of different views makes it difficult to understand all of the different priorities and preferences, and find a way to accommodate and integrate all of those views.
- There are more relationships and more diversity in the relationships, which can increase the tension and change the emotional dynamics
- It is more difficult to orchestrate and control the flow of the process through the stages noted earlier.

Managing Group Negotiations

Here are the things you need to do to manage the group process in complex multiparty discussions.

Before the process actually begins, there are many factors to consider. These include the conditions for the meeting, such as lighting, noise level, ventilation, temperature, configuration of space (e.g., where people sit, whether a large table is used), group size, and seating pattern (e.g., random, alphabetical, or with chief negotiators opposite each other). If the meeting is to be long, larger rooms provide more opportunity for people to spread out and be comfortable. Parties and members need to be identified with cards or name tags. Supplies such as pencils and paper will be needed. A chalkboard or flip chart is an excellent tool for recording ideas, structuring the agenda, and providing a focused place to propose motions, amendments, and wording of documents.

 Do You Need a Facilitator?

It is a good idea to have an impartial, neutral person to chair or moderate the negotiation meetings. The chair should be someone who has no stake in the outcome and will not be affected by it, but who can be active in structuring and monitoring the group process. This position may be filled by a consultant or mediator.

Make Sure Everyone Knows the Score

Make sure everyone understands the costs of a failed negotiation.[13] That is, does the group have a viable best alternative to a negotiated agreement (BATNA), and are parties willing to move toward it if the possible solution is sufficiently poor? It is important for each party to consider what will happen if there is no agreement. Will someone else make the decision? Or will there be none? Another important area concerns the options available to the group. Everyone needs to understand all the options. As a result, it may be useful, as the group begins to work on the problem, to list, review, and discuss all the possible available options as well as the alternatives.

Define How the Decision Will Be Made

Deciding on how the agreement or decision will be made can be fraught with difficulty. Who should decide? How should the decision be made?

Group decisions are often made by a minority of the members. If one party is stronger than the other due to greater power or status or just plain persuasiveness, then their preference may, by default, become the selected process. Or perhaps one group might convince another to join with them, forming a significant coalition, and the resulting more powerful combined group will promote their views.

The decision may be agreed on by vote. But how will it be decided? Simple majority? Two-thirds? Must there in fact be a consensus? If implementation of the decision is important, consensus is likely to be more critical, because negotiators will be more committed to a decision reached by consensus than by a simple majority.

The moderator should be sure that all pertinent information is presented to and considered by the group. The moderator will need to monitor the discussion to be sure that all parties have a chance to speak, and that they all follow the predetermined rules. People also need to be allowed to vent emotions if necessary.

To assist the moderator in managing the discussion, there are several helpful methods that enhance group decision making:

- In the *Delphi technique,* the moderator sends a questionnaire to all parties before the beginning of negotiations. The moderator summarizes the results and sends questions to all the parties again. This process can continue for as many rounds as needed, with the moderator asking questions to uncover issues, concerns, and options. The advantage of this process is that it is *not* face to face, thus saving on the emotional wear and tear that is likely to occur in group meetings. In addition, those parties who may be more timid in participating in large group discussions have an equal chance of getting their ideas into the discussion. However, because this method may lead to concessions and compromises, it may result in a Compromise solution rather than a truly Collaborative solution.

- *Brainstorming* can also be used in a group setting. The groups write down as many ideas as possible, without judging them. Then the lists of ideas are brought back to the whole group where they may be prioritized, discussed, or voted on.

- *Nominal groups* may be used after brainstorming, or they can be used separately. In a nominal group, each person prioritizes the previously generated list, then the moderator records the tally. Data are then assembled and redistributed to the group several times, to try to achieve some consensus on priorities.

KEY CONCEPT

Understand the Key Role of the Agenda

Especially in multiparty negotiation, it is very important to have an agenda and to *use* it. The agenda can be generated by the moderator, or by the group as a whole, if feasible. The agenda not only keeps people on track, it defines what that track will be. It may include:

- A list of the issues under negotiation
- A definition what each issue means
- The order of the discussion of issues (and perhaps the people to present them)
- The amount of time that will be allocated to the discussion and resolution of each issue

Agendas can be very strong control mechanisms if used manipulatively. The person who makes up the agenda can dominate the meeting by determining what gets discussed and what does not get discussed, and the order in which it is done. Therefore, if you believe that the agenda is manipulative and unfair, do not hesitate to question it and the way it was developed.

Steps in Moderating the Group Process

The mandate for the moderator of multiparty negotiation should be to manage the *process,* not the *outcome.* (The moderator of a multiparty negotiation resembles the mediator in third-party disputes.) If you find yourself in the position of moderator, you can follow specific steps to make the negotiation run as smoothly as possible:[14]

- Introduce yourself.
- Describe your role.
- Introduce the agenda and get the group to okay it, or build the agenda with the group.
- Set ground rules for meeting times, type of output the group will generate, procedures for recording minutes and decisions, breaks, location and frequency of meetings, and opportunities to consult with people not at the meetings.
- Review how group decisions will be made and implemented.
- Prepare opening remarks that set a positive, upbeat, optimistic tone for the meeting.
- Be sure everyone has a chance to speak and that no one person dominates.
- Listen for common interests, priorities, and concerns.
- Have one person restate another's position (active listening) to ensure that people are paying attention to each other.
- "Mirror" the communication. Ask *why?* Listen with your whole being.[15]

- If you ask a question, wait a while for an answer, even if there is silence. Many people cannot stand silence and will fill the silence with new information.

- Try to maintain your neutrality—do not show bias (by your words or actions) to support or oppose any particular subgroup at the meeting.

- Avoid spending too much time on one issue. Keep the pace moving. If the group bogs down, take a break.

- Bring in supporting information if appropriate.

- Allow simultaneous discussion of several issues at once, to encourage trade-offs.

- Use a chalkboard or flip chart to list issues and interests and map discussions. People are usually less competitive when they focus on a display of the issues, as opposed to focusing their comments and criticisms at each other.

- Have the group invent options. Use brainstorming and other methods to generate ideas. Use the chalkboard or flip chart to record these, discuss each, and record the pros and cons.

- Summarize often—where the group is, and where it should be going.

- Make sure standards for making a decision are fair and reasonable.

- As possible, try to move the group toward the selection of a Collaborative solution. Use techniques mentioned in Chapter 8, such as logrolling, bridging, packaging, trade-offs, and modifications.

- If an agreement at this point is not possible, aim for some form of *general agreement* or *agreement in principle* or common *statement of goals.* Plan to come back later and attempt to make it more specific and applied.

- When you have a tentative agreement, write it down. Keep a good set of notes on what is discussed at each meeting.

- Use a *one-text procedure* as you try to assemble a final agreement.[16] Write out a tentative draft of the things that have been agreed to, and circulate it so that people may continually make modifications, changes, additions, and corrections until the language is completely drafted.

- Discuss the steps that need to happen after the meeting concludes, and decide who will do what.

- Thank the participants for their time, energy, and commitment.

- Hold a postmortem to learn from the process and the results.

The final item assumes a resolution. However, this may be difficult to achieve in multiparty negotiations. If consensus appears impossible, try to move *toward* consensus by aiming for a preliminary or tentative agreement first. If this is successful, the parties can proceed to improve on the agreement, moving closer and closer to their goal with each iteration. If a lot of time has been spent getting to the first milestone, tempers may be frayed and people may be tired. In that case, take some time to cool off, then come back and try to push on. At this stage, conflict-management skills may be necessary to keep things moving along.

END POINT

This chapter gives an overview of the Negotiation game, and makes the following points:

- Negotiation is everywhere!
- There are four major concerns in negotiation:
  1. Tangible goals
  2. Intangible goals
  3. Specific, desired outcomes
  4. The relationship with the other party
- The negotiation process has relatively predictable stages and phases.
- Negotiation involves players. At minimum, these are yourself and the other party. It becomes more complex when the parties negotiate through agents, and even more complex when the parties negotiate in groups.

The next chapter describes how you begin to plan to achieve your specific goals and interests.

Your Needs and Interests

It's all too easy to fall into a negotiation without a clear idea of what you want or how you'll get it. Our natural instinct is to leap into action. Time seems of the essence. Yet the best thing you can do—absolutely the most important secret to winning any negotiation— is to start by contemplating your own position. As the old saying goes, *know thyself.*

SEARCH YOUR FEELINGS

Our first reactions to conflict are often un- helpful. The instinct to compete, the urge to lash out in anger, or the desire to run away from conflict—all are immediate reactions that may not reflect your deeper feelings or long-term goals.

Don't trust your first reactions. Instead, search your mind to explore both the emotional and rational dimen- sions of your situation.

How? This chapter will show you a powerful way to come to terms with what you want and need, and thereby to lay the foundation for successful negotiations and profitable deals in every aspect of work and life. It all starts with a clearheaded understanding of your own position.

GOOD NEGOTIATORS DON'T FLY BY THE SEAT OF THEIR PANTS

The members of a Boeing aircraft design team, working on the passenger oxygen system for a new plane, found

Is Your Initial Reaction in Your Own Long-Term Interest? (Sometimes!)

I saw a woman walking in the street, crying. I felt such compassion, I went up and asked, "What's the matter?"

She said, "What's the matter? Oh! My husband! How I'm gonna miss him! Oh, gosh! I'll miss him! True, he was bad, he used to drink and smoke and gamble, and he'd bring women to the house, and he had lipstick on all his shirts—but OH! I'm gonna miss him!"

I said, "When did he die?"

She said, "He starts tomorrow."

—Jack Carter

themselves in conflict with another Boeing design team. The first team had found a nice spot for the passengers' oxygen masks, in the back of each passenger seat. But the second team had chosen this same spot for the "gasper," the little nozzle that provides a stream of fresh air to passengers. You can't put two pieces of equipment in the same space. What to do next?[1]

If you were on the oxygen system team, you would first need to assess your team's position. Here are the kinds of questions you would ask yourself:

- Is this the only location for the mask that is likely to work, or is there room for flexibility?

- Will you suffer personal costs, such as a bad work review, if your team's design is scrapped?

- Does your team have the backing of senior managers who outrank the other team's backers?

- Even if there are alternative approaches, do you have enough time and other resources to redo your design?

- What are the costs of a change in your design to the project's overall time and budget targets, and to the ultimate quality of the plane?

- Are there viable alternatives?

- Do we want to be flexible on this one or not?

Answers to questions like these would help you and your team decide what the important issues are and how flexible you could afford to be in resolving the conflict. You would also want to know the options for dealing with the conflict. For example, are there resources within Boeing to handle this problem and minimize the costs of solving it?

In the past, this sort of problem would have been discovered on the production floor at Boeing, long after the design teams had finished their work. It probably would have led to extended bickering, escalating up the ranks of management.

The team that had to move its piece of equipment would have absorbed a lot of trouble and extra expense, and the production schedule and budget might have been compromised. Therefore, each team's positions would have been staked out aggressively. Future careers could have been at stake for the team held responsible for the mistake.

But, because Boeing is improving its methods for finding and resolving such conflicts *early* in the design cycle, a computer program quickly spotted the problem—making it less costly and embarrassing for either team to change positions. And Boeing now offers third-party help in the form of an *integration team,* which rushes in to help the two design teams come up with a win–win solution.

The early identification of this problem, coupled with the immediate use of a third party to help resolve the conflict, allowed the two teams to avoid a major conflict. And no doubt, their initial assessments of the situation showed that the costs of arguing and delaying the project were far higher to both teams than the costs of collaboration and compromise.[2] What both teams wanted was a quick, easy solution, and the company offered the resources to achieve such a solution.

Whenever you are in a negotiation situation, your first move, before you say or do anything, is to take stock of your own position and decide exactly what you want. Assessing your *position*—your arguments or your side of the story—is the first step in *successful* negotiations. It is often skipped in unsuccessful ones. It will take you 10 minutes or more to work through the systematic approach we offer in this chapter for the first time, but after you have done it formally a few times, it becomes instinctive and quick to use informally as well.

Key Questions

What do I want out of this negotiation?
Why is it important to me?

YOUR SIDE OF THE STORY

The major questions that underlie this chapter are *"What* do I want out of this negotiation?" and *"Why* is it important to me?" To find the answers to these questions, you need to conduct a careful investigation. We cannot emphasize enough how important it is to plan so that you know where you are going, no matter what negotiation strategy you ultimately select.

The care you give to exploring your position pays off in preventing unpleasant surprises. It is important to be diligent in collecting information so that you are thoroughly prepared and are not taken by surprise. *You don't want to be blindsided by the realization that you didn't recognize a personal issue involved in the negotiation until too late.*

THE SITUATION IS LIKE A THREE-STRAND ROPE

Some of the information you collect here may help you make decisions in other areas. Even though this chapter concentrates on you and your position, there is always overlap with the other party and with the situational factors. All three factors—you, the other party, and the situation—are intertwined.

For example, your behavior affects how the other side behaves, and that behavior tends to dictate the moves you make. Likewise, the location of the negotiations (their turf, your turf, or a neutral place) can affect your behavior and theirs. The extent of their power and yours will affect the outcome, too.

 **WHAT ARE YOUR GOALS?**

Goal setting is a critical aspect of analyzing and planning your position. Think about what you want to attain in the deal. List your goals in concrete, measurable terms. Try to use dollar amounts or percentages. A well-framed goal is, "I will spend no more than $5,000." Then, if a counteroffer puts a car's price at $6,000, it will be clear that you have not yet achieved your goal.

A dollar amount is a *tangible* goal. So is a benefit in salary negotiations, or a particular interest rate when you are negotiating a loan. But many negotiation situations also contain *intangible* goals, such as "making a successful transaction" or "keeping everyone in the family happy" or "looking like a good negotiator to my friends" or "being viewed as a fair and honorable person." Intangibles will be more difficult, if not impossible, for you to quantify. And you may not be able to tell whether you have accomplished them until long after the negotiation has been completed. For example, if a goal is "Reform my husband so he spends more time with me and works less at the office," you may have to wait some months to know whether his agreement to this term is for real. (If he violates it, see "Is Your Initial Reaction in Your Own Long-Term Interest?" earlier in this chapter for the next step.) Nevertheless, it is important to be aware of intangible goals and to name them whenever possible.

Tactic #1: Make Feelings Measurable

Sometimes you can make intangible goals tangible by converting them to measurable milestones. "Get my husband to come home by 7:00 every night" is more measurable than "Reform my husband," although perhaps no easier to accomplish! Other goals must remain intangible, but are still important. But always try to attach measurable outcomes or indicators to every goal, regardless of how intangible or emotional the goal may be.

If all else fails, you can always say, "I want to *feel at least 50-percent better* about my husband's overworking by the end of next month or I'm outta here." That quantifies your feelings, making it easier to think about how to achieve your emotional goal.

At the end of every negotiation, you will look back and judge the outcome by *thinking* about it, and by *feeling* about it, too. Thinking and feeling are both important. Thinking has to do with those tangible goals, while your feelings will be shaped by the intangible goals. Your rational mind focuses on the tangibles, and you need to engage your intelligence to anticipate and list these tangible goals up front. But your emotional mind focuses on the intangibles, so you need to engage your *emotional intelligence,* too, in order to list intangible goals.

 We often use a two-column format, listing tangible goals on the left (since they are *left-brain* topics) and intangible goals on the right (since they are *right-brain* topics). Figure 3.1 is a worksheet in this format for you to use.

Many, if not most, bargaining situations contain *multiple* goals. Be sure to list all your objectives for this negotiation. Likewise, eliminate any goals that do not apply to the case at hand. Loading too many objectives into the negotiation may make it impossible to achieve settlement.

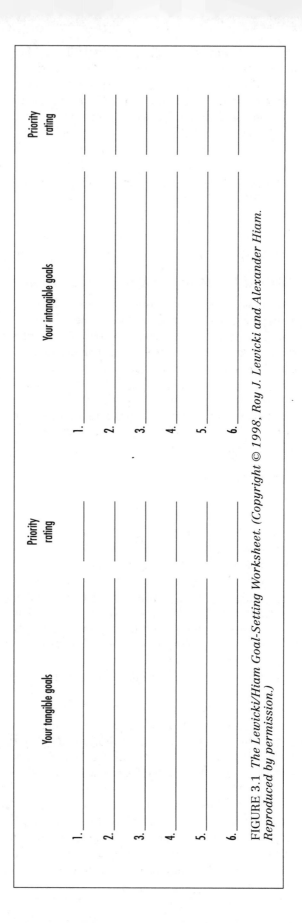

Your tangible goals

Priority rating

1. _____ _____

2. _____ _____

3. _____ _____

4. _____ _____

5. _____ _____

6. _____ _____

Your intangible goals

Priority rating

1. _____ _____

2. _____ _____

3. _____ _____

4. _____ _____

5. _____ _____

6. _____ _____

FIGURE 3.1 *The Lewicki/Hiam Goal-Setting Worksheet. (Copyright © 1998, Roy J. Lewicki and Alexander Hiam. Reproduced by permission.)*

PRIORITIZE YOUR GOALS

One way to sort out goals is to prioritize them. Ordering them in terms of their importance, assigning each one a dollar value, or using some other procedure to define value will assist you in comparing goals and deciding which are most crucial. This process may also help you eliminate the goals that are unrelated to the present situation.

Later in the negotiations, when you want to make trade-offs or concessions with the other party, you will see the value of setting priorities. At that point, you will usually be ready to *give up a less important goal to gain a more important one.* If you know the relative value of each of your goals, you will be able to evaluate the various tradeoffs.

For example, you might not insist on having four new tires put on a used car if the seller is willing to come down in price by $500 instead.

Assessing priorities allows you to establish *packages* of goals for various alternative offerings during negotiation. For example, a car CD player and automatic transmission may be more important to you than air conditioning and automatic door locks. Or intangibles like "A sporty car I really like the look of" may be your top priorities when you really think it through.

Evaluate these packages of goals with the same rating system you used for individual goals, and you will be able to compare their relative worth. When you have anticipated a package that is offered to you during negotiation, you will be able to evaluate it quickly and not lose valuable time figuring out its worth—yet another way that exploring your own needs and interests pays off at the negotiating table.

BARGAINING RANGE

The second step in negotiation is to define your bargaining range. It's the *flexibility* you feel about your goals. A bargaining range includes a starting point, a target point, and a resistance, or *walkaway,* point (Figure 3.2). Each of these points may be defined in monetary terms, or in other ways that allow you to define their relative value. The points may also be associated with *intangibles*—psychic outcomes that are harder to define, such as esteem or success, but that are nevertheless important. We will concentrate here on the *tangibles,* which are the more substantive (and usually economic) outcomes.

The *starting point* is your first offer to the other party. Where you set this point may

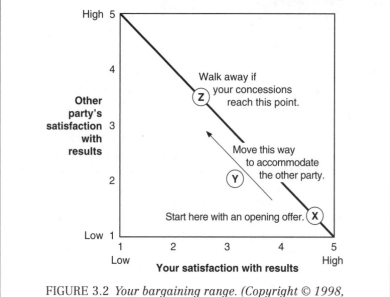

FIGURE 3.2 *Your bargaining range. (Copyright © 1998, Alexander Hiam & Associates. Reproduced by permission.)*

depend on the market rate, on how badly you want the outcome, on the time frame for the negotiation, on the other party's anticipated starting point, on concessions you may be willing to make, or on how negotiations have gone in the past. (Some of these factors depend on the context of the negotiation, which will be discussed in Chapter 5.)

Consider a simple example. You make an offer on a house that has a price tag of $175,000; therefore, the seller's starting point is $175,000. In most circumstances, buyers will not pay the seller's price, but will offer less—your starting point for an opening offer might be $140,000.

The *target* is the point where you want to settle. It is your intended outcome. In the case of the house, say your target is $150,000.

The *walkaway point* is the figure at which you will break off negotiations. The walkaway point is usually beyond your target; it is the point of no return. In the case of the house offer, it is the highest amount you will pay (or, from the seller's point of view, the lowest amount the seller will accept). Your walkaway point for the house in our example might be $155,000. Although you would prefer to pay the lower target amount of $150,000, you are willing to go as high as $155,000— but no higher.

Whether you will be able to negotiate with the other party at all will depend on the seller's bargaining range. If your range and the seller's range overlap—

that is, the most you will pay is above the least that the seller will accept—then bargaining can occur. Otherwise, there can be no negotiation. If the seller's walkaway point for the house is $160,000, then there can be no negotiation.

Bargaining range is primarily associated with competitive situations, where each side takes a stance and there is give-and-take adjustment until the two parties reach a compromise point between the two extremes. Chapter 7 will discuss the methods for setting your bargaining range if you are negotiating in a competitive situation.

ALTERNATIVES

Your negotiation analysis and planning should also include establishing an *alternative*. (Well-known authors Roger Fisher and William Ury have called this a best alternative to a negotiated agreement, or BATNA.)[3] An alternative is an acceptable alternative outcome or settlement to the issues under negotiation, such as a second but acceptable house in a nearby neighborhood, or a different car with the same equipment.

 An alternative can provide you with power during bargaining because, if the deal under consideration does not work out, you can switch to your alternative and still be satisfied. The goal "Buy a house *like* this one" is a lot more achievable than "Buy *this* house and no other."

The Advantage of Alternatives

Eventually, it came down to Charlotte and Orlando, and it didn't make much difference to me.

—Shaquille O'Neal, on his entry into the NBA[4]

Think of alternatives to the present situation that would be acceptable to you, and prioritize them if you have more than one. If you can assign each one a rating on a scale comparable to the one you used in prioritizing your goals, this will also be helpful. Then you can see exactly where your alternative fits in terms of trade-offs and limits. We feel so strongly about the importance of alternatives that we recommend using an alternatives worksheet like the one in Figure 3.3 each time you negotiate. It only takes a few minutes to fill in, and it often reveals alternatives that you wouldn't have thought of otherwise.

WHAT ARE YOUR UNDERLYING INTERESTS?

Beneath your defined goals and objectives, you may have deeper, underlying needs, interests, concerns, or fears.[5] Two examples will illustrate the importance of such underlying interests.

The wife whose goal is to get her husband to stop working too much may have such underlying interests as "Become less codependent in my life" or "Make this marriage work or get out of it before I feel too old to start a family." These underlying interests are likely to shape her view of the specific conflict over working too much. *Any resolution of that conflict needs to help her move toward her underlying interests, not just toward the immediate goals.*

For instance, if her husband's solution to his over-work problem involves her policing his behavior more carefully, that would violate her underlying interest in becoming less codependent, even though it might achieve the goal of reducing his overwork.

Similarly, a supervisor whose goal is to motivate an employee to perform at a higher level might not be happy with a solution involving tighter supervision of the employee. Why? Because most supervisors have a long-term interest in seeing their employees become more

Alternatives to consider	Priority rating
1. _____	_____
2. _____	_____
3. _____	_____
4. _____	_____
5. _____	_____
6. _____	_____
7. _____	_____

(Prioritize each alternative, from your #1 choice on down.)

FIGURE 3.3 *The Lewicki/Hiam Alternatives Worksheet. (Copyright © 1998, Alexander Hiam. Reproduced by permission.)*

self-sufficient. They want to be able to delegate work to competent, committed employees, because they don't have the time to direct everyone's performance closely. If the employee promised to work harder in exchange for more supervision and support, the manager might reject the offer. Not because it fails to accomplish the goal, but because it accomplishes the goal in a way that is inappropriate to the manager's underlying interests.

But what if the manager hadn't thought through her underlying interests? Then she'd accept the employee's proposal, and live to regret it later.

You get the idea: You'd better clarify your underlying interests along with your immediate goals or you might cook your own goose by mistake.

Just like goals, interests can be *concrete* (tangible), such as money or interest rates; or they can be more *abstract* (intangible), such as a friendly interchange with the other or the preservation of your image.

Often we have the protection of our relationship with the other party as an underlying interest. Yet it's easy to overlook this relationship interest and employ cut-throat bargaining tactics that win the battle but lose the war. In fact, in our experience as trainers and consultants in the field, we find that is one of the most common negotiating errors. Most negotiators learn the importance of the relationship with the other party the hard way—by spoiling it.

You may also be concerned about principles, such as what is fair or right.[6] You may be attentive to the *ethics* of the situation or what has happened in the past. Legal and ethical issues are discussed in Chapter 11, and we urge you to brief yourself on these two fascinating negotiating issues—if for no other reason than to make sure you don't fall into legal traps.

But you already know the basics, and you can certainly recognize underlying legal and ethical issues that matter to you. Trust your instincts—they'll tell you about any underlying legal and ethical concerns as long as you remember to listen to them. Here is a set of questions to help you surface any issues that may underlie a negotiation:

- Am I worried about any unfairness—to me *or* to the other party?
- Are there things I might find myself doing in this situation that I wouldn't want published in my home-town newspaper?
- Are there things I might find myself doing in this situation that might be illegal—such as hurting someone through an obvious deception?

The Tactic #2 box describes a method for surfacing your underlying interests using "Why do I want . . . ?" questions. It's almost as if you invited a three-year-old to question you, and the results can be equally startling.

Another good way to look at underlying needs is to ask yourself what will happen if you accomplish the goal. Then ask yourself what will happen if you *do not* achieve your goal. Sometimes the outcome is worse than you realize, sometimes better, because of the goal's relationship to underlying interests.

ALIGN YOUR INTERESTS, AND THE REST IS EASY

Researching your underlying interests will enable you to share them with the other party and thus find common interests. Although the two parties in a negotiation may appear to have conflicting goals, the underlying needs of each party may be similar. The result could be a collaborative solution that will meet both parties' goals and needs.

For example, two coworkers who are arguing over whether a window should be open or closed are unable to find a solution.[7] A third person asks each one to explain the problem. The first coworker wants the window open to get fresh air. The other person wants the window closed to avoid a draft. The third person suggests opening a window in the next room, which will provide fresh air and at the same time avoid a draft. This solution meets both coworkers' underlying interests, even though it violates one of their stated goals.

KEY CONCEPT — WHAT RESOURCES CAN YOU BRING TO BEAR?

You always have a range of resources that you can put to work for you in a negotiation. And if you are like most negotiators, *you almost always overlook some of those resources.* Most of us negotiate with one hand tied behind our backs.

It takes knowledge and creativity to recognize all the resources that might be of aid to you in a negotiation. These can be concrete assets, such as other people, files, and data to support your side. But resources also include personal traits, characteristics, knowledge, and skills that could work for you in the situation.

TiP In many negotiations, information is your most important resource. And that's great news because you can often dig up additional information at the last minute, thus increasing your strength for the negotiations ahead.

Information may be used to construct a set of arguments to persuade the other side, or to provide counterarguments to the other's persuasive efforts. For example, if you are buying a house and you happen to be a builder, you are less likely to be cheated than if you know nothing about houses. However, if you know nothing about houses but your best friend is a builder, then you have access to an excellent resource that you can use to your advantage. You can fill the information gap and greatly increase your power as a negotiator.

Your negotiation experience can also be a resource, particularly if you have had past success in the same area as the issues presently under consideration. If you are not experienced, think of experts you can call on to assist you. Or read this book.

Another resource is your creative ability in problem solving. This is particularly helpful in collaborative negotiations, where the two sides attempt to find common ground and solutions that will enhance both sides. But creativity is a help in competitive duels as well. The negotiator who can find a chandelier to swing from may win the sword fight.

If you don't see yourself as being creative, do not despair. You may be able to consult with someone else who can offer the problem-solving ability or the creativity that you need; you will also find that creativity is a muscle you can strengthen with exercise. (Alex recommends reading or training on creative thinking methods, such as are presented in his book, *The Manager's Pocket Guide to Creativity,* published by HRD Press.)

The Power of Information

If you do your homework before an annual performance review, you are better prepared for questions about your salary level.[8] Know what the average salary level is for people with your training and experience in jobs like yours. Document your accomplishments carefully to show how much you are worth to the company. Otherwise, you might say something stupid when your boss asks you how much of a raise you deserve—like "Whatever you think is fair," a response guaranteed to net the lowest possible raise.

When you inventory your resources, identify your strengths and weaknesses. Because weaknesses represent areas of vulnerability, the other side will try to identify them and take advantage of them in a negotiation. You need to protect such weaknesses or offset them with other strengths, particularly if the other party is competitive. Stay alert—weaknesses will surely take you by surprise later if you do not account for them now.

HAVE YOU BEEN HERE BEFORE?

A factor that dramatically affects negotiations is whether the parties regularly relate to each other. In organizations, many negotiations are recurrent; the parties have regularly dealt with each other in the past and will continue to do so in the future. A purchasing agent routinely negotiates with a supplier over prices and delivery; a manager regularly negotiates with her boss about budget and personnel. In such cases, your knowledge of the other party becomes a strength. On the other hand, their knowledge of you may be a weakness. Try to identify any specific knowledge you've gained that might give you an advantage—such as an insight into their underlying interests.

Other negotiations may occur only once, as when the company buys a real estate parcel to build a new manufacturing plant. For a one-time negotiation, your approach may be different than for a series of meetings. The stakes may seem higher in a one-meeting bargaining session, and this may affect your strategy and tactics.

HOW DO YOU BEHAVE?

The easiest way to predict how you'll hold up under fire is to recall your own reactions to similar situations in the past. What is your personal negotiation history? Are you conflict averse? Do you lose patience too quickly? (See assessment in Chapter 1.) And what about your communication style—are you too slow-paced, or perhaps too fast, for the other party?

Such questions help you anticipate your own natural behavior patterns. If your natural instincts are appropriate, list them as strengths. If not, list them as weaknesses—but weaknesses you can do something about. As you'll learn later in this book, you can and must learn to flex your negotiating style and communication habits so as to adopt winning methods in any situation.

It is also wise to research previous cases in which similar issues were under negotiation. The outcome of such cases may be instructive to you as you prepare your negotiation plan. You aren't the only one who has negotiated for a raise in your company. Nor are you the only one to get into an argument about responsibility with a member of a project team. And you certainly aren't the first person who has wished to modify a loved one's behavior. Look around, talk to friends, and find some helpful precedents.

WHAT ARE YOUR BELIEFS ABOUT NEGOTIATION?

Do you hold basic beliefs about what negotiation is and how to go about doing it? Most people do—and, in most cases, are limited by these beliefs. We hope that you are gaining new ideas and points of view to take into the negotiating arena, but you may still cling to a picture of the "typical negotiation," where two warring parties battle each other verbally until one gives up and gives in, and the other gets all the goodies. That is not a helpful image to bring to your preparations.

A typical assumption about negotiation is that a fixed amount is available (the fixed pie) and that you have to get as much of it as you can. While this may sometimes be true, holding such a point of view can cause you to miss opportunities to negotiate solutions that could make both parties happy.

WHO CAN YOU TRUST—AND WHO TRUSTS YOU?

Trust is one of the trickiest and most important aspects of negotiating. Since the topic of this chapter is you, the first question to ask is "How trustworthy are you?" If you value trust and tend to behave in a trustworthy manner, then you will likely expect to be trustworthy yourself and to trust the other party as well. That means a high level of trust is important to you, and should be a goal in your negotiations. It also means you may be at risk. Here's how.

DANGER! If you prefer to operate in a trusting, open manner—as most people say they do in our studies of negotiation in the workplace—then you may be easy to take advantage of. Your trusting nature is both a strength and a weakness. It's a strength because it allows you to move off the line of win–lose solutions and work toward a shared, collaborative win–win outcome. But it's a weakness because you may be easy to con. The trick is to build trust carefully in the negotiation, making sure the other party reciprocates. Don't put yourself at far greater risk than your opponent.

Be fair with others, but then keep after them until they're fair with you.

—Alan Alda

If you value trust and want to use a collaborative approach toward a conflict, then you need to signal this desire to the other party. Let them know you expect them to be trustworthy. Expectations can influence situations of all kinds. For example, if a teacher expects poor behavior from a student, it often occurs. If the teacher looks for good behavior, the student frequently lives up to the teacher's expectations. A bit simplistic, perhaps, but human behavior is an amazing blend of the simple and the complex.

What should you expect? Well, if you do your research carefully, you will have a good sense of the situation and know how trustworthy you can expect the other party to be. Whatever you expect will direct your moves. If you are distrustful (even for good reason), your behavior will probably be less than open. But trust can be built, based on observed behavior. And if you expect the relationship between you and the other party to continue into the future, then you will have to establish a degree of trust.

WHO'S IN CHARGE OF WHAT?

Another key variable is the *authority* or *power* you have as a party to decide on the actual outcome of the negotiation. Are there policies in place that will govern your actions, either protecting you or restricting you? Are there rules or regulations by which you must abide? In a corporation, are you negotiating at the request of someone higher up? Will you be able to resolve the disagreement yourself, or will others have the final say in the outcome? Such questions help you figure out who's in charge of what—and how these authorities might affect your negotiations.

"Higher-ups" and "others" who may affect negotiations are called *constituencies*. These individuals or groups may be physically present at the negotiations or not, but they maintain accountability over you and hold you responsible for the outcome you achieve. Whether a constituency is large, such as all the members of a labor union, or small, such as the members of your family, it exerts some kind of positive or negative influence on you as a bargainer.

In some cases, negotiators simply have to take into account the position and concerns of the constituency. In others, the constituency has the final say in the negotiations. For example, in union labor negotiations, the agreement has to be voted on by the union membership (the union negotiator's constituency) and okayed by the board of directors of the corporation.

When a supervisor and an employee meet for a formal performance review, they generally do some negotiating. The final report reflects a give and take in which, on average (at least in U.S. companies), the employee talks as much as the supervisor. So a performance review is a negotiation. (Most people don't realize that, and so fail to prepare for it properly.) And in the performance review negotiation, there are important constituencies who don't sit at the table with the employee and supervisor. And most of these constituencies influence supervisors to overrate employee behavior—a widespread problem according to experts on the topic, but a boon to employees.[9]

 For instance, in most performance reviews the supervisor's boss will rate his or her performance in part based on how well his or her employees perform. Employees who see this constituency's role can use it as a lever to encourage supervisors to rate their performance in a highly favorable light.

KEY CONCEPT For planning purposes, it is necessary to know how much bargaining authority you will have and how supportive your constituency is likely to be. In some cases, everything you negotiate will have to be cleared and approved by some higher authority; in others, you may have carte blanche to find a resolution.

SHOULD YOUR STRATEGY BE FIRM OR FLEXIBLE?

If you want to remain flexible during negotiation, you might think that having a plan would be restrictive. You might be tempted, therefore, to go into a negotiation without a plan and just wing it. The problem is, you could be caught short by an unanticipated proposal or countermove by the other party. If you have not set goals and prioritized them for your side, it will be difficult to evaluate whether a new offer moves you closer to your intended outcome. If you have done your homework, you will have a good idea of what to fight for and what to let go.

The best approach is to build some flexibility into your plan by establishing goal packages and alternative scenarios.

Your flexibility will also be influenced by your constituencies, and by your own style. Although some people are comfortable to just let nature take its course, that might not work if you have a strong, directive constituency. A relaxed style may send signals to the other party that you are either poorly organized or a pushover. You could open yourself to aggressive tactics by the other party.

Flexibility implies a willingness to be open to the other party and to invest time in the proceedings. If you cannot spend time on analysis and planning, then the negotiations will proceed differently than they would with the application of time and effort. If you display flexibility and openness during negotiation, your willingness to share information may encourage the other side to do likewise. Both your appearance and your degree of flexibility can influence the situation.

WHAT DOES WHO YOU ARE HAVE TO DO WITH WHAT YOU MUST DO?

Some of your personal qualities and attitudes will be called into play during negotiations, so it is important to assess these traits ahead of time also. For example, how do you feel about *rules* and *fair play?* How concerned are you about your *reputation* and *image?*

Your standards, principles, and values will affect the proceedings. If your position is to take care of yourself first and foremost, then that will dictate the negotiation strategy you select and how you carry it out. If you value fairness, you may make a concession to be fair but not be happy about it. How you behave will also affect how the other party behaves.

You should also beware of displaying any stereotypes or biases. Prejudices of any sort can work against you if the other party sees these weaknesses and decides to take advantage of them.

Negotiation step	Check if done.
1. Define the issues.	_____
2. Assemble the issues and define the agenda.	_____
3. Analyze the other party.	_____
4. Define underlying interests—yours and theirs.	_____
5. Consult with others who have relevant input.	_____
6. Manage the goal-setting process—openings and targets.	_____
7. Identify your own limits—walkaways and alternatives.	_____
8. Develop supporting arguments and consider possible options for settlement.	_____

FIGURE 3.4 *Negotiation planning guide. (From Roy J. Lewicki, Alex Hiam, and Karen Olander,* Think Before You Speak, *[New York: John Wiley, 1996]. Copyright © 1996, Roy J. Lewicki, Alex Hiam, and Karen Olander. Reproduced by permission.)*

Characteristics such as persuasiveness and tenacity can affect the outcome of negotiations. Integrity and character may be hard for you to evaluate in yourself, but you probably have a good idea of your reputation. Rest assured that the other party will be checking on these aspects of your personality. The other party will be reticent to negotiate with you if you appear to be a deceitful person.

END POINT

We cannot stress enough the importance of assessing yourself as accurately and honestly as possible. The objective of this personal assessment is to plan an action for each possible action that can occur during negotiations. With a firm plan formulated before the negotiations begin, you will be prepared for most eventualities.

Although it is tempting to just go ahead with negotiations, beware! An early start could be harmful to your case.

The next chapter will show you how to gain valuable insights into the other party.

Step-by-Step Analysis

It can be helpful to put the information surfaced by a self-analysis into a structured analytical framework. We recommend the following method for complex or high-impact negotiations. Allow plenty of time for this process. (see Figure 3.4.)

As you go through the analysis steps, be sure you thoroughly understand your strengths and weaknesses at each stage. This will help you make convincing arguments for yourself or against the other party.

Step 1: *Define the issues.*   Analyze the conflict situation from your own point of view. Look at the issues, and decide which are major issues for you and which are minor. Experience can be helpful. Take into consideration the research you have done, including your history in negotiation. Based on the issues, make a list of experts in the field who may be able to contribute advice, information, or expertise.

Step 2: *Assemble the issues and define the agenda.*   List all the issues in the order of their importance. This should be relatively easy because of the work you did earlier on prioritizing goals. You may find that some of the issues are interconnected and therefore have to be kept together.

Step 3: *Analyze the other party.*   Although it may be difficult to obtain information on the other party, researching the other side is vital to planning a good strategy. At this stage in your analysis, you should start to think about your relationship with the other party, for this will affect all your ensuing moves as you design your negotiating plan. In particular, your history with the other party and the degree of interdependence between the parties will affect your interactions. All the research you have done thus far will influence how you work with (or against) the other party.

Step 4: *Define underlying interests.*   To define the interests and needs that underlie the issues you specified, remember the question "Why." *Why* do you want this item or goal? Why is it important to you? When you investigate the other party's goals in the next chapter, you will again use the *why* questions to get at the underlying reasons for the other party's preferences. This will help you understand where they are coming from and will enable you to find common interests and differences.

Step 5: *Consult with others.*   Unless this is a very simple negotiation, other people will probably be involved. For example, if you are negotiating a bank loan, the loan officer probably has to clear it with higher-ups. Or perhaps you are buying a car to use primarily to drive to work. If your spouse will be driving it occasionally, you will probably need input on the choice of car.

You will also consult with the other party, perhaps on issues, or even on how you will negotiate. Talks with other parties can be amicable or hostile, depending on the situation. Nevertheless, any parties to the negotiation should be brought into the proceedings as early in your analysis and planning as possible so you can begin to see the whole picture.

(Continued)

Step 6: *Set goals for the process and outcome.* Be sure you have a clear picture of your preferred schedule, site (location), time frame, who will be involved, and what will happen if negotiations fail. You will need to take into account the other parties' preferences that surface in your consulting with them. Be sure you know which items are important enough to fight for and which to be flexible about. Such prenegotiation talks will tend to set the tone for the bargaining session itself.

Step 7: *Identify your own limits.* It is very important to know your own limits. These will arise from having a clear picture of your goals and their priorities, your bargaining range points, and your alternatives or BATNAs. If you know your limits you will be able to adjust your plan as necessary. For example, if an item is rejected by the other side during bargaining, you will more readily be able to reevaluate it and decide what your next move should be.

Be sure your limits are realistic. It is fine to have an absolute minimum or maximum acceptable point, but consider having a range for flexibility. The priority ratings you gave to your issues when you were defining them will also help you set limits. You want to do better with the more important issues and be more flexible on the less important issues. You will be in an even better position for negotiating if you have anticipated possible packages that might be offered by the other party, and assigned them values on a scale similar to the rating scale you used for your own packages. They will help you make comparisons.

Step 8: *Develop supporting arguments.* Once you know your goals and preferences, think about how best to provide supporting arguments for those goals. You need facts to validate your arguments. You will have accumulated many of these during your research. Methods for presenting facts include visuals, such as charts, graphs, and other visual aids; people, such as experts; and records or files, especially from respected sources. Other similar negotiations can provide clues for how to proceed.

Use them regularly to help your negotiation planning. In the next chapter, when you look into the other party's views and interests, you may be able to find a common basis for negotiation as a result of understanding their position.

4

The Other Players

Few sports are played alone, and few negotiations take place without other players.

What? You didn't think *any* negotiations took place without other players? Well, have you ever tried to lose weight, quit smoking, or initiate an exercise program? If so, you've negotiated with yourself, attempting to balance conflicting goals and desires in order to change your own behavior. And, if you are like most people, you've lost those negotiations with yourself more often than not. Negotiating with yourself is like attempting to perfect the skills of archery. There's just you and the target. Nobody else matters. But still, it's fiendishly hard to do it perfectly.

So don't ever discount your own importance in a negotiation. As we hope you learned in the first few chapters, you compete first with *yourself.* Even where there are dozens of others involved, your own clarity of thought and emotion is a necessary prelude to effective negotiation with others.

 Once you are clear with yourself about what you want and how you feel, you are ready to handle an opponent or cooperate with a teammate. You are truly ready to turn your attention to the other players in the negotiation game.

Sometimes negotiation is like a sword fight, in which each of your opponent's thrusts must be met with a parry until you find a weakness and can drive your own point home for the kill.

Other times it can be a less brutal competition, like a tennis match in which each point is hotly contested but both players can reasonably expect to walk away from the court with their health and dignity intact.

Still other times, negotiation is a cooperative endeavor, as when a crew of sailors struggles together to make their craft beat a speed record for a transoceanic crossing.

In all these games, however, your understanding of the other party is key. You need to "get into their head" and be able to anticipate their moves and desires. Don't assume they will be honest with you—or even with themselves!

STEPPING OUTSIDE YOURSELF

To achieve the requisite insight into the other players, you must first achieve a certain personal objectivity. You need to look at them openly and honestly, without letting your vision be colored by your own desires and fears. Otherwise you will fail to gain any real insight into the other players.

Some negotiators achieve this state of objectivity toward their opponents or teammates by thinking of themselves as teachers, working constructively to help the other players achieve success. Others do it by telling themselves that they are students, and this negotiation is but one of many life lessons—something to be experienced fully but without fear of failure because there will always be another opportunity to apply what is learned in future negotiations.

WHAT *DO* THEY WANT?

While it can be difficult to diagnose your own needs and position, understanding someone else's position is far harder.

Many negotiators assume it is just too difficult to figure out what the other players want, and do not even bother. Their strategy is simply to take care of their own needs, and let the other players take care of theirs. This is a mistake! While appealing at first glance, in practice it is likely to produce undesirable results ranging from suboptimal outcomes to failure to agree or, worse, to conflict escalation. A look at a real-world negotiation situation helps clarify the importance of understanding the needs and positions of other parties to the negotiation.

MAKE OPPORTUNITIES TO STUDY OTHER PLAYERS

During negotiations, you will have many opportunities to learn about the other party and you should seek out

To See Your Opponent Clearly, You Must Be without Fear

Burke Franklin named his successful software company JIAN, from a traditional Japanese term for Zen masters, and his advice on how to handle competitors is certainly in the Zen tradition—a perspective he appreciates since he devotes many hours a week to face-to-face combat as a black belt in Tae Kwon Do. Here is his advice on how to handle competitors:

Compete without fear. When you have the wisdom to do business without fear, you also have much more time to think because your mind is not locked by fear. Why fear your competitors? Instead, use them for training, focus, and motivation. Why try to beat up your competitors? Just have the strength not to get beaten up by them.

—Burke Franklin[1]

and use these opportunities. "Face time" with the other party is particularly important. So is the opportunity to debrief someone who has negotiated with this party before. Or the chance to do some background research to find out more about the other party's position and needs.

If you can manage to "take a long walk" with them, so much the better. But you do not have to be friends to learn what you need to know about the other party's position. You should be able to find plenty of ways to expose yourself to the key players and to research their backgrounds before you negotiate.

Imagine you are preparing for a tough tennis match with someone you've never played before. Rather than simply walk onto the court, you'd want to find out how they've played in the past, who they've beaten, and who's beaten them. You'd also seek opportunities to watch them play, and even to warm up or practice with them. And you would certainly treasure any tips or insights others could give you, like "Stay away from her backhand." The same is true for negotiation.

TO UNDERSTAND OPPONENTS, THINK AND FEEL AS THEY DO

Knowledge of the other party's concerns and issues will come from both what is said and what is *not* said. If

Tom Stoner started Highland Energy Group to help organizations convert to energy-efficient technology. But the work required large investments in technology and staff, and Stoner had to raise venture capital to get the business off the ground. That meant negotiating with any potential investors who would give him an audience.

In any negotiation, and especially in negotiations over future plans, the other party's position can offer the key to a successful strategy. Tom Stoner's experience reflects this principle. He recognized that the systems he wanted the firm to bring to market were untested. Large-scale conversions to newer, more energy-efficient technologies were not in the mainstream. Most investors knew little about the technology, and his firm had no track record to convince investors that the technology would work. He knew his own position and needs; that was the easy part. But the fund-raising task required him to understand the motivations of investors.

Stoner recalls the result of his analysis of potential investors: "I needed to create the belief [in the investor] that these systems would work." But how? Most investors were too busy and skeptical to take the time needed to learn about the technologies. So Stoner targeted HFG Expansion Fund, a venture capital firm founded by Tim Joukowsky, an old friend from college who was willing to learn about the idea. Stoner recalls, "Tim and I went for nice long walks. You can learn a lot about another party's position by going for a long walk with him—and he can learn a lot about your company's technology and plans." (Recall the famous "walk in the woods" that President Jimmy Carter took with President Anwar Sadat of Egypt and Menachem Begin of Israel, resulting in the Camp David accords.)[2]

The plans made sense to Joukowsky, but he still had reservations about Stoner's ability to carry them out because of their highly technical nature. Knowing this, Stoner agreed to bring in a technically oriented business partner, and finally HFG was ready to invest. After more than a million dollars in venture capital, followed by a private offering for second-round financing, the company finally won its first major bid in 1993 and is now one of the major contractors to utilities in its industry.[3]

This success story would not have been possible without Stoner's commitment to understanding the needs of the other party in his early planning negotiations, because—as Stoner realized—the *other party* is the key to your success.

you are a good reader of body language, for instance, you may learn a lot just by watching the other party.

Anxiety is easily betrayed by defensive postures, for example. Crossing legs or arms, turning to sit diagonally to you, putting distance or furniture between you, avoiding direct eye contact—all are signs that a player is anxious in the situation.

How you use this insight depends upon your goals, but you certainly should use it. If you are competing hard, you might want to push hard now in the hope that this anxiety will lead to a mistake. If you are trying to build cooperation, you would instead attempt to make this player feel more secure. But however you choose to use your insight, it will prove key to your success.

Your skill at reading nonverbal cues is remarkably important during negotiations, and you should take every opportunity to *practice* it. An easy way is to work on your empathy (your emotional understanding of others' feelings) in your daily relationships.

Want to know how to practice reading nonverbal cues? Here's one simple way. Try asking a spouse, friend, child or associate if you understand their feelings at a particular moment when you think you've picked up a good nonverbal cue. Were you right? See how many times in a day you can "diagnose" their feelings. Research indicates that emotional intelligence skills like empathy can be improved at any stage of life, so it is a realistic goal to practice and improve your ability to read others' feelings.

DANGER! PLAN THE OTHER PARTY'S NEGOTIATION

While essential, it is not enough to find out about the other party as you go along. You need to anticipate their needs and reactions and adopt a strategy based on them.

That's one reason why you need to create an effective plan for any negotiation. The other reason, of course, is that you have some needs and feelings that must be accounted for.

But planning a negotiation based only on your own needs *won't work*. You need to plan it from the other player's perspective, or else they won't go along with the plan.

To do so—to plan a negotiation game the other party will want to play—you need to do some up-front research and thinking about the other party's long-term needs. The more you know about them ahead of time the better.

Daniel Goleman on Empathy

Goleman, a psychologist and author of the best-seller *Emotional Intelligence*, provides the following insights of aid to negotiators:

Just as the mode of the rational mind is words, the mode of the emotions is nonverbal. Indeed, when a person's words disagree with what is conveyed via his tone of voice, gesture, or other nonverbal channel, the emotional truth is in how he says something rather than in what he says.

and

Empathy requires enough calm and receptivity so that the subtle signals of feeling from another person can be received and mimicked by one's own emotional brain.[4]

    Try to apply these insights in your next conflict-oriented interaction and see if you can tune into the emotional message behind the other party's words.

That doesn't mean you can learn everything the first time through—planning is an ongoing activity, and as you learn things about the other party—their interests, preferences, primary concerns, areas where they are committed or flexible, and so on—you will want to revise your plans accordingly.

SPY VERSUS SPY?

Remember that while you are researching the other party, they may be checking up on you. Giving and obtaining information can be a somewhat delicate matter, especially if you feel that you need to guard some details, such as weaknesses, for fear that they might be used against you. This behavior is typical in the competitive negotiation process, which is discussed in depth in Chapter 7. In contrast, in the more open communications that characterize collaborative negotiations, both parties share information openly and extensively: The objective is to find a common ground and a solution that will satisfy both parties. The Collaborative strategy is the subject of Chapter 8.

DO SOME RESEARCH

Before you begin your detailed research on the other party, think once again about your relationship with them. How important is it? Your relationship (or lack of one) will direct the process of data collection and influence your choice of negotiating strategy.

DANGER! We need to repeat again the importance of research before you enter a negotiation. Do not skip this step! While it may seem much harder to get information on the other party than it was to figure out your own position, it is (at least) equally important. The better idea you have of what to expect, the better prepared you will be, and the more successful you can be. As stressed earlier, you need to know not just the information but the *why* behind it.

What if you cannot find any hard facts in time? It happens. If you are unable to obtain material beforehand, do not worry. Here are two *substitutes* for formal research:

- First, decide whether you can make any reasonable *inferences* or *assumptions* about the other side. For example, if you are buying a used computer, you can assume that the seller will start with the price that was advertised or posted on the computer.

- Second, you can pick up details as you go along (are you practicing your empathy skills?). And even if you have perfect information on the other party to begin with, you will probably see changes and adjustments as negotiations progress. This is the result of interaction between two parties and the growth of a relationship, whether positive or negative.

WHAT TO RESEARCH

You will need to conduct research about other players in the following areas:

- Their objectives
- Their interests and needs
- Their alternatives
- Their resources
- Their reputation, negotiation style, and behavior
- Their authority to make an agreement
- Their likely strategy and tactics

Let's look at each of these separately in the following discussion and set of worksheet questions.

Their Objectives

Questions to ask yourself:

- What does the other player want to get out of this negotiation game?
- Are there definite outcomes they must achieve?
- Are there definite relationship goals they want to achieve?

It is easy to make assumptions about the other party's objectives. Although they may be true, be careful not to jump to conclusions. For example, if you are considering buying a used guitar, you may believe that the seller is trying to get as high a price as possible. That may be true, but aim to learn specific information rather than relying on guesswork. Perhaps the seller has to sell it, but would rather do business with someone who will take good care of the guitar. Perhaps the seller is in a hurry and just wants to sell it fast.

If you discuss the negotiation with the other party, you may discover their objectives in what they say, or emphasize, or do not say. Or, perhaps, at this early stage, the other party may not have carefully formulated objectives. And if they reveal several objectives, you may not know which ones are more important. Once negotiations begin and progress, you will be able to formulate a general idea of the other party's objectives, and you may be able to infer by the type and size of their concessions what appears to be more (or less) important to them.

Likewise, you may not be able to ascertain the other party's bargaining range before you begin negotiations, but once you get underway, their starting point will become clear. If you hit their walkaway point, you will know it from their words and actions.

TiP Some commodities are so widely exchanged that you will be able to find informative books and articles about them. For example, numerous books on purchasing an automobile present negotiating advice as well as a great deal of information about dealer costs, the price of options, and so on. Similar information is available about houses, antiques, and artwork. If you want a basic idea of what to expect before starting your negotiations, read about commonly accepted ranges in similar transactions. You can consult with experts in this area, or ask other negotiators about their experiences. Bear in mind that each negotiation is different because of the different people involved and the different array of goals and concerns.

Indirect methods of obtaining information include observing the other party, looking through documents and publications, and asking sources who know the other party. The direct method is to ask the other party, but you may not receive an accurate response because they may wish to keep you in the dark. They may limit what they say, so you will not know whether you have a full picture of the situation. However, even partial information and some good guesses are enough to give you an advantage in most negotiations.

Their Interests and Needs

Questions to ask yourself:

- Why does the player care about his/her outcome and relationship goals?
- What underlying interests does this player have?

We considered *your* underlying interests and needs in the previous chapter. The *other party's* interests and needs are no less important. In fact, if you expect to find a common ground with the other party and to create a collaborative solution, then you *must* know the underlying factors of the other party's position. Without knowing their needs, you might assess the situation as being competitive when in fact there may be some common ground that can serve as a basis for finding a good collaborative solution, for example.

If you can, ask the other party the *why* question: Why are these objectives important to you? And related questions: How did you come to this position? What if you cannot accomplish your goals? Have your needs changed since our previous discussion?

Tactic #3: Probe for Insight

Ask value-free, informational questions to find out what the other party's underlying needs are. Avoid judgmental styles of questioning—even though your first instinct is to use them. How you *word* these questions will help or hinder you in obtaining responses. For example, if you say, "How did you ever think you could get *that* objective?" you will simply put the other party on the defensive. But if you say, "I'm not sure I understand why that objective is so important to you. Can you explain your concerns?" you are far more likely to obtain useful information about the other party's underlying concerns.

DANGER! And remember, keep your mind free of antagonism and judgment since your tone of voice and body language will "leak" any negative feelings and contaminate even the most politely worded question!

Be sure to ask probing questions (see Tactic #3) in order to explore the other party's underlying interests. And after you ask a question, listen carefully to the answer. For one thing, you will be gaining information. For another, you will be indicating to the other party that you are truly interested in hearing what they have to say. This will certainly open them up to your future questions, and it may encourage them to listen to your needs.

Try to find out the other party's walkaway point. This is usually difficult, but it can give you a sharper sense of the other party's bargaining range and how well it meshes with yours. One way to do this is to ask directly, although you will probably get an ambiguous answer.

But again, remember that the *real* message may be revealed in the nonverbal component of the answer. If you ask, "Honestly, tell me, would you ever be at all open to a major reduction in price, like, say, twenty-five percent off your asking price?" the other party will probably say no. But do they really *mean* no? If they seem to be controlling anger, outrage or disappointment, perhaps they do. But if they seem emotionally cool, they may be giving you an accidental yes.

Their Alternatives

Questions to ask yourself:

- What alternatives do they have?
- How appealing is the best of their alternatives compared to working with you?

You need to know whether the other party has any alternatives and, if so, how strong or weak they are. If the other party has a strong alternative, they do not have to continue bargaining with you. If they have a weak alternative, then you may be in a better bargaining position. If the other party is unwilling to share information, it may be difficult to find out such details before you begin negotiations. But don't be afraid to ask. Again, you may learn something from *how* they answer, even if they don't tell you exactly what you want. And continue to explore their alternatives during negotiations. You will probably learn more over time.

Their Resources

Questions to ask yourself:

- Are they expert negotiators?
- Do they have more time, money, power or other resources than you do?

Knowing about the other party's business and background will assist you in gauging what to expect in negotiation. Therefore, you need to research the other party's business history, previous negotiations, and financial data, as appropriate. You can make phone calls or site visits, assuming that it is not a hostile relationship. If it is, then you may prefer to use less direct methods of fact finding. Public companies will be listed in stock reports, reported on in the media, and described in legal documents.

You may want to investigate any past negotiations by the other party.[5] Historical information about negotiation successes and failures with this party will help you assess your own chances of success. History gives you some indication of the resources they can bring to bear in any negotiation.

You will want to learn as much as you can about the bargaining skills and experience of the other. The more experience they have, the stronger their position. (But you can counter this strength by boning up on your own negotiation skills, so read on.)

Their Reputation, Negotiation Style, and Behavior

Questions to ask yourself:

- What does the rumor mill say about this player?
- What style do they usually take in conflict situations?
- Is there anything unusual or distinctive about their interpersonal behavior?
- How trustworthy is this player?

Although historical information about the other party's successes and failures in negotiation may be informative, you cannot be sure people will behave as they have in the past. However, this information, in combination with their preferred type of negotiation, may give you a good picture of what may occur. For example, if they have a reputation as hard bargainers, then you may expect a difficult competitive negotiation.

As previously mentioned, beliefs and expectations affect how we go into negotiation. Thus, if you believe that there can be only one winner, you will behave accordingly during negotiation. Likewise, if the other party holds a particular belief about how negotiation should work, then this will affect both their behavior and the outcome.

 Perhaps the most important assessment of the other party is their trustworthiness. Can you trust them? How *far* can you trust them? (Should you even negotiate with them in the first place? Not unless you can count on at least a minimum level of trustworthiness.)

If I trust you to be open and honest, and you are, we have one sort of communication. If I trust you and you are *not* open and honest, then I will adjust how I respond to you, and our communication will change. Open, trusting relationships cannot be built with players who are suspicious and tricky in their attitudes and behavior. Trust is a necessary foundation for cooperative negotiations. In fact, a certain level of trustworthiness is necessary even to compete, as you have to trust the other party to play *by the rules,*—for example, by not going back on concessions. So make sure you have a *realistic* view of the level of trustworthiness of the other party.

Their Authority to Make an Agreement

Questions to ask yourself:

- Am I negotiating with the right decision maker?
- Are there other players who will be part of this negotiation game at some point?
- Are there other parties who have strong underlying interests in the outcome of this negotiation?
- If so, to what extent can they constrain this player's negotiations?

You need to know whether the other party will be working alone, or with others, and whether a constituency will influence their agreement-making capability. Further, do they have the authority to make agreements or are they limited by other parties, or by company rules and regulations?

An opponent with limited decision-making authority can often turn this against you. For example, they might use limited authority to advantage by saying, "It is out of my hands" (when it may or may not be). So it's best to clarify who makes the ultimate decision—and get them involved up front before you waste time on a senseless negotiation.

Sometimes it seems that you are working with the right person, until they become stuck on a concession point they haven't the authority to concede. Then you must give up on that desired concession, or else backtrack and try to involve other parties. For instance, if you are negotiating with an entrepreneur who values his wife's opinions highly, you may suddenly find that negotiations have ground to a halt because the wife disapproves of the direction they are taking. Because you failed to recognize that she has a strong influence on her husband's final decision, and didn't consider her bottom-line requirements, the deal is bound to fail.

TiP When we negotiate with executives of privately owned businesses, we always ask them point-blank if they have spouses or other family members whose concerns we should know about, too. Often the answer is yes, and then we ask for a casual preliminary chat with the spouse, brother, or other stakeholder in order to find out what their perspective is.

Their Likely Strategy and Tactics

Questions to ask yourself:

- What are their favorite negotiating tactics?

- Do they have a reputation for any particular tactic or ploy?

Different people have different responses to conflict, as seen in Chapter 1. You need to anticipate the other party's likely response and think about their preferred negotiating style in order to anticipate how they will behave. Try to estimate and characterize in general how the negotiations will go, and prepare for the other party's behavior.

On the one hand, the other party may be conciliatory and open to accommodations and flexible solutions, suggesting that they prefer to collaborate. On the other hand, the other party may be hard-nosed and appear to be ready to fight you tooth and nail, suggesting that a competitive style is most likely.

And there are a number of other possibilities between these two extremes. Some parties prefer the simplistic rules of a compromise, others are so averse to conflict that they generally try to withdraw during the process, and so on. As you do your research, you

Oops! Lost My Cool

If you don't anticipate and prepare for an angry opponent, you can easily be drawn into playing his or her game instead of your own. Listen to this exchange between Nixon and Khrushchev in 1959. Nixon initiates it by trying to explain that the United States and the USSR shouldn't get engaged in angry threats and ultimatums. But Khrushchev's immediately angry response throws Nixon off balance and soon they have exchanged threats—precisely what Nixon meant to avoid![6]

NIXON: The moment we place either one of these powerful nations, through an ultimatum, in a position where it has no choice but to accept dictation or fight, then you are playing with the most destructive force in the world.

KHRUSHCHEV (flushed, wagging a finger near Nixon's face): We too are giants. If you want to threaten, we will answer threat with threat.

NIXON: We never engage in threats.

KHRUSHCHEV: You wanted indirectly to threaten me. But we have means at our disposal that can have very bad consequences.

NIXON: We have too.

---

will develop a good picture of how the other party is likely to operate. This will not only help you select an appropriate negotiating style, it will also prepare you to deal with their style.

For instance, if they are prone to angry outbursts, you can prepare yourself to ignore the outbursts, or even to use them to your benefit by insisting on a concession in exchange for overlooking their rude behavior.

One to Wish For: Foreknowledge of Their Concessions

It can be useful to know what points the other party might be willing to concede during negotiations, but this is fairly difficult to find out beforehand. You probably will *not* know until the concessions actually occur. However, once there is a concession, you can make some educated guesses about whether there may be others and their probable magnitude. You will be able to base your expectations on the behavior and interplay you have seen demonstrated thus far in the negotiations.

A few words on concessions: Each side will most likely make at least one concession. Once one party makes a concession, it is more or less expected—negotiation protocol, if you will—that the other side will follow suit. If they don't, you can usually count on one of two explanations: They want to achieve 100 percent of what they are asking for (their opening bid and walkaway point are identical), or they are very competitive and are trying to force you to make more concessions before they give anything.

KEY CONCEPT — TRY ON THEIR SHOES

At this point, if the relationship between the parties is important (and even if it is not), you may want to try to get into the other person's shoes by using role reversal. This can help you understand the other person's motivations and needs.

Role reversal involves taking the side of the other person and arguing for that side. Although you can do this mentally and informally, it is more effective to actually do it with a friend or colleague when you are preparing for a communication. The method is to first develop your own point, then to look at the possible counterarguments and develop responses to them—somewhat like walking in the other person's shoes for a while.[7]

Role reversal is a great skill to have when you must focus on someone else's problem, and help them out. Thus, a customer service representative would see what it is like to be a customer frustrated with a product, or a laborer could get a feel for the kinds of decisions management must make. Patients often criticize a doctor for having a bad bedside manner, meaning that the physician fails to listen and really understand how the patient is feeling.

TIP You can use role reversal to psyche out an opponent by acting out a make-believe negotiation in which you pretend to be them. You can also play yourself, of course, but it can be fun to enlist a friend or associate to play you.

Actively arguing the other person's position as though you really believed it can be very helpful in the following ways:[8]

- It can help you understand the other party's position.
- It can help you see similarities between the two positions.
- It can improve outcomes if the two points of view are basically compatible. However, it is usually less successful when the points of view are fundamentally incompatible.
- It can reduce distortions in communication.

Role-playing exercises based on role reversal are a great active research technique for preparing to negotiate. And if you've done your homework on the other players, it should be easy to step into their shoes.

END POINT

Understanding the other party is vital to planning a good strategy. By thinking about the other players and doing some homework, you can anticipate what they want and how they will go about trying to get it. Your up-front research and your ability to apply emotional intelligence in order to gain real-time insights will add up to that most precious of negotiating skills—the ability to plan and manage *the other party's negotiation*.

The next chapter will move on to the third and last aspect of your preparation, the negotiating context or situation. It's the playing field upon which you and the other party will engage. And the good news is, you can *design* this playing field to a large degree.

Sizing Up the Field

We have compared negotiation to playing a game. But unlike other games, the negotiation game can be defined by the players. You can start out with a round of boxing, decide you don't like it, go on to racquetball, decide you don't like that either, and, finally, switch to chess. Or you can make up your own game as you go along.

And negotiation offers an even greater advantage over other games. You can, if you so choose, design the playing field, court, ring, board or whatever arena you wish to compete within.

Granted, most negotiations come with a context. But you don't have to live within that context if you don't like it. You can make many small changes to it. Or you may even be able to exchange it for a new one.

Most negotiators fail to take advantage of their potential power over the playing field. They tend to take it for granted—because, after all, the playing field must be accepted in most games. But not in negotiation.

In negotiation, you can learn to *redesign the context* to put yourself in a more favorable position. Your strength in the negotiation is relative to the other players, within the context of the playing field. That means you can increase your relative strength by tilting the playing field your way. Or not. It's up to you. If you choose to become a student of context, you will soon become an architect of your own negotiations.

The Importance of Position

Each advantage, no matter how small, is important because a few small advantages added together can mean a winning position.

—Chess Master Bruce Pandolfini[1]

I'm living on a one-way dead-end street. I don't know how I got there.

—Comedian Steven Wright

This chapter will show you how to take advantage of the many contextual factors that affect the negotiation process. These fall into two broad categories—situations and relationships (see Figure 5.1).

Situational elements, such as deadlines, constituencies, options, and rules and regulations are important to understand because they frequently affect which side has more power in the strategic negotiation process. As you look at these various factors, try to assess whether they are positive or negative for your party—and alter them in your favor whenever possible. Following the discussion of situational elements, we will examine the *relationship* between the parties and its impact on your negotiations. Again, you should read this with an eye to how you can use relationship factors to increase your strength.

RECOGNIZING POWER FACTORS IN THE SITUATION

Situational factors have subtle but important impact on negotiations. They are often called *power factors* be-

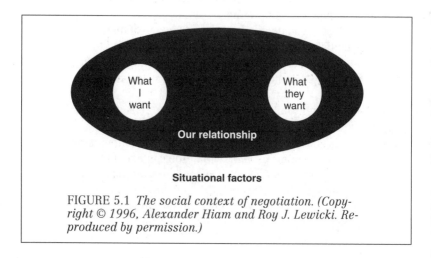

FIGURE 5.1 *The social context of negotiation. (Copyright © 1996, Alexander Hiam and Roy J. Lewicki. Reproduced by permission.)*

cause using them in a particular way can contribute a distinct advantage to a party's negotiating position.[2] In contrast, if situational factors are effectively balanced, both parties can employ their negotiation power to assure a mutually effective agreement. Power gives you leverage over *both* the outcome and the relationship.

In competitive situations, then, you want to use power factors to your advantage by creating pressure on the other player or players. And in cooperative situations, you want to use power factors to help align your interests with the other players by balancing the power as fairly as you feel is practical.

HARNESSING THE POWER OF INFORMATION

The key source of power in negotiation is information. Your planning is based on the information that you have, or can obtain from various sources. Once you know your own objectives, you need information to support and buttress them. Once you know the other party's objectives and the underlying factors for their point of view, you will need information to refute their position or to support it. Much of negotiation is simply an exchange of information, and using information to convince the other party that you have a better, stronger, or more valid case.

When negotiation begins, you will make an opening offer, with a limit in mind. You will have set the opening, target, and walkaway points based on such information as the going market rate, the time frame, the other party's range, possible concessions, and generally accepted standards for a particular negotiation, all of which you will have assembled and determined beforehand.

To be prepared with a good plan, you need good information. Having a good plan will move you toward a positive outcome.

Since we have discussed at length the information you need to collect for your side and for your assessment of the other party, we now turn to some of the more general aspects of information and how they can provide power in negotiation.

Accuracy. You will base your negotiation requests on the information you gather, so it must be as accurate as possible. The more accurate the information, the greater the power it gives you. If it is not accurate, you can lose face with the other party. There is nothing more embarrassing than trying to build a strong and compelling case, only to have the other side correct you and tell you that your facts are wrong.

Unfortunately, you may not be able to get accurate information from the other party, especially if they are trying to maintain power by withholding or altering data. As a negotiator, you also have to decide whether you want to do the same thing—whether you want to conceal information from the other party to give yourself an information advantage.

Expertise.   Being able to assemble the facts into a coherent, coordinated presentation can help your image of being skilled in the area. One way to emphasize your pertinent skills and abilities is to offer information that only an expert would know. Likewise, you can refer to people who can vouch for your expertise. If the negotiation takes place in your office, the presence of diplomas, certificates, and other validating materials and credentials can add to your image of expertise. As mentioned earlier, you can balance lack of knowledge to some extent by engaging the services of an expert to assist you.

In addition, expertise in negotiation itself is extremely helpful. The more experienced you are in negotiation, the more power you wield.

Communication skills.   In addition to the quality and accuracy of information, how that information is communicated can also contribute to your power. For example, how you structure the message to the other party affects their response. It can put you at an advantage or a disadvantage. It can support your position, or it can undermine the other party's position. It can make them feel more or less confident in the information they have already assembled. Similarly, your style of presentation can affect the other party's response. Personal characteristics, which are treated later in this chapter, can assist you in getting your message across. Even your body language may help you appear credible and trustworthy.

Resources.   You can obtain power through a variety of nonhuman resources, especially if these are scarce. (If I have all the oil, or own all the real estate in a key neighborhood, then I am in a powerful position.) Supplies and equipment can provide power. Money, in all its varieties (insurance, stocks and bonds, and benefits, to name a few) is a powerful tool. Time, which is treated separately later in this chapter, can also be a powerful tool in negotiation.

Even control over the agenda is a valuable resource—sometimes, in fact, far more valuable than hard assets. Agendas can be used to control the information on the table, to alter the focus and pacing of the negotiations, and to manipulate many other power factors as well. As a result, expert negotiators often spar over who will control the agenda.

CASE IN POINT: SOUTH KOREA AND THE IMF STRUGGLE OVER AN AGENDA

The context: November 1997 negotiations between the International Monetary Fund and South Korean government officials concerning the IMF's terms for bailout loans to turn the Korean economy around.

The players: Lim Chang Yuel, Finance Minister, South Korea, and Michael Camdessus, Director, IMF

The issue: Control over the agenda

The gambit: "As Mr. Camdessus headed down a walkway at the Seoul airport, accompanied by Mr. Lim's deputy, he was handed a schedule: a quick press conference, followed by 45 minutes of negotiations, followed by a visit with the president, followed by a signing ceremony."

The response: "Startled by its brevity, Mr. Camdessus promptly canceled some of these meetings—sending markets tumbling on news of 'failed' talks—and insisted that the sheltered economy accept more foreign investment. 'Unless you agree with all the items I have on my piece of paper,' Mr. Camdessus says he informed Mr. Lim, 'there won't be a bailout.'"

—Quotes from the *Wall Street Journal*[3]

In summary, a negotiator can gain power if he or she has more information than the other, has more accurate or unique information, has greater expertise, has better and more persuasive communication skills to present this information, or can control the flow of information in the negotiation agenda. In contrast, if both parties possess this information or have these skills, then the power of information will be balanced between the parties.

HARNESSING THE POWER OF CONSTITUENCIES

In a simple two-party negotiation, as when you and a friend are deciding which movie to see, there are no other parties to influence your decision. The two of you discuss your preferences, come to an agreement, and go to the movies. But in most negotiations, there *are* multiple parties. Behind you as a negotiator, there may be a department or a management group, a spouse or family members, or some other group that has goals and objectives of importance to you.

 These constituencies are an important source of power. Most obviously, if you can bring players who support you into the negotiation game, they lend their power to your position.

When you or the other party have constituencies, you need to recognize their interests, too. They will play a role in the negotiations, but what exactly that role is depends upon their interests and also partly on how you handle them. Understanding the role of constituencies helps you master the art of using them to your advantage.

Taking Sides
A friend is a man who has the same enemies you have.

—Stephen Leacock

Constituencies serve two major roles. First, a constituency helps to define the objectives of the group. Even if you are the sole negotiator for the group, if you have a constituency, then the chances are that the constituency has had some input in shaping your objectives. Second, a constituency evaluates your work. How influential or powerful the constituency is can affect how well you are able to negotiate. The evaluation by the constituency will affect your reputation as a negotiator, both now and in the future. As a result, negotiators with a strong constituency must negotiate in a way that pleases that group of people and keeps them happy; if they are not happy, then they can embarrass you in negotiations, or may even dismiss you from your negotiating responsibilities.

DANGER! If the constituency is powerful, yet removed from the negotiation process, they may expect extravagant results from you as the negotiator without fully understanding the situation. In fact, that is frequently the experience of negotiators with powerful constituencies. Because these groups are out of touch with what can actually be accomplished, they tend to form unrealistic expectations. Then, instead of giving you powerful support, your constituency questions and weakens you. To minimize this problem you need to *educate* your constituency about the difficulties of negotiation and exactly what the possible outcomes are. Take the initiative with your constituencies by giving them plenty of information about the negotiation. It's a good preventative.

A powerful constituency can be a positive or a negative. It can be limiting to the negotiator to have to go back to the constituency for permission to make an agreement or a concession. On the other hand, insisting on a review process by the constituency is a way to the gain additional control over the situation. You can always say to the other party, "I'd like to give you that, but I can't make a decision right now. I have to talk to my superiors."

TiP Or you can say, "I think your offer is reasonable, and I appreciate your willingness to negotiate. If it were me, you know I'd accept. But I continue to have trouble getting ____ to go along. In fact, I doubt they'd still be bargaining if it weren't for me. So I'm going to need another week to discuss this with them and see what I can get them to do." That approach generally wins you the space to demand an additional concession, so it is a very powerful tactic. And note how it uses the constituency as an excuse for dragging out the negotiation, too—which puts the power of time on your side.

In an ideal relationship, a constituency is supportive of the negotiator's work and worth, and will back the negotiator on whatever needs to happen. Yet it is often useful to convey to the opponent that you do not completely have this control; in this way, you can use the constituency as an excuse to not give in on the other party's concerns. For example, you and your spouse may have talked about the car you want to buy and the price you are willing to pay before you went to the dealership. But if the dealer presses you to complete a deal you are unhappy about, you can always say, "I have to talk to my spouse first before I can make an agreement."

 Clever competitive negotiators try to achieve complete agreement with their constituencies, but nonetheless *portray* their relationships as difficult. This tactical deception, like many in competitive negotiating, is widely accepted in most societies. If you don't like playing deceptive games, then you need to use what power you can muster to steer the negotiation toward a collaborative style instead of a competitive one.

USING TIME WISELY

He who hesitates is sometimes saved.

—James Thurber

Half the agony of living is waiting.

—Alexander Rose

Time is a powerful thing in the game of negotiation. Imagine if you were playing a tough basketball game, your team was down by 4 points with 20 seconds remaining—and you had the power to add 2 more minutes to the clock! Well, you can't do it in basketball, but you often can in negotiations.

 You can use time by either *rushing the pace* or *slowing it down.* Which will help you? It depends upon the situation, but invariably one or the other *will* help you. Let's look at the various ways that time affects the game of negotiation so that you can master the art of using it to your advantage. (Oh, and by the way, stop looking at your watch and worrying about time. Most negotiations worth pursuing have outcomes worth waiting for. He who hesitates *is* sometimes saved!)

 Timing affects the rate of concessions, so you can speed up the other player's concessions by creating time pressure. There is a "Murphy's law" of negotiations: They tend to take as long as the time period that is allotted for them. This means that concessions usually do not occur until close to the end of the allotted time, or just before the negotiations are due to end.[4] There are three main reasons why timing drives concessions:

- The parties tend to stall when they have time in the hope that the other will make concessions first.

- A deadline gives a party a "reason" to offer a concession, whereas they would not have wanted to do so earlier in the negotiations for fear of appearing weak.

- A deadline can serve as an excuse to one's constituency: "We held out as long as we could, but time was running out and we had to come to an agreement." You can use a deadline to give the other party an excuse for conceding so that they won't look weak and their constituents won't think they caved in.

As long as both parties are operating under the same deadline, then neither side has a power advantage. However, if one party does not have a deadline, or has a less urgent deadline, then the more flexible party gains some power. The party with the deadline will feel forced by the urgency of the situation to make concessions.

A classic example of the power of deadlines is negotiation between labor and management, where each side has a lot to lose if negotiation is not completed on time. The union will go out on strike and management will have to find ways to cope with the loss of labor.

The other players will feel time pressure if they believe your deadline is more flexible than theirs. In other words, they react to their *perception* of your time pressure, not the reality. And guess what? You can shape that perception fairly easily. Make up your mind to *act* in an unhurried manner and you may be able to seize the high ground, even if you are secretly in a hurry.

What about the opposite situation, in which you have a deadline and the other party does not (or claim they do not)? One way to try to balance the power is to set some kind of deadline for the other party, such as by offering a very attractive negotiating package, but then requiring a decision in 24 hours.

Thus, even if time was not important to them before, now *you have made it important.* For example, an automobile dealer will often attempt to close a sale with a hesitant buyer by offering a price reduction that is available "only today!" The salesperson has a daily or weekly quota to achieve, and so is in more of a hurry than the average buyer who simply wishes to replace an old car at some point in a period of several months to year.

Similarly, companies often make job offers to graduates that are only effective for several weeks, so that students cannot accumulate several good job offers and then play the companies off against each other.

USING THE LEGITIMATE STATUS OF CUSTOMS AND RULES

In our everyday lives, we are governed by formal rules, laws, and regulations that set certain limits for our behavior. We are also constrained by societal norms and cultural expectations. Parents set rules of the house for their children; teachers set rules for classroom behavior.

And in organizations, policies, regulations, and rules give the organization power and authority, and shape the behavior of employees and customers. If we want to remain a part of an organization (or society) and do business with that organization, we are obliged to follow its rules. These rules often limit what is negotiable and how it can be negotiated.

It is hard to challenge something that is "policy." Challenges takes time, money, and persistence, often ending in frustration. Thus, bureaucracies often have a lot of power, simply because they make it difficult for anyone to do anything outside the established rules, regulations, and procedures. We call this the *power of legitimacy.*

Star For example, in accepting a new job, you might ask for a higher salary than is being offered. The manager might say to you, "If it were up to me, I would gladly give you a higher salary. But it is our company's policy to offer this amount. It cannot be adjusted." In this example, the manager may well be using the organization's policies as a source of negotiating power.

What might a savvy negotiator do to counter a policy-based rejection of his or her request? If the policy has been accurately cited, then an end run around it is usually the best ploy. For example, one could request other benefits that are not part of the policy. However, if the policy is ambiguous or weak enough to permit a frontal assault, then one might ask how the policy can be modified, and insist on speaking to the person who has the authority to do so.

Other types of legitimacy include formal authority, usually granted by the institution to senior managers, and the authority earned through past performance. If you have the authority to make an agreement, for example, you have more power than someone who has to keep returning to a constituency for authorization to proceed.

Tactic #4: Control the Written Record

The theory behind this tactic is that, while you can't put words in the other players' mouths, you *can* put words in their notes.

Many negotiations require written notes or minutes. Team, project, or committee meetings often need someone to wrap things up by writing a summary of what was discussed and decided. And many people like to duck that assignment, since they don't see themselves as note takers or secretaries and don't want the extra work. But you *should,* because this gives you a wonderful opportunity to make sure the written report represents the results accurately and fairly. (And maybe even a little *more* fairly from your perspective than theirs, if it was a competitive negotiation.)

So seize the opportunity to get the last word in by volunteering to prepare the minutes of the meeting, the draft of the report, or the summary of the discussion.

Even when a written report isn't required, you can still take it upon yourself to play this role by simply writing a follow-up letter or e-mail to the other party.

For example, if you've just had a telephone discussion with a supplier, follow it up with a quick e-mail starting, "Nice to speak with you today. Here's a quick note to help me remember what we decided in our phone conversation." Unless they refute the written version, they've tacitly accepted it.

By the way, this is a great tactic for dealing with difficult bosses. So long as the written follow-up is polite and respectful, your boss will probably let you get away with documenting things like your job assignments and performance feedback that you have an interest in securing. Then you don't have to say later on, "But I thought you said. . . ." You—and your boss— will *know* what was said.

USING POSITIONAL POWER

Position in a company or organization can also provide legitimacy and power for negotiating. Organizational charts, and the job descriptions that accompany all the boxes in the chart, grant the occupants of various positions greater or lesser authority. The higher your box is in a chart, the more likely it is that you have more *positional* authority. If you do, you can use it to gain more concessions than you give, or (if you wish to collaborate) to push the other party toward an open, cooperative style.

These days, positional power can be unclear in businesses. As organizations have undergone tremendous transformations in the past 10 to 20 years, the power that goes with position has changed dramatically. Whereas once we might have looked at an organizational chart to see where the power lies, nowadays responsibility, authority, and position look more like an interconnected network or spiderweb of relationships than like the traditional chart with boxes.[5] On the traditional organizational chart, authority (and power) usually lies at the top.

But to see where the power lies in businesses dominated by teams and networks, look for the parts of the network where critical information or resources are assembled, exchanged, or disseminated. If you are in one of those critical gatekeeping positions, you may have considerable information positional power you can bring to bear. If not, perhaps you can enlist constituents who do have informal power in order to give you the strength to negotiate with those who outrank you in formal authority.

CONSIDER THE ALTERNATIVES

Alternatives are so important that we've already mentioned them in earlier chapters. And we'll bring them up again and again, because they are a wonderful source of leverage in any negotiation. What makes options so powerful? We thought you'd never ask!

The key benefit of alternatives is that they allow you to avoid feeling compelled to complete the current negotiation. If you have good alternatives, you are not obliged to pursue the negotiation at all costs. Once a negotiation gets started, the players naturally feel a commitment to it. They have made a public commitment and invested time, possibly money, and certainly their energy in it. No wonder negotiators generally behave as if they *have* to see the game through to completion.[6] But in truth, you can walk away from the majority of negotiations. Keep that in mind and you will have a serious advantage over other negotiators.

And it's easiest to walk when you have developed a good alternative. That's why alternatives give you power. The other party realizes (you make *sure* they realize) that you will pursue the current negotiation only so long as it is better than your alternative. If it is not, then you can simply walk away and accept your alternative. Hence, having alternatives—even ones that aren't very good—gives you more power than having no alternative at all. The threat that you will exercise other options can help you persuade the other party to make a deal that meets your needs.

Tactic #5: Develop Alternatives

It's so easy to develop alternatives, but most negotiators never do. Which means you can gain a significant advantage by specializing in this simple tactic.

For example, let's say you call a resort hotel to make a reservation for a conference that requires you to stay for two nights over a weekend—only to find that the hotel's policy requires a *three*-night stay. (This just happened to Alex, so we know it is plausible.) You could grin and bear it, paying for the extra night you don't need. Many guests do—that's why the resort persists in the policy. But why not develop alternatives? Alex did, by first asking to speak to a supervisor (who presumably would have the authority to negotiate), and then asking her politely to give him the names and numbers of other hotels nearby in case he couldn't get the reservation he wanted.

This innocent question, followed by a momentary pause in which he wrote down the numbers, put him in a better opening position by letting the point sink in that he could very well take his business elsewhere. And it took only a moment and no additional calls since the information about alternatives was *solicited from the other party*. When the dust settled, he got what he wanted—an exception to the policy—probably because he invoked the threat of exercising his alternatives.

You, too, should always take a moment or two to think of alternatives. Often it is as simple as asking a few questions. And if you haven't had time to develop alternatives before the negotiation begins, try asking the other party during your negotiations. Amazingly, they will frequently supply the information you want.

USING YOUR PERSONAL POWER

There are several personal qualities that can give a negotiator power. To help you remember to use them, memorize this simple memory device:

The three Ps

- Persuasiveness
- Persistence
- Personal integrity

Let's take a closer look at each of the three Ps of negotiating.

Persuasiveness

People differ in their ability to be persuasive. Success in negotiation will depend to a large extent on your ability to persuade the other party. You may persuade them to see things your way. You may convince them that their approach is all wrong. Or you may persuade them to try a collaborative approach. No matter what your intent, if you have persuasive skills, it will help your case immeasurably. Persuasiveness is power.

And you can gain persuasiveness by focusing on it and practicing your skills. In your next negotiation, think about how persuasive you are being from the other party's perspective. Ask yourself what you could do to be more convincing. Try a change of approach— for instance, by listening for longer periods, echoing back what you just heard, and then making your next point *relate* to what the other party is saying or feeling. This tactic often makes negotiators more persuasive.

Persistence

A second personal quality necessary for successful negotiation is persistence. A negotiator must be able to persevere through ups and downs to accomplish the objectives. And persistence is even easier than persuasiveness to acquire.

To become a more persistent negotiator, determine that you will stay with it. Don't give up. Vow to yourself that you will ask for something 10 different ways before you accept "no" for an answer.

As any child trying to coax a parent into doing something knows, "no" doesn't necessarily mean *no*. "No" can mean maybe, try again later, keep asking, and so on. Persistence will often yield something! This may mean sticking it out through emotional exchanges, or patiently waiting while the other party consults with their constituency. Tenacity can be a source of power if used gently but firmly.

Personal Integrity

Character has a lot to do with power. Your reputation for personal integrity and trustworthiness can go a long way toward giving you a powerful position in bargaining. If the other party knows that you will stick by an agreement, and that you share information honestly, then they need not fear underhanded tactics. They will definitely be more willing to negotiate. If you are known for your integrity, the other party will generally trust you.

Usually high trusters believe that the other party will be trustworthy and that they need to be so themselves. Low trusters expect untrustworthiness, so they are less inclined to be trustworthy themselves. As was said earlier, what you expect tends to be self-fulfilling. This can be a powerful tool in negotiation if you manage to convince the other party that you are to be trusted. However, if your actions and behaviors during a negotiation change—for example, if you give incorrect information or use underhanded tactics—the other party will likely become less trusting.

If a party has been in a situation with you or with someone else where their trust was broken, then they will be less willing to trust you in the current situation. This, of course, is a disadvantage. If it isn't your fault, you may be able to disassociate yourself with the other party's earlier traumas by encouraging them to talk about it and by expressing genuine sympathy. The other party may start out associating you with earlier opponents but you can probably get them to see you as being on their side of those earlier negotiations.

Your personal reputation can provide power if it is positive. Someone with a reputation of being honest, or of always being successful at negotiation, has power over someone who does not have an established reputation or who has a poor one. Your past performance can add to or detract from your reputation. What this means is that you accrue negatives or positives for future negotiations as you negotiate right now. "What goes around comes around," so remember that in the long run it is in your personal interest to negotiate with integrity.

KEY CONCEPT — PRECEDENT

Another powerful tool is the record of previous outcomes, especially in similar situations. Whenever possible, cite precedents that support your position in a negotiation.

If an issue has been negotiated by other people in similar circumstances, the results of those negotiations can set a precedent for the current dealings. And the more frequently an issue has been negotiated before, the more those negotiations will limit the range of possible outcomes in the present situation.

When precedents exist, they will define the most likely outcome. For the current negotiation to produce a different result, it would have to be demonstrated that this situation is different, unique, or in some way exceptional, and hence not subject to the previous precedents.

Depending on whether precedents are going for you or against you, they will strengthen or weaken your negotiating position, so always bone up on relevant precedents. And if they favor the other party, prepare an argument for why they don't apply now. But remember, when precedent is not in your favor, don't bring it up. Save your arguments in case the other party thinks to mention it. They may overlook it, because many negotiators fail to use power factors.

CHOOSING THE SITE FOR NEGOTIATION

The nature of the problem will govern some of the decisions made about choosing the site for the negotiation. If it is a simple one-issue, one-event negotiation, there may not be a need for finding a location or setting up an agenda. If it is a new car bargaining session, for example, you probably will not need to find a location—it is usually at the car dealership. On the other hand, in a salary negotiation you might be able to select the location, say your boss's office or yours. You will have to decide where it would be better to meet, and have a voice in the selection of the site if it is important to you. Perhaps you will want to use a neutral location, given the nature of the negotiation.

Star For instance, if your boss says it's time for your semiannual performance appraisal, which is always held across a big, mahogany desk in his "power office," you may wish to reframe the negotiation in order to change the venue. How? Maybe you could say that you have been tracking your own performance goals and plotting them on a chart in *your* office, and therefore that it makes most sense for your boss to come see you in order to have a look at your new system. If he goes along with this (and why not— he probably hasn't read this book) you will be able to have the appraisal meeting on your turf instead of his. And home turf offers a subtle, but often significant, advantage.

Sometimes it is helpful to hold negotiations on your own turf. Your resources are readily available there, you feel comfortable, and you have considerable control over configuration issues, such as who sits where.

At other times, you may want to select a neutral site. And, on occasion, you will have to meet at the other party's site. Each of these situations has advantages and disadvantages.

KEY CONCEPT In general, negotiators tend to do better on their home turf, so you need to decide whether you want to take the advantage for yourself, give it to the other party, or call for a neutral site where neither has an advantage. For example, Geneva, Switzerland, is often used for international disarmament talks; the United Nations is often used for debating international treaties; and championship sporting events are usually held in neutral stadiums.

 Maybe you can't afford to go to Geneva for a neutral site, but there are many practical ways to go to Geneva in principle, if not in practice. Companies often use off-site conference rooms for *retreats* where they bring together groups or teams of people with competing interests to develop mission statements, plans, or solutions to difficult problems. The advantage of the retreat is that it puts all players more at ease. The level ground of a neutral site helps everyone share needs and information more fully, moving the group toward solutions faster and often producing better outcomes by minimizing distraction and politics.

You can "go to Geneva" for smaller groups and problems, too. A project team can go out to lunch at a comfortable restaurant to discuss a problem. And the couple that chooses dinner and a movie as a venue for resolving a problem is more likely to succeed than the couple that stays home in the kitchen and pitches plates at each other.

KEY CONCEPT — CONFIGURING THE SITE

The arrangement of the room can also be a power factor. Frequently in diplomatic negotiations, there is lengthy discussion of site and configuration factors, such as the shape of the table and the seating arrangement. Certain positions tend to hold more power in terms of the process, while other positions are important for highly symbolic reasons. For example, the person who is running the meeting will usually select a location at the head or the center of the table. The person sitting straight across from the leader usually holds some power, which can be used positively or negatively. A person to the right of the leader has more power than the person to the left.[7] You can apply these principles in your own meetings at work as you set up a conference room or office for a meeting.

Tactic #6: Beat Them to the Seat

Working sessions in conference rooms offer many opportunities to take advantage of the power of seating arrangements. If you wish to control the information flow in a meeting, but lack positional power over all the other participants, then you'll need to establish *Seat power* instead. The seat at the head of a nonround table is the obvious one to take. If you don't have enough authority in the group to get away with this, try taking the seat at the foot of the table instead. It isn't hard to flop the group and get them oriented toward you from this seat.

Or, even more subtle, try capturing the seat nearest the flip chart or board (or move the chart to be nearest your seat). Sometimes people set up a separate seat next to the board and volunteer to take the outwardly low-

(Continued)

status role of note taker. However you do it, the note-taker's seat gives you the opportunity to stand up and take over the meeting as a facilitator. Then you can use this power factor to prevent the meeting from becoming dysfunctional, to block an expected political attack from other participants, or to advocate for your department or team's needs.

How can you get control of a power seat? Easy! Just arrive for the meeting 20 minutes early. Nobody else will be there, so you can set the seating up however you choose.

SCHEDULES AND AGENDAS

The agenda for a negotiating session or series of sessions is also a potent power factor. The structure of the undertaking and the process can favor one party or the other. Time and information are of course potent power factors, as we've already seen. And your control over the schedule gives you opportunities to play with both.

For instance, if you think the other party has a great deal of information to present that may work against you, you can limit the time available to them in order to make it harder for them to use their information. Or, if you think the other party has an urgent deadline, you can push for a relaxed schedule designed to put them into crisis mode so that you can force last-minute concessions from them.

Power is also contained in the process of developing the agenda. If one party would like to have issues talked about in a particular order, sequence, or time frame, then it is to their advantage to dictate and control the agenda. Anyone who has seen a meeting manipulated by parliamentary procedure—what items are to be discussed, in what order, and whether they are discussed at all—knows how much power can be contained in dictating and controlling the agenda. In contrast, if one wishes to share this power, then both parties ought to collaboratively structure the agenda.

RELATIONSHIPS

Your use of power factors can influence your relationship with the other players, and it is certainly affected by that relationship. Always think about the relationship, asking yourself if it constrains your use of power factors or (hopefully) if it enables you to use certain power factors effectively.[8]

CONCEPT Much of the interpersonal behavior in a negotiation will depend on what the two parties view as most important: the outcome or the relationship. If the outcome is more important, and relationship issues do not count for much, then most personal qualities will not really provide you with much power. If the relationship is important, power may figure more, but it will not be used in a strategy of one-upmanship.

DANGER! Remarkably, negotiation research reveals much less about how to define what the key relationships factors are, and how they affect (or are affected by) the ongoing negotiation process. Yet much of the negotiation that actually takes place—between coworkers, spouses, parents and children, suppliers and customers—occurs *in the context of an ongoing relationship.* Negotiation researchers lack understanding of this issue because it is much more difficult to study these relationship factors in a research laboratory; as a result, much negotiation research has studied negotiation processes between strangers who do not know each other and will not have a relationship in the future. As a result, we suspect that *much of the standard advice about negotiating can be harmful to relationships,* and we urge you to avoid tactics that you feel might hurt the feelings or destroy the trust of the other party. Your instincts may be better than the "party line" when it comes to maintaining valuable relationships.

DANGER! Be especially distrustful of negotiation experts who emphasize aggressively deceptive competition. That's usually an unhealthy way to run a relationship.

Several researchers have begun to study relationships and their impact on negotiation.[9] These studies have identified a number of key factors that will either directly affect the negotiation process between parties, or will be affected by those negotiations as the parties sustain their relationship after the negotiation is over. If you are aware of such issues, you will be more likely to notice them and put them to service in your efforts to keep the negotiation process healthy and profitable for all involved.

- *Trust.* Trust was discussed in earlier chapters with regard to your own trustworthiness and the trustworthiness of the other party, and again in the this chapter with regard to personal integrity. While trustworthiness is a key quality of individuals, the level of trust between parties is a key factor in a relationship. The more people trust each other, the easier it will be for them to take risks with each other, to know what they will do and understand how they will react, and be able to coordinate with each other to achieve a good outcome.[10] However, if the parties are competitive with each other, then the trust level is likely to decline.

- *Commonality.* The more the parties have in common, the more likely they are to be able to build a relationship and sustain it. Commonality also leads to predictability and understanding each other.

- *Respect.* Parties who have respect for each other are likely to treat each other better. Respect contributes to a desire to treat each other fairly and honorably, and attend to their needs and concerns.

- *Cooperation or competition.* The parties differ in their level of cooperation or competition with each other. This may be a function of different goals, personalities, or many of the other situation factors described earlier. This factor may also directly affect the strategic choice process described in Chapter 6.

- *Exchange or transactions.* This element reflects the basic outcomes or resources that the parties want or expect from each other. This may be information, products, goods and services, contracts, budgets, assistance, and so on.

- *Scope.* This element describes how many different *facets* there are to the relationship. A husband and wife have a relationship with a broad scope—they work and relate to each other in a variety of different ways. In contrast, a supplier and customer may relate to each other in only one or two ways, based on the simple exchange of products or services.

- *Affect.* This element reflects how the parties feel about each other—their emotional reactions and feelings. Strong relationships are likely to have a great deal of affect, which may also lead to a high level of intimacy and romantic attachments. Using affect—being emotional—can also be an effective tool in negotiation.

- *Acceptance.* This element reflects how much the parties accept each other. It can also relate to the amount of conflict in the relationship, such as the frequency of fights, disagreements, or inability to get along with each other.

- *Empathy.* Being sensitive to the other party's needs involves the ability to look at their perspective.[11]

- *Power.* This is a key element of a relationship. Is one party more powerful than the other, in that they almost always get what they want while the other party seldom achieve their preferred outcome? In contrast, are the parties relatively equal in power, so that, on balance, both parties win a number of their transactions?

PERSONALITIES

The personality characteristics of the individual nego-tiators are often difficult to separate from relationship characteristics. A number of personal qualities, such as the following ones, can affect the relationship dynamics in negotiation:

- Attitude toward conflict (their personally preferred style of managing conflict, which parallels the strat-egy options outlined in Chapters 7 to 11)
- Degree of assertiveness and cooperativeness[12]
- Level of cognitive complexity (ability to think about issues in more or less complex terms)
- Level of self-esteem[13]
- Belief in their ability to negotiate effectively
- Belief that events are controllable (or not)
- Personal need to be in charge or in control of situations

For example, if a person's style tends to be competi-tive, then that person will be less of a risk taker, will demonstrate more internal control, will show a high need for power and control, and will be less concerned about the other person's possible reactions of dislike or anger. On the other hand, a person who tends to oper-ate collaboratively will be more cooperative, more trusting, more creative, and more capable of dealing with complexity.

Although many researchers have studied the poten-tial impact of personality factors on negotiation, the true impact of these factors remains elusive.[14] In gen-eral, and over the long term of the negotiation process, the situation and relationship factors will have far more impact than individual personality elements.

A practical approach to personality factors is to use a personality profile such as INSIGHT, a questionnaire marketed by HRD Press. It identifies differences in personal style that are often at the root of communica-tion or relationship problems; Alex has used it in a variety of trainings and finds that it can help negotia-tors learn how to communicate more effectively with each other. It is especially helpful for teams, siblings, union–management groups, and others with long-term relationships to use a questionnaire such as this to stimulate discussion of communication styles and preferences, because a deeper understanding of such matters often leads to improved working relationships.

Tactic #7:   Tilting the Playing Field

This tactic uses lots of small advantages in order to create a negotiation context that favors you strongly. Think of each context issue as one of the many pawns on a chess board. Alone, they are powerless. But together, they can create a *bind* that limits the other party's movements and enhances your power. Here's how the strategy works in chess, according to chess master Bruce Pandolfini:

When one side's pawns and pieces are so well positioned that they prevent the enemy from moving freely, a bind is created. A player who is in a bind is not only cramped and unable to make freeing pawn moves but is also vulnerable to attack.[15]

In negotiations, your pawns are all the details of the situation, from timing and agendas to selection or design of the location. If you offer to write up the minutes of a meeting, you have just placed one pawn in a position favorable to you. Place four or five more, and the other player may find him- or herself in a bind.

 GENER DIFFERENCES

There are some generalized differences between how men and women negotiate (although there are exceptions to all rules in this area). As a result, you may find it helpful to consider whether another player's behavior may be predictable in part based on his or her gender. Also, you may find ways to use gender differences to your advantage—if only by taking advantage of common perceptions about how *your* gender negotiates in order to get away with something.

It is easy to generalize that men and women negotiate differently, forgetting that there are individual differences within the population of each gender. Not all males are alike, nor are all females; nevertheless, differences have still been observed in the way that men and women approach negotiation.[16] There are four basic areas of difference:

- *Relationships among the parties negotiating.* Women are more apt to be concerned about the broader situation, and the feelings and perceptions of the participants, than are men, who usually want to resolve the matter at hand without considering the larger view.

- *View of the negotiation.*   Men tend to see a bargaining session as a finite, separate event, whereas women see it as part of a larger relationship with the other party.

- *View of power.*   Women tend to want to see everyone in the bargaining situation be equally empowered, whereas men tend to use power as a way to achieve their own goals.

- *Dialogue.*   Women tend to use interaction and dialogue to achieve understanding, whereas men tend to use it for their own ends—to persuade the other party of their point of view.

The point about men's and women's approaches to negotiation is not that one approach is better than the other, but simply that they are different. Women may perceive negotiation differently than men.[17] And this may explain, in part, why they have been found to be treated differently in negotiations.

DANGER!   In fact, women were found to be treated differently in the bargaining situations of buying a car and negotiating salary.[18] Opening offers made to women were worse than those made to men, and the outcomes were worse for the women buyers, too. When women used the same tactics as men, they appeared to be penalized for doing so. One way for a woman to counter this problem is to tell the man she is negotiating with about the study finding that women receive worse opening offers—and then ask him to provide a better offer in order to redress the problem!

END POINT

So what can you do when you know there are one or more power factors at work in the negotiation? It depends to some extent on how you view power or the lack of it. If your objective is to find a solution that will keep everyone happy, then you probably want to equalize the power. However, if you want the best outcome for yourself and you do not care about the other party, you will probably want to do everything you can to increase your power advantage. In either case, power factors are important to the outcome of the negotiation, and it will pay off for you to study them carefully.

Power also has a lot to do with perception. The other party may see you as having more power than you do. Further, they may believe that you have the ability to use it. So, just the *image* of power can be effective in accomplishing your goals. Many will argue, in fact, that the image of power is more important than real power.

In addition, the use of power is to some extent based on experience. As you learn what works in a particular situation, you will adjust your behaviors accordingly.

Some people use power more successfully than others. It can be used positively or negatively, as noted previously. Remember also that negotiation is usually a changing situation, with the parties making moves and countermoves, so that the behaviors and actions provide a moving target that is sometimes hard to zero in on.

Now you are ready to consider various strategies to use for negotiation. Chapter 6 will show you how to choose the right style for any negotiating situation, and subsequent chapters will help you master each of the possible styles.

Choosing Your Game

What game do you want to play? This is the key strategic question for anyone wishing to make a favorable deal.

In negotiations, you can play their game, or your own. Needless to say, you do dramatically better when you pick the game.

Imagine you have been challenged to an old-fashioned duel. In the movies at least, you always are given the opportunity to "Choose your weapon." Will it be short swords or broadswords? Pistols or staves, or perhaps hand-to-hand combat? Your choice would be designed to give you an advantage, to favor you over your opponent in the circumstances at hand.

Similarly, in the great game of negotiation, you should always take a moment to *think about what type of negotiation you want.* Don't just start negotiating! If you haven't chosen the game, you'll find yourself playing their game. Big mistake.

There are many ways to negotiate—you'll become a master of five different negotiation games by the end of this book. A thoughtful selection of the best negotiation game is as important as choosing the right weapon. It has a dramatic impact on the outcomes of every deal.

GOOD NEWS: YOU'VE DONE YOUR HOMEWORK

Your preparations in previous chapters have readied you to make the right choice. You're prepared to choose the negotiation game that you are most likely to win. Your *knowledge of your own and the other players' positions* gives you the insight needed to choose the right negotiation game.

Sometimes negotiations become involved and drawn out, requiring a series of exchanges over time. That's certainly true of a formal labor–management negotiation. And—something few of us recognize—it is equally true of one's long-term relationship with a boss or supervisor. In which case, you will find it advantageous to change games periodically.

 A *combination* of strategies makes sense for complex negotiations that involve a mixture of issues, each of which may best be handled with a different strategy. For instance, in your many negotiations over time with a coworker or teammate, you should certainly plan to vary the game from time to time as circumstances demand.

 Similarly, when a single negotiation continues over a considerable time, each side will make adjustments that may call for shifts or changes of strategy by the other side.

But even where the situation is multifaceted, the basic principle applies: You should choose the game you want to play.

 The wrong strategy guarantees failure!

CHOOSING YOUR GAME

To choose the right game, you need to decide how important two factors are:

1. The *outcome*—what you might win or lose.
2. The *relationship*—how the negotiation will affect your relations with the other players.

 Outcome and relationship—that's your mantra as a negotiator. Every time you approach the beginning of a negotiation, think about the outcome and think about the relationship.

This is such an important point that we need to illustrate it with an example. Imagine you are negotiating to rent an apartment for a year. The apartment is in a desirable building and a good location, and you really like it. The agent representing the landlord has quoted a painfully high rent figure, but you gather there is some room for movement if you press the point. You have learned from another tenant in the building that the landlord is in a hurry to rent this unit and has had trouble finding someone appropriate.

Okay, let's look at this case from an outcome and relationship perspective. How important is outcome to you? Fairly important. On a 1-to-5 scale, for example, it might rate a 4, since you definitely want this unit, and you are eager to see the price come down.

How important is relationship? Well, you aren't dealing directly with the landlord, and the whole thing seems to be done on a professional rather than a personal basis. Further, you may not need to deal with this agent again, and even if you do, the rental rate you negotiate now will set a precedent. So on a 1-to-5 scale, relationship probably gets only a 2.

What you have then is a situation in which outcome is pretty important and relationship is not. Knowing this, we can tell you that the best game is a competitive one. You'll want to compete hard to get the lowest possible rent. We can also guess that the other party, the landlord's agent, will feel the same way. The agent's job is to rent units, not make friends, so he or she will be ready and willing to play a competitive game, too. And that's a good thing for you. Your chances of a good outcome are often better if both parties agree to play by the same rules.

Victory often goes to the army that makes the least mistakes, not the most brilliant plans.

—Charles de Gaulle

NEED AN INSTANT ANSWER?

We know you are impatient to find out how to choose the right negotiating game. If you are in a hurry because you have to negotiate right now, then simply use the strategy selector in Figure 6.1. It will tell you which type of negotiation to pursue in any given situation.

However, in the long run you will want to master this decision by understanding the outcome and relationship issues fully on your own. And so we recommend that you read on in this chapter to find out more about these two essential factors. If not now, then as soon as you've keyed out that pressing negotiation.

Examining Relationship Concerns

How important is your past and future *relationship* with the other party? How have the two of you gotten along in the past, and how important is it for the two of you to

Situational Negotiation Strategy Selector

Here is a simple way to diagnose any negotiation in order to decide what negotiating style to use. Just answer the questions in Figure 6.1 and key out the style. This tool is used in corporate training sessions to help turn participants into crack negotiators—see if it will do the same for you.

INSTRUCTIONS

This assessment tool is designed to help you determine the optimal negotiating style to adopt in a strategic negotiation planning effort. Its underlying premise is that different negotiation strategies, based on each of the five legitimate negotiation styles, are indicated in different situations.

Following are 10 pairs of statements. Each pair describes a negotiating situation. To complete this assessment, first think of the strategic negotiation you are planning; then circle the letter of *the one statement from each pair* that you think fits your negotiation situation best. (Don't worry about the meaning of the letters right now; that will be discussed later.)

Even if neither statement fits your situation exactly, *you must choose one statement over the other.* Weigh the statements as accurately and honestly as possible.

Example:
P. I don't really care what the other party thinks of me after the negotiation is over.
R. It is important that I have a good relationship with the other party once the negotiation is over.

Situation Assessment Statements
P. I don't really care what the other party thinks of me after the negotiation is over.
R. It is important that I have a good relationship with the other party once the negotiation is over.

M. It won't be the end of the world if I lose this negotiation.
O. I have vital interests at stake in this negotiation.

P. I don't have a significant personal or business relationship with the other party.
R. My relationship with the other party is important for business or personal reasons.

M. The time and trouble needed to negotiate may not be worth it in this case.
O. I expect the negotiation to be worth my while if it goes reasonably well.

P. In my relationship with the other party, there is very little sharing of feelings and information.

(Continued)

(Continued)

R. My relationship with the other party is based on shared feelings and in-formation.

M. I don't expect this negotiation to affect future negotiations.

O. I won't be surprised if this negotiation sets the pattern for many future negotiations.

P. My communication with the other party has been quite limited.

R. My communication with the other party has been extensive.

M. I will not feel any worse about myself if I end up thinking I lost the negotiation.

O. I won't feel really good unless I do well in this negotiation.

P. I am not dependent upon the other party.

R. We have common interests because of the ways in which we are thrown together.

M. The issues at stake here are clear and straightforward.

O. I suspect there are important hidden factors at stake in this negotiation.

SCORING

Instructions
Please count your letter scores and fill in the blanks below.

How many P's did you circle? _____ P's
How many R's did you circle? _____ R's

Check one:
_____ I circled more P's. Relationship **IS NOT** important.
_____ I circled more R's. Relationship **IS** important.

How many M's did you circle? _____ M's
How many O's did you circle? _____ O's

Check one:
_____ I circled more M's. Outcome **IS NOT** important.
_____ I circled more O's. Outcome **IS** important.

INTERPRETATION: SELECTING A STRATEGY

You have now assessed a specific negotiating situation in terms of the im-portance of your long-term relationship with the other party, and the impor-tance of the outcome of the negotiation. Select your strategy by using the **Negotiation Strategies** grid that follows, or by finding the best match among the following descriptions.

- A situation in which neither outcome nor relationship matter to you calls for an **Avoiding** strategy.

(Continued)

(Continued)

- A situation in which outcome and relationship are both very important calls for a *Collaborative* strategy.

- A situation in which outcome is important but relationship is not calls for a *Competitive* strategy.

- A situation in which outcome is not important but relationship is calls for an *Accommodate* strategy.

- A situation in which outcome and relationship are both somewhat important to you calls for a *Compromise* strategy. To diagnose this strategy, check your letter totals under "Scoring." Were both sets of scores almost tied (3/2 or 2/3 scores)? If so, then you should consider a *Compromise* strategy as an alternative to the one you obtained from the raw scores.

THE FIVE LEGITIMATE NEGOTIATION STRATEGIES

Plot your scores to determine the negotiation strategy that best matches your situation.

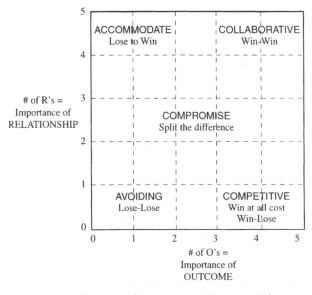

FIGURE 6.1 *Situational Negotiation Strategy Selector.* *(Copyright © 1997, HRD Press. Reproduced by permission. This assessment is part of the* Flex Style Negotiating *product line by Alexander Hiam.)*

get along, work together, and like each other in the future? Perhaps it is very important. Perhaps it does not matter at all. Perhaps it is somewhere between these extremes. If maintaining a good relationship with the other party is important to you, then you should negotiate differently than if the relationship is unimportant.

If you need to be more analytical about a relationship—as when it is complex or difficult to assess—it will help if you understand that your assessment of the relationship between two parties can consider the following factors:

- Whether there is a past relationship
- Whether that relationship is generally positive or negative (whether the two of you have gotten along well or poorly in the past)
- Whether a future relationship is desirable
- The length of the relationship and its history, if one exists
- The level of and commitment to the relationship
- The degree of interdependence in the relationship
- The amount and extent of free, open communication between the parties

For example, if you are negotiating the purchase of a new car, you may never have met the salesperson before and may not expect to have a continuing relationship. Therefore, your relationship concerns are low. However, if your business uses a fleet of cars and you expect to work with this person on deals in the future, your relationship concerns are high, and this will affect negotiations.

Or if you are buying the car from your neighbor, and want to continue to have a good relationship with that person, you may negotiate differently than if you were buying it from a stranger.

In the case of a party with whom you have an ongoing relationship, it may be congenial, or it may be antagonistic if earlier negotiations have been hostile. If it is a congenial relationship, you may wish to keep it that way, and avoid escalating emotions.

If the relationship has a history of hostility, you may prefer not to negotiate, or you may want to lower the emotional level in the negotiations. Lowering the emotional level is important if you expect the relationship to continue in the future.

Negotiating has a powerful impact on any relationship—for good *or* for bad, depending on how you choose to handle the negotiation. Be careful not to poison good relationships by choosing overly competitive negotiating games.

Outcome Concerns

How important is it for you to achieve a good outcome in this negotiation? Do you need to win on all points to gain the advantage? Or is the outcome of only moderate importance? Or does the outcome not really matter in this negotiation?

For example, let's return to the car-buying scenario. If you are buying a car from a dealer, price may be the most important factor, and you may have absolutely no interest at all in the relationship. If you are buying the car from your neighbor, and you want to keep a good relationship with your neighbor, then you might not press as hard to get a good price.

In other situations, neither outcome nor relationship are important—in which case, the time and effort of negotiating may be wasted. Avoidance is sometimes the best policy—and it is always the best if the outcome and relationship are trivial.

Yet many of us are drawn into senseless conflict situations because we rise to the bait, even though we would have realized, upon reflection, that the outcome and relationship issues matter little. Many a bar fight or intraoffice rivalry starts this way. Remember, you aren't a fish. You don't have to rise to the bait. In fact, you don't even have to *play* the fishing game. Just swim away when the outcome and relationship issues are of no real consequence.

 THE FIVE NEGOTIATING GAMES

By considering the relative importance of both outcome and relationship, you are able to adapt your game to each negotiating situation. Untrained negotiators, and those who have taken a simplistic course in competitive tactics, generally use the same approach in every conflict situation. Yet each deal is different, and you definitely get better results by flexing your style to suit the situation.

> The Queen had only one way of settling all difficulties, great or small. "Off with his head!" she said without even looking around.
>
> —Lewis Carroll, *Alice in Wonderland*

If we show the relationship and outcome concerns on a graph, with high and low priorities for each represented, it looks like Figure 6.2. The vertical axis represents your degree of concern for the relationship, and the horizontal axis represents your degree of concern for the outcome. Looking at the various quadrants created by different levels of concern for relationship and outcome, five distinctly different strategies emerge:

1. *Avoiding (lose–lose).* This strategy is shown in the lower left of the diagram. In this strategy, the priorities for both the relationship and the outcome are low. Neither aspect of the negotiation is important enough for you to pursue the conflict further. You implement this strategy by withdrawing from active negotiation, or by avoiding negotiation entirely.

2. *Accommodating (lose to win).* This strategy is represented in the upper left of the diagram, where the importance of the relationship is high and the importance of the outcome is low. In this situation, you back off your concern for the outcome to preserve the relationship; you intentionally *lose* on the outcome dimension in order to *win* on the relationship dimension.

3. *Competitive (win–lose).* The lower right of the diagram represents high concern for the outcome and low concern for the relationship. You use this strategy if you want to win at all cost, and have no concern about the future state of the relationship.

4. *Collaborative (win–win).* The upper right part of the diagram defines a strategy where there is a high priority for both the relationship and the outcome. In this strategy, the parties attempt to maximize

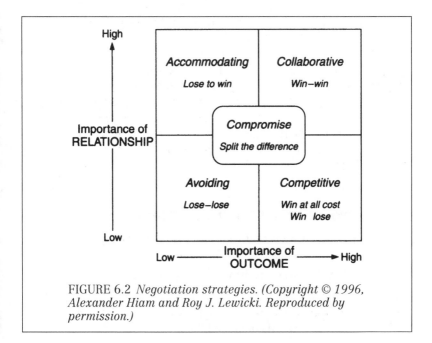

FIGURE 6.2 *Negotiation strategies. (Copyright © 1996, Alexander Hiam and Roy J. Lewicki. Reproduced by permission.)*

their outcomes while preserving or enhancing the relationship. This result is most likely when both parties can find a resolution that meets the needs of each.[1]

5. *Compromise (split the difference).* In the middle is an area we will call a Compromising, or "satisficing," strategy. It represents a combination approach that is used in a variety of situations. For example, it is often used when the parties cannot achieve good collaboration, but still want to achieve some outcomes and/or preserve the relationship. Then a Compromising strategy can be effective. It is also often used when the parties are under time pressure and need to come to a resolution quickly. Each party will give in a bit to find a common ground.

One of these five negotiating games will be best for you in each situation. And you can decide which one by considering outcome and relationship issues, then selecting the approach that matches your needs. Pick the right one for the circumstances and you are already way ahead.

WHAT GAME WILL *THEY* PLAY?

You will find your analysis of the other party helpful when you are selecting the appropriate strategy for a particular situation, because you may want to adjust your strategy choice based on what you expect the other party to do. If the parties are able to agree on one strategy, negotiations will be easier. In real-life situations, however, each party may start with a different strategy.

If you don't like the game they're playing, you'll need to steer them toward your game. Tell them you don't like their approach and why you think your game is better for everyone concerned. And stick to the rules of your game, not theirs. Often, they will follow your lead and you'll be able to switch their game to one of your choosing.

ADVANCED SELECTION CRITERIA

By now you know that you can chose the best negotiating game by considering two key factors:

1. How important is the outcome to be gained from this negotiation?

2. How important is the past, present, and future relationship with the opponent?

Collaborating with a "Family" of Contractors

Should you compete hard for the best deal from suppliers, or look for a win–win and a more long-term relationship?

To Robert L. Bodine, founder and president of Synesis Corporation of Roswell, Georgia, the choice is clear. His firm brings in contract workers to help the full-time staff develop custom training materials for his clients during peak periods. "Our business owes much of its success to the contributions of contract workers," he explains.[2]

And so he "treats contractors like family," paying them promptly instead of asking them to wait until his clients pay. And in his company, contract workers are treated "like partners." Bodine explains that "We are open in sharing our tools and procedures." And his company is willing to teach contract workers more than the minimum they need to know to get a job done. As a result, Synesis has strong relationships with contract workers, and is likely to be chosen over competitors when a contractor has to make a choice between competing offers.

"Ideally," Bodine explains, "your relationship with a contractor should be like a marriage of equals, based on full disclosure."

It is clear that Bodine values the long-term relationship just as much as the short-term outcome and, as a result, takes a collaborative instead of competitive approach to dealing with his subcontractors. He does not compete as hard as he could to get the cheapest rates, but he benefits amply in the long run because he has preferential access to subcontractors.

The following paragraphs describe ways to decide about these two questions and other factors to consider in answering them. You've seen this two-factor model used to prescribe which of the five styles to use—Avoid, Accommodate, Compete, Collaborate, and Compromise. You won't go wrong with this simple but powerful two-factor model, but on the other hand, there are times when you might want to refine it by considering some additional factors, as well. We'll look at them briefly before ending this chapter.

Situation

Look at the *situation* and try to figure out which strategy might be best in those circumstances. Do you care a lot about the outcomes in this situation? If you do, are you willing to sacrifice your relationship with the other person? Or, conversely, is the relationship so important that you are unwilling to endanger it by pursuing the outcome? Alternatively, consider the conditions under which each strategy is most effective (see Figure 6.2). Which of these conditions apply to the present situation?

Remember that each strategy has both advantages and disadvantages. One strategy is more or less appropriate depending on the type of conflict and the situation.

Preferences

Analyze your personal *preferences* for the various strategies. You will probably be more successful using a strategy that feels comfortable. Research has shown that people in conflict have distinct preferences for employing certain strategies in conflict situations.[3] These preferences lead individuals to develop distinct *styles* with which they approach many situations. Based on experience and history, some people have strong biases toward being competitive, collaborative, compromising, accommodating, or avoiding in conflict situations.

 The stronger your preference for a particular conflict management strategy (or style), the more often you will choose it, the more biased you will become in seeing it as an advantageous strategy, and the more likely you will be to see that strategy as appropriate in a variety of situations. Thus, if you normally respond to conflict (and negotiation) situations in a competitive manner, then you are more likely to see the Competitive strategy as being widely appropriate—even when it may not be. Similarly, the less likely you are to avoid conflict, the more likely it is that you will not choose the Avoiding strategy—even when it may be the most appropriate thing to do.

Therefore, understanding your preferences and biases is critical, because they will affect your tendency to overselect or underselect strategies in particular situations.

Your preferences for a particular strategy are also influenced by such subtle issues as your *values* and *principles.* These may be harder, in some ways, to define than your goals, priorities, or limits. But how you evaluate the following will have a great impact on your willingness to use (or not use) certain strategies:

- How much do you value truth, integrity, manners, and courtesy?

- Is respect an important issue for you?

- How important is fair play? (And, for that matter, how do you define *fair?*)

- How much of your ego is involved in this—your reputation, your image? How concerned are you about how you will see yourself—or how others will see you—if you get what you want, or don't get what you want?

Experience

Next, consider your *experience* using the various strategies. The more experience you have, the better you become at using that strategy—and, probably, the more likely you are to use it. Experience is one of the key factors that works to shape your *preferences.*

Style

Think about your own style as it interacts with the *other party's style,* and consider the possible consequences. What will be the effect of such a combination? For example, two competitive parties might have more conflict in their negotiation than a competitive party negotiating with a party that usually yields. While it would be too complex to explore all the possible interactions between each of your five possible styles and the styles of the other in detail, we have summarized the possible combinations in Table 6.1. (Some of the cells in the left side are blank because the information is contained in the matching cell on the right side.)

Perceptions and Experience

Consider your *perceptions and experience* with the other party. How you feel about the other party, and what you want to have happen in that relationship in the future, will drive your strategy. How well do you like each other? How much do you communicate? How much do you need to work with the other party in the

TABLE 6.1 LIKELY INTERACTIONS BETWEEN NEGOTIATORS OF DIFFERENT STYLES

	Avoiding	Accommodating	Competing	Collaborating	Compromising
Avoiding	Both parties avoid pursuing their goals on the issues, and do not take any action to endanger the relationship.	Accommodator shows strong concern for the Avoider, particularly the relationship; Avoider attempts to minimize interaction.	Competitor will dominate or Avoider will escape. Avoider attempts to minimize interaction, while Competitor tries to engage.	Collaborator shows strong concern for both issues and the relationship while Avoider tries to escape. Collaborator may give up.	Compromiser shows some concern for both issues and relationship; Avoider tries to escape. Compromiser may give up or Avoider may engage.
Accommodating		Both parties avoid pursuing their goals on the issues, give in to the others' goals, and try to smooth over relationship concerns.	Competitor pursues own goals on the issues, while the Accommodator tries to make the Competitor happy. Competitor usually wins big.	Collaborator shows strong concern for both issues and relationship; Accommodator tries to make the Collaborator happy. Relationship should be very strong, but the Collaborator may achieve better outcomes.	Compromiser shows some concern for both issues and relationship; Accommodator tries to make the Compromiser happy. Relationship will improve, Compromiser may entice the Accommodator to pursue some issue focus.

	Competing	Collaborating	Compromising
Competing	Both parties pursue their goals on the issues and ignore any concern for the relationship; create conflict, mistrust, and hostility.	Collaborator shows strong concern for both issues and relationship, while Competitor only pursues issues. Competitor usually wins, and both parties become competitive.	Compromiser shows some concern for both issues and relationship, while Competitor only pursues issues. Competitor usually wins, and both parties become competitive.
Collaborating		Both parties pursue their goals on the issues, show strong concern for the others' goals *and* sustaining trust, openness, and a good relationship.	Compromiser shows some concern. Collaborator shows strong concern for both issues and the relationship. Minimally, good compromise or better.
Compromising			Both parties pursue their goals on the issues in a limited way and attempt to "do no harm" to the relationship.

SOURCE: From Roy J. Lewicki, Alexander Hiam, and Karen Wise Olander, *Think Before You Speak: A Complete Guide to Strategic Negotiation* (New York: John Wiley & Sons, 1996). Copyright © 1996, Alexander Hiam and Roy J. Lewicki. Reproduced by permission.

future because you are dependent on what they can do for you? How much do you trust them? Your level of trust with the other party will be based on your experience with them, and on the history and results of other negotiations they have conducted with you or with other parties in the past.

Can You Choose "No Strategy"?

Some people whom we have taught in negotiation have argued that it is possible to adopt *no strategy:* You refuse to make an explicit strategic choice, and let the chips fall to determine what you will do next. This allows you *maximum flexibility* to adjust your approach based on what your opponent does first, or as the proceedings change.

The "no strategy" approach has some distinct advantages. You get a chance to find out how your opponent wants to negotiate first, which may tell you a lot about your opponent. It also keeps you from making a commitment to a strategy that may not work or may not be able to be completed—for example, being accommodative while the other party is being competitive.

However, a "no strategy" choice is often the lazy negotiator's way of avoiding a key part of the planning and preparation process. We do not think this is a good choice. While a "no strategy" choice may give you some negotiating leeway, it could also put you in a precarious position if you have not planned well. The result will be that the opposition will gain an advantage over you before you realize what is going on.

If you know that you care about the relationship, or the outcome, or both (or neither), select a strategy and begin to plan around it. If you are proactive about strategy choice, you are much more likely to get what you want than if you wait for the other party to initiate action. As has been pointed out, you can always adapt your strategy later as necessary.

END POINT

After you decide which strategy is best for you, it is time to take all the information you have gathered and proceed to implement that strategy. The following chapters discuss the implementation of the five most important negotiation games. While you have already studied them in this chapter, and know enough to perform them adequately, there are many additional points you may wish to master. We suggest that you read each of these chapters to familiarize yourself with the characteristics of the strategies.

CHAPTER 7

The Competitive Game

Competition is the strategy most of us associate with negotiation and deal making. It is the classic bargaining or haggling style used in open-air markets throughout much of the world (although sometimes bargaining follows the rules of compromise instead). Competition is also the style used most often to negotiate the price of a car or house. And within companies, rivalries over access to resources, power, and promotions often follow the rules of competitive negotiating.

In our corporate training work, we find that many employees prefer a collaborative style instead of a competitive one. Perhaps this is true of you, too. But regardless, you still need to master the competitive game because you cannot always avoid it.

The competitive game is played frequently, so it is important to understand how it works, even if you do not plan to use it yourself. But you *will* use it, well or poorly, at least on occasion, because others will often try to draw you into it—and sometimes it is the right game to play. Sometimes it is your best choice, and a collaborative approach won't work.

In a competitive negotiation, the outcome is more important than the relationship. Because the outcomes (resources, gains, profits, etc.) are seen as finite and limited in amount or size, the person engaging in competition wants to get as much of those outcomes as possible.

 We will use the term *competitor* to denote the person using competition because the players in this game are definitely playing a competitive sport—and a contact sport in many cases!

We call this strategy *win to lose* because it is likely that while competitors may gain on the outcome, they will strain and endanger the relationship between the parties. The thinking and goals in this strategy are short term: to maximize the size of the outcome right now, rather than to care about the long-term consequences of this strategy on the relationship.

You may want to use competitive negotiating if the relationship with the other party does *not* matter. For example:

- This may be a one-time negotiation with no future relationship.
- The future relationship may not be important.
- The relationship may exist, but was poor to begin with.
- You don't care if other people find out about your competitive behavior.
- The other party may have a reputation for hard bargaining or dishonesty, and this strategy is adopted for defensive reasons.

At any rate, this strategy is undertaken with the assumption that the future relationship with the other party is unimportant, but the specific outcome *is* important.

DANGER! Competition tends to emphasize the differences between the parties, promoting a *we/they* attitude. Thus, the relationship during negotiation in a competitive situation will be characterized by lack of trust and even by conflict. This contrasts with collaboration, in which differences are minimized and similarities are emphasized. Collaboration builds trust, but competition does not build trust and sometimes degrades it.

TAKE AS MUCH AS YOU CAN

The goal in competition is to get the other party to give in, in order to satisfy your own needs now. It is based on the "I win, you lose" concept. Each competitor will do anything to accomplish the objectives and obtain as much of the pie as possible. This can include a variety of behaviors, including hardball tactics, such as the use of a "straw man" issue that you put forth as if it's key, then concede on—in exchange for a deep concession on an issue that *is* important to you.

THE RISKS OF COMPETITION

Negotiations that rely on competition can be costly and time-consuming, especially if each party holds out for

Don't Try This at Home!

Here's an amusing (if not totally honest) anecdote from a comedian who found a creative way to cope with a landlord's expectation for a bribe. His competitive style didn't do much for the relationship—but it got him what he wanted at a bargain price.

They got some new apartments down on Riverside Drive, so I went down to get me an apartment. I said, "I'd like to have five rooms," and the man said, "Sorry, Mr. White, but we've got to put you on the waiting list. It'll be about two years before we can get you in this apartment house."

I said, "Two years? Okay, get me in as soon as you can." I ran my hand in my pocket, dropped a thousand dollars in the trash can. I said, "If you find anything, let me know. Here's my phone number."

I go home. About a half hour later the phone rang. "Mr. White, we do have one apartment left." So I go back down and sign a five-year lease. About four days later I get a phone call from the same guy. He said, "Mr. White, that money in the trash can—it was counterfeit. It was no good."

I said, "I know, that's why I threw it away!"

—Slappy White

all its demands. Much time is spent researching, pressuring, and psyching out the other party. Further time is consumed making moves and countermoves, trying to figure out what the other party will do. Competitive strategies are often compared with strategies used in chess, poker, military warfare, and other tactical games. The time spent in these activities is very different from alternative uses of that time; for example, in the Collaborative model, this same time could be spent on mutual exploration of issues, sharing of information, and an attempt to find mutually acceptable solutions.

Time and goodwill may also be lost if the competitor anticipates that you will be competitive and prepares to compete too. If you had not intended to be competitive, you may switch strategies when you discover that they have decided to be competitive, thus escalating emotions and increasing conflict. Not only does such confusion lose time, but it may hurt the relationship and toughen competitors so that they become willing to give far less than they might have originally.

 A major problem with competition is that it is frequently used by inexperienced or untrained negotiators who believe that competition is the only viable strategy. They may be missing opportunities by automatically selecting competition. It is important to select a strategy only after thorough investigation of the issues, coming to an understanding of what strategy the other is likely to pursue, and making some clear decisions about the relative importance of the outcomes and the relationship with the other party.

Likewise, it is possible to underestimate the other parties in a competitive situation. Remember that they, too, have adopted the mission to win at all costs. When using competition, we tend to underestimate the strength, wisdom, planning, and effectiveness of the other party and assume that even though they are preparing to be competitive, too, we can beat them at their game. If you do not pay close attention to their behavioral and verbal clues, you may set yourself up for manipulation by the other party.

ARE YOU FORCING OTHERS TO COMPETE?

Finally, you need to beware of something called the *self-fulfilling prophecy*. A self-fulfilling prophecy is something you believe so strongly that you actually make it come true. It often happens in negotiation when one party expects the other to behave in a particular way, and as a result, actually makes the party behave that way. This tends to come true if the other party is using competition because they think you are.

Anticipating that the other is going to be competitive, we prepare to be competitive ourselves. The cues we give off in this preparation—our language, tone of voice, gestures, and behaviors—let the other party believe that we intend to be competitive. So they behave competitively, which only assures us that our initial assumptions were right.

HOW TO SET YOUR BARGAINING RANGE

In a competitive situation, the focal point is the bargaining range. It consists of three points, as previously seen: a starting point, a target point, and a walkaway point. Each party's bargaining range is different. An important part of planning your moves for competitive negotiation is to define these points for your side and to do the best you can to deduce those for the other side (see Figure 7.1 for a diagram representing these points).

The *starting point* is where you commence bargaining. It is your initial offer to the other party. You will need to do a lot of research to define your starting point. It will depend on the market rate; the urgency of the situation, both for you and for the other party; the anticipated range (starting and walkaway points) of the other party; the number and value of concessions you are willing to make; and the time frame for the negotiations. For example, on a car with a price tag of $15,000, you might offer $12,000 as a starting point. Or, in labor negotiations, a firm might start out by offering labor a 3-percent wage increase, when they expect the union to ask for 8 percent. In house buying, it might be customary in negotiations to offer 80 percent of the asking price.

You may or may not know the other party's starting point. Cars usually have sticker prices; houses have advertised prices. In labor negotiation, labor usually has stated goals, and often the parties are familiar with each other's tactics. In many cases, these "price tags" have anticipated that bargaining will take place, and thus the price may have even been inflated by some percentage, in the expectation that the other party will make an offer that is less than 100 percent of the price.

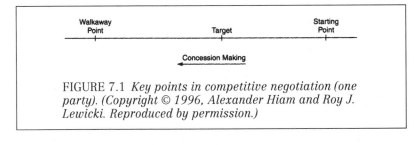

FIGURE 7.1 *Key points in competitive negotiation (one party). (Copyright © 1996, Alexander Hiam and Roy J. Lewicki. Reproduced by permission.)*

Situations Where Competition Is Effective

Here are the appropriate circumstances for competitive negotiating:

1. First, the goals of the parties are *short term.* There is no desire to establish or nurture a long-term relationship.

2. Second, the parties assume that their goals are *incompatible.* The issues under discussion are seen as a *fixed pie;* what one gains, the other loses, and there are a limited number of ways in which it can be divided. Your objective is to maximize your piece of the pie. If there is more for you, there is less for the other party. And vice versa. So the aim is to get as much as you can.

3. Third, the *tangible,* or more quantifiable, objective benefits are the most important to you—factors such as price, interest rate, number of items, delivery terms, and wording of a contract. The price is the most common tangible benefit in competitive negotiations. *Intangibles,* or psychological factors such as esteem, principles, precedents, or the overall well-being of both parties (now and in the future) are less important in competitive negotiations, though they need to be taken into account as well.

4. Finally, you are likely to use competition when you *expect the other party to take a competitive stance.* From your research on the other party you probably have a good idea of what strategy they will employ. If you know that the other party is going to be Competitive, then competition may be appropriate. However, if you are only guessing, and the other party uses a different strategy, whatever you have planned may not work. And even if the other party is likely to employ competition, you may still find it desirable to try to shift them to a Collaborative negotiation in order to increase the outcome possibilities for both sides.

TiP

But often, starting points for the other side are not so clear. For example, you may not know or be able to find out how much your boss has been authorized to increase your salary. Even if you do not know the starting point of the other side, you will know it after you make your opening offer or bid; when the opposing party comes back with a counteroffer, it represents their starting point. The two parties' starting points are rarely the same—if they were, there would be no need for negotiation.

The *target* is the settlement point you want to attain. It is your hoped-for outcome. The target may be defined in monetary terms, or in other tangibles such as benefits, shorter working hours, and the like. There may be *intangibles*—psychological factors such as esteem—associated with the target as well. As was mentioned earlier, intangibles are harder to define and may seem less important because they are less concrete. Nevertheless, you should define them during your planning.

The *walkaway point* is the point at which you will break off negotiations, either temporarily or permanently. The walkaway point may be somewhat beyond your target, but it will be the absolute maximum you will agree to pay if you are the buyer (or the minimum you will agree to if you are the seller). In the case of a car deal, it is the highest amount the buyer will pay, or the lowest amount the seller will accept.

KEY CONCEPT

Sometimes you can figure out the *other party's* target point. For example, if the other side does not expect to negotiate, their target point is the stated price on the car or the advertised house price; if they *do* expect to negotiate, the target is probably some percentage less than the stated price. However, you may never know the other party's walkaway point. It is not usually the same as the target. If the negotiations are broken off, you can suspect that you were in the neighborhood of the other party's walkaway point, but you cannot know for sure (see Figure 7.2).

As long as the bargaining range for one party in some way overlaps that of the other party, then there is room for bargaining. (By *overlap,* we mean that the most the buyer is willing to offer is above the least the seller is willing to accept.) If the ranges do not overlap (and this may not be known at the beginning of the negotiations), then there may be no successful negotiation. The parties will need to decide whether to adjust their bargaining ranges, or to end negotiations. To illustrate overlap, if the maximum you will pay for a used car is $13,000 and the dealer will not take less than $14,000, then your bargaining ranges do not overlap. In this case, you need to reevaluate your bargaining

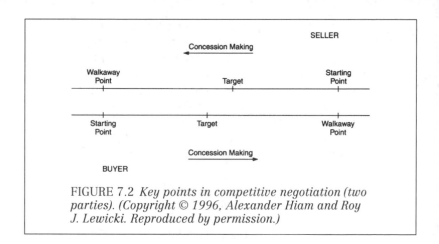

FIGURE 7.2 *Key points in competitive negotiation (two parties). (Copyright © 1996, Alexander Hiam and Roy J. Lewicki. Reproduced by permission.)*

ranges, especially your resistance points, and either adjust them or end the negotiations (see Figure 7.3).

DO YOU HAVE A BATNA?

Your planning should include establishing an alternative or BATNA, if possible.[1] The role of a BATNA—the best alternative to a negotiated agreement—was discussed in Chapter 3. An alternative is a viable option to the current settlement or agreement to the items under negotiation, which can provide you with power in the bargaining process. Without an alternative, your position in bargaining is much weaker. Returning to our used car illustration, there might be a second car, with a price tag of $12,000, that you believe to be of equal value. If you cannot come to an agreement on price for Car 1, then you could cease negotiation and switch to your alternative, Car 2.

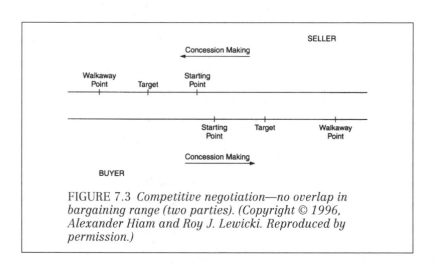

FIGURE 7.3 *Competitive negotiation—no overlap in bargaining range (two parties). (Copyright © 1996, Alexander Hiam and Roy J. Lewicki. Reproduced by permission.)*

Alternatives interact with walkaway points to influence the choices you make. For example, say you currently make $25,000 in your job and you are job hunting. You decide that you want to find a job that pays at least $30,000. What do you do if you find a job you like, but it only pays $28,000? Do you take it or not? If there are no other such jobs available (no alternatives) because the economy is sluggish, then you might take the $28,000 job. However, if many alternative jobs are available for the taking, then you might hold out for a higher salary.

On the other hand, suppose you lose your $25,000 job and you are offered $24,000 for another similar job. Will you take it? Perhaps under sluggish circumstances, you will be more likely to do so. In any negotiation, it is wise to be well informed of your alternatives and, wherever possible, to use them to your advantage.

Suggestions for Defining Your Bargaining Range

❏ *Define your walkaway point in advance.*   Know ahead of time the point at which you want to stop bargaining. If you do not, you may have to drop out of the negotiation when the price gets too high, or else you may end up spending more than you had intended.

❏ *Have a good alternative.*   An alternative provides you with a bargaining chip in negotiations. Without an alternative you will be in a weaker bargaining position. If there is no good alternative, be sure you know this during your planning (but also be careful not to tell your opponent this). It will help the process of setting points on your bargaining range.

❏ *Focus only on this deal.*   To maximize the results of this deal, you need to ignore your relationship with the other person, and other peripheral or low-priority issues. Staying focused on the matter at hand allows you to keep control and therefore gives you power in the negotiation. Note again that this may not be a good approach if you are bargaining with a party with whom you will have future negotiations or relationships. A prime example is if both parties work for the same company, and will need to work together at some time in the future. And it also means accepting that this deal is not worth it unless you achieve or exceed your alternative.

❏ *Get as much information as you can without giving much (if any) away.*   The more information you have, the better. This is also true of the other party. Research the other party carefully; talk with them if possible; ask questions. Try not to share much information about your own position. Knowing all you can about the other party's position and bargaining range will help you set your own position. More will be said about researching the other party in a moment.

❏ *Set the opening as high or as low as possible.* If you are a seller, set your price as high as possible; if you are the buyer, set your offer as low as possible. How you set your opening will be based to some extent on how urgent this deal is for the other party. For example, if the other party needs to sell in a hurry, you start with a much lower price than if the negotiation is of little importance to the seller or if there are many other potential buyers.

Setting the opening offer is often a tricky process. First, as was said, you want to set your opening as high or low *as possible*. What we mean here is high or low enough to get a good agreement without being so high or low that the other party simply laughs, walks away, or declares that you are insincere and have no credibility. (Warning: They may do this even if your opening offer is reasonable, just to make *you* think they will never give in to your opening demands.)

A second reason why this is a tricky process is that opening offers tend to set the range for negotiation. Once both sides have declared opening offers, psychological principles dictate that both parties begin to look to the middle of the range as the place where settlement is likely to occur. So if your price is $15,000 and I offer $12,000, both of us begin to look at $13,500 as a reasonable place to settle. If we want to settle lower than that, we need to make a lower opening offer (e.g., $11,000) and still have the other side accept this as a credible opening. This is why opening offers should be as high (or low) as you can go, without completely losing credibility with the other side.

Do You Have Multiple Issues?

We have been describing a simple negotiation, where there is one issue and two parties are trying to resolve it.

Planning becomes more complex when you must resolve a *collection* of issues. In planning for a multiple-issue negotiation, you will need to list all the issues that need to be discussed in the negotiation, and then prioritize them. You may need to focus on only the major issues and save the items of lesser importance for another negotiation session. The lesser issues can often be used as "throw-ins" on which you can make concessions during the closing stages of the negotiation.

Do You Know Your Costs?

In negotiation planning, we almost always estimate the gains that we may achieve if negotiations are successful. Yet few negotiators give as much thought to their costs.

 Costs play an important part in negotiations, especially if there are delays. And significant costs are usually incurred if the negotiations are broken off. Both time and money are lost. Therefore, you shouldn't attempt to use a competing strategy unless you are also prepared to lose and incur the estimated costs.

 Many people think that when they try to compete, they are automatically going to win. This is not true. So anticipate the costs of losing and make sure you are willing to accept them before starting a competitive negotiation.

Are Their Costs Higher? Aha!

It is important to know the costs not only for your side but for the other party as well. If the other party's costs of delay are high, you can use a foot-dragging tactic to create pressure for a resolution. This sort of manipulation is discussed further in the sections on various tactics later in this chapter.

Did You Remember to Do Your Homework?

You only know something useful like the other party's costs of losing if you've done the homework as advised in earlier chapters. When you are planning competition, it is very important to research the other party. Although you may pick up a lot of information as the negotiations proceed, it is important to obtain as much information as possible *before negotiating.* This information will help you set your bargaining points and other aspects of your strategy. You need to know what *value* the other party places on the outcome, something about the limits of their *bargaining range,* and their *level of confidence and motivation.* Based on this information, you can plan your position and strategy for bargaining.

HOW TOUGH IS YOUR OPENING POSITION?

Whether to take an *extreme* position at the outset is a difficult question, as this stance has both advantages and disadvantages.

First, an extreme position sets a tone for the negotiations. It suggests that you are a tough, no-nonsense negotiator and that the other party will probably have to make many concessions (see the sections on concessions later in this chapter).[2] An extreme offer leaves a lot of room for adjustments, which may give you more time to figure out the other party, but can also mean more lengthy negotiations.

DANGER! In contrast, a major disadvantage of an extreme offer is that the offer may be rejected out of hand, thus bringing negotiations to a halt. In many situations, the opponent party will simply refuse any further negotiations and will walk away—particularly if they have a good alternative.

Therefore, while you may wish to convey toughness, an extreme opener can be a drawback if there is ever to be a future relationship with the other party. The premise in competition is that the relationship concerns are, at best, low and short term. But if you destroy the relationship completely with your opening position, then you obviously cannot reach a deal.

TiP A civil relationship is necessary in order to proceed, so your opener mustn't insult the other players. Since the extreme offer can be problematic, you should use it only if you also have a good alternative.

SETTING A TONE AT THE OPENING

Your opening offer sets the tone for the negotiations. The other party's behavior will frequently mirror yours, so if you set up an adversarial situation at the outset, then the other party may expect to fight on each point of the negotiation. Both sides' behavior may become belligerent. A less strong opening stance can result in the other party having more reasonable expectations, which may lead to reasonable concessions and compromises. The other party will be confused if you start out with a reasonable offer and then take a tough stance, or make an outrageous offer at first, and then appear to be compromising and reasonable.

It is difficult to know what is more important here—toughness or consistency. If you have the choice, you are better off being consistent—whether consistently tough *or* flexible—than being erratic in your messages. Toughness can produce better outcomes, but consistency in strategy helps your credibility with the other party.

If you start off being tough, you probably need to *stay* tough unless that behavior produced such a negative response in the other party that you decide to be more flexible—at the cost of consistency, and therefore some of your credibility.

HAVE YOU PLANNED YOUR CONCESSIONS?

A series of concessions will follow each side's opening. Concessions are trade-offs that a party is willing to make, usually with the expectation that the other side will respond in kind and in the same magnitude. For example, if you go up by $100 in your offer for a used car, the dealer may be willing to come down from the asking price by that amount. But if you only go up by $10, it is unlikely that the seller is going to come down by $100.

Concessions are usually built into the bargaining situation by the distance between your starting and ending points and those of the other party. There is enough space between your offer and the other party's that each side can make some adjustments to their offers.

Concessions affect not only the tangible outcomes but also the intangibles, such as esteem or reputation. When you make a concession, you are acknowledging that the other party is a worthy opponent. If you make a concession, however, and the other party either does not make one or else makes a very small concession, you may lose face and thus appear to be the weaker party—particularly to your constituency. The intangible—your reputation and image—thus figures in the negotiations prominently, particularly when constituencies are present.

If you find that the other side's concessions do not match the ones you offer, you may want to negotiate about how concessions are made. For example, you may say, "I need you to give me some indication that you are willing to negotiate in good faith, by indicating where concessions may be possible." Or, you can link concessions together: "If you agree to throw in that roof rack for the car, I'd be willing to offer you another $200." Another approach is to package concessions: "I will do A and B if you do C and D."

DO YOU SEE A PATTERN TO THEIR CONCESSIONS?

The competitive strategist can learn a lot about the progress of the negotiations by looking at the pattern of concessions. In the discussion of consistency, we implied that the pattern of concessions is important. It is!

In general, negotiators begin by making large concessions, and then make smaller ones as they get closer to the target point, and even smaller as they get closer to the walkaway point. In addition, the tougher the negotiator, the fewer concessions they will make, and the smaller these will be in all stages of the negotiation.

Thus, if the other party's concessions are becoming smaller during each round, it is probably because they are close to their walkaway point and have less space for movement toward a resolution.

A pattern of shrinking concessions can develop early on if the negotiations started at a point very close to their target or walkaway point, thus leaving little space for concessions. To avoid this situation when *you* are making concessions, you may find it helpful to *save one small concession for the last round.* Then you have something to use when you think the other player needs a final incentive to close the deal.

IS THE CONCESSION PATTERN IRREGULAR?

If the size of the other party's concessions vary—first large, then small, then large again—it may be hard to discern what is happening. Watch for behavioral clues from the other party. Or ask them what they are doing, if their behavior confuses you. (There may be times when you want to confuse your opponent, and this is certainly one way to do it!)

DANGER! There is generally a point of no return beyond which the other party has nothing left to concede (get enough concessions from them and you reach their BATNA). However, the other party may try to convince you that they can't make any more concessions, when they really can. You have to decide whether this message is really true, or just an effort to have *you* make the concessions, not them.

COMPETITIVE RULES OF THUMB

Once you get past the opening offers (or demands) of each side, and into a pattern of concessions, a number of things can happen. So from this point, it is a bit more difficult to state exactly what will happen next. But if you follow these rules of thumb, you should be able to plot a successful course through the dangerous middle ground of a competitive negotiation.

1. *Stick to your planned target and walkaway points.*
   Try not to be manipulated by the other party. Watch
   out for the tendency to find a midpoint between the
   other party's asking price and your first offer, and to
   settle there too quickly. Once both sides have stated
   their opening, there is a tendency to jump to the
   middle of those two points and offer a settlement.
   This is often called the *1-2-3 and it's over* process.
   They say $15,000, you say $12,000, and they say,
   "Why don't we just settle for $13,500?" Don't say
   yes unless $13,500 is really your target (or better).
   Stick to your planned goals. Remember that you
   may be able to make a better deal if you make
   smaller moves.

2. *Do not reveal your target point too early.* Provide
   minimal information to the other party. If you let
   your target point be known, you will be open to manipulation, particularly if you think you can do better than your target point. So only let them know
   your target point if you can't possibly do better.

3. *Never reveal your walkaway point.* Never let them
   know your limits. If you let them know this, they will
   try to settle as close to your walkaway point as possible. Say as little as possible—even if they keep
   asking you questions about how far you are willing
   to go.

4. *Get the other party to make big concessions.* If you
   believe that the pie is limited in size, then you want
   to get as much of it as you can, while allowing the
   other side to get as little of it as possible. Keep trying to persuade them that it is up to them to make
   big moves in their position.

5. *Keep your concessions few and small.* If you have
   to give in, do it in small increments, one item at a
   time. Be patient. Remember that time is on your
   side.

6. *Know the other party's level of concern for the outcome and the costs of ending negotiation.* You may
   learn this through direct information—for example,
   if a company claims it cannot withstand a strike, or
   if there is a push to settle quickly. To learn about
   their concerns while masking your own, ask them
   questions, but avert their questions to you. This information can be useful in planning your tactics.

KEY CONCEPT — SENDING AND READING COMMITMENT SIGNALS

In competitive negotiations, you cannot always be
certain about the other player's level of commitment.
Sometimes people will just shrug and walk away from

a negotiation because they don't like it or feel it is becoming too costly or emotionally stressful. Sometimes negotiators will send messages about their commitment level in order to signal a lack of commitment so the other party feels obliged to make big concessions in order to make the deal more attractive.

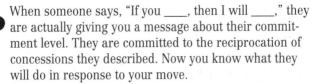 When someone says, "If you ____, then I will ____," they are actually giving you a message about their commitment level. They are committed to the reciprocation of concessions they described. Now you know what they will do in response to your move.

There are two kinds of commitment statements—threats and promises. A *threat* specifically states what happens if the other does *not* do what you want. Thus, a threat is, "If you do not ____, I will ____." This sort of statement puts the other party on the defensive, while clearly establishing your commitment. Your own esteem and need to maintain credibility (that you do what you say you will do), coupled with public pressure, can be strong motivators to make good on such a statement. In contrast, a promise is, "If you do ____, I will ____." Since you are usually offering to do something good for the other, these are more likely to help the other party open up and make them less defensive.

Like threats, however, promises can cause problems, particularly with credibility. Just as with a threat, you may get stuck with a promise and actually have to deliver on the terms. It may put you in a difficult position. If you promise your son that you will buy him a new computer game if he cuts the lawn, you will have to follow through on your promise when he does it!

Both types of commitments—promises and threats—decrease your flexibility but enhance the likelihood that the other party will give you what you want. If you decide that a commitment statement would help your position, make it. To have it carry more weight, make it public. State it in front of several people, or a group, to make it public. To add support to your statement, find allies who will back you on it. Be sure that you can carry it out.

AVOID COMMITMENT GRIDLOCK

If you make a bold promise or threat, the other party may retaliate with a similar commitment of their own. Or you may be tempted to respond to your competitor's threat with one of your own. "If you do A, I'll B." "Oh yeah? Well if you do B or C, I'll do D."

The trouble with this type of exchange is that it quickly locks the players into hard-line positions. In these situations, both sides are usually declaring that they are locked into their statements and are unwilling to change their intentions. And if both sides become entrenched in their commitments, neither may feel able to back down. And then the negotiation is likely to stall or fail. So be careful with commitment statements, whether threats or promises. It's best not to say too much about what you plan to do, since you may want to change your mind later.

FINAL OFFERS

A final offer is also a form of commitment. Final offers are declarations that one party has made all the concessions they are going to make, and it is up to the other side to make the rest of the movement to close the gap between them.

It is usually pretty obvious when the other party has made their final offer. Often they state it explicitly: "This is our final offer." They may include with the final offer a concession of fair size, as it is a common practice to save one concession until the end. Your decision now is whether to give in and move to that point, or make a final offer of your own and hope that they will decide to make more concessions. It is not uncommon for two negotiators to make concessions that cover 95 percent of the distance between their opening moves, only to deadlock with final offers that leave the remaining 5 percent on the table.

HOW TO GET OUT OF A COMMITMENT

Since commitments decrease your flexibility, you may need some sort of escape hatch or alternate plan to get out of such a commitment. Having committed yourself, what do you do if you need to get out of it? Here are several ways:

- One way to "uncommit" is to say that the situation has changed or you have new information.

- Another is to let it die quietly by never mentioning the commitment again.

- A third way out is to modify your commitment—for instance by changing the statement to more general terms.

- Phrase commitments generally so that you can modify them later. Choose the language of your commitments carefully, so that there are "escape clauses" in your words: "I never said I would buy you a video game *this week*." (You can try this on your child but it probably won't work!)

USING TACTICS

Have you planned your tactics? Competition is also characterized by a number of tactics calculated to enhance the competitor's position and place the other party at a disadvantage. These include behavioral tactics such as bluffing, being aggressive, and threatening, which can give the competitor power over the other party. While these tactics sometimes work, they also can backfire on the person using them, so they must be employed carefully. (Some of the most effective of these tricky tactics are shared later in the chapter.) However, not all competitive tactics are tricky and dangerous. Tactics #8, #9, and #10 describe methods that help win a competitive negotiation without deceit. Even though they are focused on the outcome, they don't do damage to the relationship.

Tactic #8: Helping the Other Party (or How to Get a Raise)

Here's a useful tactic from sales expert Kathy Aaronson. It's used when your boss delays discussing your raise or promotion—a common ploy. Bosses often claim they "don't have the time right now" to talk about it, but you know you can't make any progress until you can get them to the negotiating table. How?

Aaronson recommends preparing an analysis and presenting it in table or grid form in order to give your boss the information needed to justify your raise. If you can show that you've brought in a high volume of business and that the company is profiting from your work, then it is far easier for your boss and the company to justify that raise. But why should your boss do that analysis? You're the one who cares the most, so you should do the work. Then Aaronson recommends giving the information to your boss:

> Give your supervisor a copy of this material and say, "I know you have to go through channels, so you could just attach a memorandum to this if you like." You have empowered him with information.
>
> It's a good strategy, not just for this situation but for any situation in which you think you can build a good rational argument for your cause using objective information.
>
> —Kathy Aaronson[3]

Tactic #9: Shut Up

You can't give anything away if you don't talk. In fact, how much you give away is generally proportional to how much you talk. That means *the one who talks the most, loses.*

So why is it so hard to shut up and listen in a negotiation?

It isn't hard for everybody. Many Japanese negotiators are comfortable with long periods of silence—a cultural difference that gives them a natural edge over more talkative Americans.

Let's think quietly about that for a minute.

Okay. We're back. Did you squirm a little while we were sitting here silently? Were you tempted to fill the void? Most people are. Leave a thoughtful gap in the conversation and they will fill it with their thoughts. You might get an extra concession. You might simply hear some useful information about their concerns.

Whatever you hear, it is likely to help you understand the other party and design your next move. And even if you *hear* nothing of value, you can still have the satisfaction of knowing that by being quiet you *gave away* nothing of value.

 WANT TO PLAY HARDBALL?

CONCEPT   Playing the tough guy, starting out with an extreme offer, refusing to make concessions, making tough demands, and making final offers are examples of hardball tactics. They are calculated to put pressure on the other party. And they work especially well against anyone who is poorly prepared.

Tactic #10: Ask and Then Shut Up

Here's a variant on the "shut up" tactic that works well when you need more information.

Use silence to *bracket* a question, focusing the attention of the other party on a topic of your choice. All you need to do is to be quiet for a moment, then ask a question, and then wait silently for an answer, or (often) a string of answers as the other player fills the silence.

Tactic #11: Help the Other Party Save Face

If the *other party* made a commitment that it now needs to abandon, it is usually an astute move on your part to help them save face. This is where you will need to be less competitive than you might expect. If you keep the pressure on them, they are likely to either lock in to their unreasonable position and refuse to budge, or they will feel so embarrassed that they may plot to get even with you later.

Instead, we recommend that you help them save face. You might allow them to change their offer, find a way for them to be flexible without looking foolish, say that this is being done for the greater good, or make some other generous and supportive statement. If constituencies are involved, you might actively compliment the other party so that their constituency can overhear.

But other parties can be moved to revenge by your aggressive play. Then the negotiations become a series of hardball moves and countermoves, all of which may be unproductive or time-consuming. And there are other risks associated with hardball tactics, too, including loss of reputation, negative publicity, loss of the deal, and becoming the brunt of the other party's anger about what has happened.

With that warning, we want to take a look at some of the classic hardball tactics. You should learn these even if you don't plan to use them, since you may well have to defend against them in a future negotiation.

The Good Guy/Bad Guy Tactic

We have all seen this tactic in cop movies, where two investigators are questioning a suspect. First the bad guy leans heavily on the suspect, pushing him or her to the limit. Then the bad guy gets exasperated, storms out of the room, and the good guy takes over, trying to persuade the suspect to confess before the bad guy comes back.

In negotiation, the job of the good guy is to try to cut a deal before the bad guy returns. A variation on this theme is for the bad guy to talk only when the negotiations are faltering—to soften the other up—and the good guy to take over when things are progressing smoothly. The disadvantages of this tactic are: (1) it is usually obvious to everyone, (2) it alienates the other party, and (3) energy is spent on the tactic rather than on the negotiations. Nonetheless, it can be quite effective.

The Highball/Lowball Tactic

The point of this tactic is to make a ridiculous first offer, either very low or very high, depending on the situation. The intent is to force the other party to reassess its position.

If someone is selling a used computer and the buyer offers half of what the seller has asked, the seller who hasn't done his or her homework may very well think this is a fair offer and accept it. On the other hand, the seller may simply end the negotiations, thinking that there is no possible overlap. A skilled competitor may be able to turn the situation around and get the negotiations moving again, but there can be residual bad feelings that will be hard to counteract.

The Bogey

In this tactic, you pretend that an issue is important when it really is not, then trade it off later in the negotiations for something that really is important. (It is called a *straw man* issue by many negotiators.)

To use the bogey, you need to know the priorities of the other party. For example, if price is the most important element in a sale, while a good warranty is a second concern, you may make some outrageous demands on the warranty (which you know they will not give you), and then offer big concessions on the price instead.

In the bogey, you have to pretend that something is very important when it is not, and this can be difficult and confusing. If the other side is employing the same tactic, it may be impossible to sort out what is being negotiated.

The Nibble

In this ploy, you wait until the end of the proceedings when everything is almost decided, and then ask for something new. Just before the deal is ready to be signed, you try to press for one more concession: "Oh, gosh, I forgot to mention, can you have this ready for me to pick up in three hours?"

The nibble often works—unless the other side feels they are being nibbled on purpose, in which case they will resent it and may try to go back on some of their earlier concessions.

Playing Chicken

Chicken is another familiar negotiating game. It is similar to the driving game in which two teenaged drivers race directly at each other, each driver waiting for the other to "chicken out" and turn away.

 Chicken is used in competitive negotiation by bluffing and threatening in order to get what you want. The objective is to hold your ground and intimidate the other party into giving way so you can win. For example, you might make an extreme promise or threat and then wait out the other party, hoping your competitor will chicken out and cave in with a huge concession.

 The problems with this strategy are: (1) it has very high stakes, and (2) you must be willing to follow through on your threat. Escalation of war between countries is often a game of chicken. But you don't have an army or the power to raise taxes in order to fund one, so you need to be careful with this tactic.

THE POWER OF COERCION

Some negotiators behave very aggressively in an effort to intimidate or otherwise coerce the other players.

 Many intimidation ploys can be used to force an agreement in competitive negotiation. One is anger, real or feigned. Another is the use of formal documents such as contracts that force certain responses or postures. Yet another is to press someone to do something by appealing to their sense of guilt.

Aggressive behaviors—such as being pushy, attacking the other person's view, asking for explanations of positions—all can be used to coerce the other party.

 Coersive tactics such as these add up to an in-your-face style of negotiating that the other players will probably find offensive. If intimidated, they may be caught off guard and give up more than they meant to. On the other hand, they may become angry and respond with unreasonable demands. Or they may simply decide they dislike your style so much that they withdraw from the negotiation, preventing you from achieving any outcome. We don't recommend these tactics because they backfire so often.

 TACTICAL USES OF TIME

There are many ways to use deadlines, scheduling, and delays in competitive negotiations. In general, the principle is to create time pressures on the other party.

Scheduling can affect the outcome of negotiations, from the day of the week (Monday as opposed to Friday), to the hour of the day (early morning, late afternoon), to the final hour of a schedule. If a party has to travel some distance to the site of the negotiation, factors such as jet lag may affect how well the negotiations proceed. If a final negotiating session is scheduled for the hour before a party's plane departs, this may have a strong effect on the outcome. If you are the traveling party, be careful when you are setting up your flights and schedules. In labor negotiations, there may be a pressing time schedule because labor is due to go out on strike at a particular hour, or a plant is scheduled to close. You can take advantage of these situations and manipulate the scheduling to affect the course and outcome of negotiations.

Delays can be a good ploy to force a concession or resolution, particularly if time is not essential for your side but is a strong concern for the other. Stalling and slowing down the process gives you a means for manipulating the other party. Not showing up on time, asking for a rehash of the proceedings, postponing a meeting, talking endlessly about issues, and other such maneuvers can be used to advantage as long as they do not result in the breakdown of negotiation.

Some competitive tactics move into the realm of questionable ethics (see Chapter 1). While these more aggressive ploys can be successful, it is also possible that the other party will see through them. If a competitive tactic backfires, negotiations may break off because the other side is angry, feels duped, and is unwilling to deal with you. Unless you are persuasive enough to get the other side to resume negotiations, or have a good alternative, *these tactics can lead to complete negotiation breakdown.*

Some Thoughts on the Importance of Timing

After all, tomorrow is another day.

—Scarlett O'Hara in *Gone With the Wind*

I have noticed that the people who are late are often so much jollier than the people who have to wait for them.

—E. V. Lucas

MANIPULATING THE OTHER PARTY'S IMPRESSION OF YOUR CONCERNS

You can manage the other player's view of where you stand and what you want out of the negotiation if you use the following tactics:

- *Use body language or be emotional to convey your attitude, whether real or feigned.* Make them think you are angry when you are not.

- *Give the impression that you do not have the authority to make a decision.* Use someone else as a team spokesperson, or use a lawyer or agent. They may think the outcome is of less importance than it is.

- *Bring up lots of items for negotiation, many of which are unimportant.* Increase the "fog index" and confusion in the negotiation. Do not let the other side know which items are important. This is often easy to do when negotiations are over technical or complex information, or involve experts—accountants, lawyers, and engineers—who are not good at explaining technical issues to laypeople.

- *Present selectively.* Give only the facts necessary to your point of view. This allows you to lead the other party to a particular conclusion.

- *Misrepresent your information.* In some cases, exaggeration and argument lead to outright distortions of facts and misrepresentation of issues. In the extreme, this is outright deception and lying. We are not advocating this (as is said very strongly in Chapter 11), but it does happen as parties get wrapped up in the competitiveness of the process.

- *Make the costs of the negotiation seem higher.* Manipulate facts and behavior to make the other party think the proceedings are more costly than they are.

- *Manipulate the actual costs of delay or ending negotiation.* This can be done by prolonging the negotiations, by introducing other issues, or by asking for other parties to be brought in.

- *Conceal information.* Omitting information pertinent to the negotiation can manipulate the outcome, but may have dire results.

- *Use emotional tactics.* Negotiators often try to manipulate the other party's emotions to distract them and to get them to behave in a less rational manner. Get them angry or upset, flatter or amuse them—then try to get concessions while they are not paying attention. Highly emotional ploys, such as threatening to end the negotiations, sometimes achieve your purposes. Another tactic is to appear angry when you are not, to get them feeling contrite or guilty.

Disruptive actions may have the desired effect but may escalate the emotional climate and thus block your efforts. Refusal to concede sets a tone for the proceedings. So does silence.

- *Ally with outsiders.* Political action groups, protest groups, the Better Business Bureau, and other supportive groups may be able to assist you in putting pressure on the other party for a resolution. Simply threatening to talk with such groups may prod the other party to action.

ARE YOU PREPARED TO COPE WITH TOUGH TACTICS?

The best way to cope with competitive tactics is to be prepared. *Know* the various tactics, why they are used, and how they are used. Have a firm understanding of the other party's position, and keep in mind your own alternative.

In addition, here are a number of ways to handle the other party's tactical moves:[4]

- *Ignore them.* Pretend you did not hear what was said; change the subject; call a break in the proceedings and when you come back, change topics.

- *Confront the issue.* Discuss what is going on and what you see. Say something like, "I don't use the nibble tactic, and I don't want you to either. If you forgot about something while we were negotiating and you can't live without it, we'll just have to start all over again."

Negotiate about *how* you will negotiate. Suggest changes. This is easy if you remember to keep the people separate from the problem.

- *Retaliate.* Respond in kind. This can escalate the emotions, and result in hard feelings. However, it may be useful if you are being tested by the other party.

- *Sidetrack it before it happens.* For example, start out the negotiations with a discussion of how the negotiations will be conducted. Offer to behave in a specific way, and ask them to comply with your request.

END POINT

This chapter has discussed competition and its related tactics. In competition, your intention is to maximize what you can achieve on the outcome dimension, while not being concerned about the relationship dimension. As a result, you should be willing to use the strategy and tactics outlined here without any concern for what it might do to the relationship between you and the opposing negotiator.

But as you can see from many of the things discussed, if someone uses tough competitive tactics on you, it is likely that you will not see the other as nice, friendly, or someone you want to deal with in the future. As a result, if you *do* have concerns about the relationship, then this is *not* the strategy to use. (Try a Compromise strategy, or if the relationship is long term and vital, use a Collaborative approach.)

In addition, a number of things that you can do to protect yourself from an opponent who uses these tactics have been suggested. Make sure you know all the competitive tactics even if you don't like to use them. That way, you'll be ready and able to defend yourself against them.

The Collaborative Game

A collaborative negotiation is one in which both parties consider the relationship and the outcome to be important, and so work together to maximize both.

KEY CONCEPT

The collaboration game is also referred to as *cooperative* or *win–win* because it permits *both* sides to achieve winning positions.[1] How? By collaborating, you can put your energy into *creative problem solving* instead of into competitive tactics. And by so doing, you often find new ways to think about the conflict—ways that make it possible to replace trade-offs with mutually desirable outcomes.

When Goals Align
Any kid will run an errand for you, if you ask at bedtime.

—Red Skelton

In collaboration, the parties to the negotiation either begin with compatible goals or are willing to search for ways to align their goals so that both can gain. This is in sharp contrast with competition, where the parties believe their goals are mutually exclusive, so that only one side can win.

Which view is right? Are conflicts either-or, or is it possible to reframe them so that everyone wins? Remember, in negotiations, you have the opportunity to decide what game you want to play. If you want a win–lose game, you'll get it. But if you want to seek win–win opportunities, you'll find them instead. Most conflicts of interest can be viewed from *either* perspective. It's up to *you*.

DO YOU WANT TO BUILD THE RELATIONSHIP?

In successful collaborations the relationship between the parties is often an ongoing one, with some established history of give and take, so that the parties trust each other and know that they can work together. In addition, collaborative strategies are often initiated when the parties know that they want to establish long term goals for particular outcomes and for the relationship.

To make the Collaborative game work, *both* parties to the negotiation must be willing to collaborate; if one side employs it and the other uses a different one, the chances are that both parties cannot achieve good outcomes.

WHEN COLLABORATION IS KEY

Collaboration is particularly appropriate in the following situations:

- Within an organization
- When two parties have common ground
- In situations where two parties have the same customers, same clients, same suppliers, or same service personnel

In any of these cases, the parties have or want to establish a working relationship and want to keep it working smoothly.

In addition, we strongly recommend collaboration whenever the obvious outcomes of a negotiation are *undesirable* to the players. If you are all fighting over a small pie, the temptation is to compete all the harder. But what's the point of fighting over a small pie?

As the old saying goes, it's far better to figure out how to bake a bigger pie, or at least lots more little pies. Collaboration switches you from dividing the spoils to searching for more. If you use your collaboration to search for new and better approaches to the conflict—

treating it as a puzzle rather than a fight—then you are likely to improve the outcomes for both parties. And so we want you to remember the following principle:

Collaboration is the best response to conflicts in which there doesn't seem to be enough to go around.

By collaborating, you can redefine the problem so as to make more desirable outcomes possible. Why accept limits when you have a chance to redefine them?

 A FOUNDATION OF TRUST

For a collaboration to work, there must be a high degree of trust, openness, and cooperation. The parties look for common needs and goals and engage in mutually supportive behavior to obtain them. Both parties realize that they are interdependent and that their cooperative effort can solve the problems and meet the needs of both sides.

HONESTY IS THE KEY

In collaboration, communication between parties is open and accurate. This contrasts greatly with the Competitive strategy, in which the negotiators have a high level of distrust and guard information carefully to prevent the other side from obtaining the advantage.

 Deceit is often the key to competitive deals, but collaborative deal making requires honest sharing of positions. The kind of information you seek in analyzing your own and the other players' positions should be put on the table for collaboration to work. That way, each player can help the other think about how to meet their goals in creative ways that satisfy other players' goals too.

The players in a collaborative game need support from their constituencies. The constituencies must trust the parties to find common ground and support them in doing so. Doing so may mean not achieving absolutely everything the constituency wanted on the substantive issues, and the constituency has to accept this as valid. In contrast, in competition the constituencies usually push the negotiator to get everything he or she can, regardless of the future of the relationship.

Collaborating parties respect deadlines and are willing to renegotiate the time frame if necessary to achieve everyone's goals. Contrast this with competition, where time is used as an obstacle or as a power ploy to accomplish one's own ends.

Collaboration is hard work, especially if the game is new to you, but the results can be rewarding. It takes extra time and creativity to build trust and to find win–win solutions. But the outcome and relationship results are usually better for both parties.

KEYS TO SUCCESSFUL COLLABORATION

Collaboration has traditionally been underutilized, because most people do not understand the fine points of the strategy and because collaborations are less familiar than competitive negotiating methods. Many negotiations are based on the Competitive model, which is the way most people view negotiation—as a competitive situation where one is better off being suspicious of the other, and the fundamental object is to get all the goodies.

For collaboration to work—to find those "out of the box" solutions that give both parties more than they initially expected—both parties need to be committed to the following objectives:

1. Understanding the *other* party's needs and objectives

2. Providing a free flow of information both ways

3. Seeking the best solutions to meet the needs of both sides.[2]

KEY CONCEPT   **CAN I HELP YOU GET WHAT YOU WANT?**

Understanding the other party's goals and needs is critical to collaboration. We suggested that this is important in a competitive negotiation as well, but for very different reasons. In competition, you may know or think you know what the other party wants; but your objective in learning this is to facilitate your own strategy development, and also to strategize how to beat the other side by doing better than them or denying them what they want to achieve. In collaboration, your objective is to understand their goals and needs so that you can work with them to achieve their goals as well as your own.

Good collaboration frequently requires not only understanding their stated objectives, but also their underlying needs—*why* they want what they want. In a collaborative negotiation, both parties must be willing to ask questions and *listen carefully to the answers,* to learn about the other party's needs.

To provide a free flow of information, both parties must be willing to *volunteer* information. The information has to be as accurate and as comprehensive as possible. Both sides need to understand the issues, the problems, the priorities, and the goals of the other. They need to fully understand the important context factors in the negotiation. Compare this with competitive negotiations, in which information is closely guarded, or, if shared, often distorted.

Finally, having listened closely to each other, the parties can then work toward *achieving mutual goals* that will satisfy both parties. To do this, the parties will need to minimize their differences and emphasize their similarities. They will need to focus on the issues and work at keeping personalities out of the discussions.

BECOME A COLLABORATIVE PROBLEM SOLVER

Collaborative goals differ from competitive goals. In competition, the goal is obtaining the largest share of the pie, at any cost, without giving away any information or conceding on any issue. In collaboration, each party must be willing to redefine their perspective in light of the collaboration, knowing that the whole can be greater than the sum of the parts. In this light, having a strong knowledge of the problem area is a definite advantage. While a lack of information can be overcome, starting out with the knowledge is definitely an asset.

To achieve success, each party *from the beginning* must send signals to the other that will help build trust between and among those negotiating. Be careful not to send mixed messages if you want to collaborate. There is no point in putting half your cards on the table. It precludes collaboration *or* competition.

OBSTACLES TO COLLABORATION

Both parties to a negotiation must be willing to collaborate if this strategy is to be successful. It will be difficult, if not impossible, to employ collaboration under the following circumstances:

- One party does not see the situation as having the potential for collaboration.
- One party is motivated only to accomplish its own ends.
- One party has historically been competitive; this behavior may be hard to change.
- One party expects the other to be competitive and prepares for negotiation based on this expectation.

- One party wants to be competitive and rationalizes this behavior.

- One party is accountable to a constituency that prefers the Competitive strategy.

- One party is not willing to take the time to search for collaborative items.

- The negotiation or bargaining mix includes both competitive and collaborative issues. (Sometimes, the two parties can collaborate on collaborative issues and compete on competitive issues. Our experience, however, is that competitive processes tend to drive out collaborative processes, making collaboration harder to achieve.)

Most of these obstacles reflect a lack of commitment to collaboration on at least one player's side. Again, commitment is the core issue if you want to make collaboration work.

ARE YOU SERIOUS ABOUT COLLABORATION?

Some negotiators think they are collaborating when in fact all they have done is wrap their competitive strategy in a friendly package. Thus, they put on the *image* of collaboration, only to move in for a competitive grab near the end of the negotiation. This is not collaboration—it is competitiveness in a Collaborative disguise. True collaboration requires the parties to move beyond their initial concerns and positions and go on a joint quest for new, creative ways to maximize their individual and joint outcomes.

In collaboration, both the relationship *and* the outcome are important to both parties. The two parties usually have long-term goals that they are willing to work for together. Both parties are committed to working toward a mutually acceptable agreement that preserves or strengthens the relationship. Because each party values the relationship, they will attempt to find a mutually satisfying solution for both parties. Working together effectively in a Collaborative negotiation process can itself enhance the quality of the relationship. This approach is very different from the Competitive strategy, where both sides want to win so badly that they pursue their goal at all costs and ignore all the factors that might allow a Collaborative process.

 PAY ATTENTION TO THE SOFT STUFF

In the collaborative model, intangibles are important and accounted for. These include such items as each party's reputation, pride, principles, and sense of fairness. Because these concerns are important, the negotiations must stay on a rational, reasonable, and fair level. If the parties get angry at each other, the collaborative atmosphere will degenerate into a competitive one. Allow for plenty of venting time if you or the other party begins to get irritated, and be sure to listen to complaints about your behavior with an open mind to avoid conflicts that can derail collaboration. There must be a great deal of trust, cooperation, openness, and communication between the parties to engage in effective problem solving.

ARE YOU READY TO MAKE CONCESSIONS?

To collaborate the parties must be willing to make *concessions* to accomplish their goals. These concessions should be repaid with creative win–win solutions, but they represent a risk for each party that the other party must be careful not to abuse. If you aren't willing to run some risks, don't bother with collaboration.

USE TIME AS A RESOURCE, NOT A WEAPON

Collaboration relies on deadlines that are mutually determined and observed. They are *not* used for manipulation, as they are in competitive negotiations. Information flows freely and is not used to control the situation or guarded to maintain power. The objective is to find the best solution *for both sides.* Similarities between the two parties, not differences, are emphasized.

A FOUR-STEP PROCESS

There are four major steps in carrying out collaboration: (1) identify the problem; (2) understand the problem; (3) generate alternative solutions; and (4) select a solution. You need to master each step, so let's take a closer look at them.

Step 1: Identify the Problem

Identifying the problem may *sound* like a simple step, but it's not.

In the Collaborative model both sides are involved equally in the process of problem definition, and both need to agree fully on what the problem is.

When you were gathering information you focused on *your* point of view, but for collaboration to work, you will need to work closely with the other party to find a common view of the problem.[3]

When defining the problem, try to use neutral language and to keep it impersonal. For example, you might say "We are not able to get our work out on time" rather than "You are preventing us from doing our work and getting it out on time." It is important to define the obstacles to your goals without attacking other people.

Try to *define the problem as a common goal.* Keep the goal definition as simple as possible. Try not to load the situation with peripheral issues that are not really related to the central concern. Stick with the primary issues.

Each party needs to be assertive, but cooperative at the same time: You need to be clear about what you want to achieve, yet not at the expense of dominating the other side. Because the relationship is important, you need to see the problem from the other party's perspective—to walk a mile in the other person's shoes, as the saying goes. Understanding and empathy help you find the common issues.[4]

Watch out for a tendency to define solutions before you have fully defined the problem. In fact, you should *avoid discussing solutions* until you have thoroughly defined and understood the problems. The point of collaboration is to treat the outcome as variable, not fixed. So don't fix it up front.

Be Creative

And remember, the more creative the problem definition, the more likely you are to discover a new, beneficial win–win solution. Throw caution to the wind, brainstorm wildly, and hope for a creative insight that will make it fun and easy to solve the problem.

Step 2: Understand the Problem

In this step, you try to get behind the issues to the underlying needs and interests.[5] As noted earlier, an *interest* is a broader perspective that is usually behind a position. You need to learn not only about the needs and interests of each party, but also about their fears and concerns. The reason for getting behind the positions is that they tend to be fixed and rigid; modifying them requires the parties to make concessions either toward or away from the target point.

In contrast to positions, interests define what the parties care about more broadly, and there are often multiple ways to resolve the conflict between these competing interests.

In addition, a focus on interests tends to take some of the personal dimension out of the negotiation and shifts it to the underlying concerns.[6] Since there is bound to be a difference in thinking styles, people will approach even similar issues in different ways. Positions offer only one way to think about an issue; interests offer multiple ways to think about it. Thus, you can find out where they are coming from more effectively by discussing interests than by stating positions. By using *why* questions, you can dig deeper into the reasons for each party's position.

Collaborators Must Stand on Shifting Ground

Remember that even if you define interests carefully, they can change. Because the negotiation process is an evolving one, you may need to stop from time to time to reconsider interests. If the conversation begins to change in tone or the focus seems to shift, this may be a signal that interests have changed.

Collaborative negotiators with changing interests should be encouraged to share their shifts in needs. The other party may be able to help achieve new needs by expanding resources, extending the time frame, or changing the details of the negotiation to accommodate the changed interests (more is said about some of these tactics in the next section).[7]

Step 3: Generate Alternative Solutions

Once you have defined the issues to the satisfaction of both parties, you can begin to look for solutions. Note that this is plural: solution*s*. You want to find a group of possible solutions, then select from among them the best solution for both parties. In collaborations, the more solutions the merrier!

There are two major ways to go about finding solutions. One is to redefine the problem so you can find win–win alternatives for what at first may have seemed to be a win–lose problem. The second is to take the problem at hand and generate a long list of options for solving it.

To illustrate the different approaches, we will use an example suggested by Dean Pruitt, about a husband and wife who are trying to decide where to spend a two-week vacation.[8] He wants to go to the mountains for hiking, fishing, and some rest; she wants to go to the beach for sun, swimming, and night life. They have decided that spending one week in each place will not really be adequate for either person, because too much time is spent in packing, unpacking, and traveling between the two locations.

- *Expand the pie.* If the problem is based on scarce resources, the object would be to find a way to expand or reallocate the resources so that each party could obtain their desired end. Knowing the underlying interests can help in this endeavor. For example, the parties could take a four-week vacation, and spend two weeks in each place. While this would require more time and money, each person would get a two-week vacation in the chosen spot.

- *Logroll.* If there are two issues in a negotiation and each party has a different priority for them, then one may be able to be traded off for the other. For example, if Problems A and B are common to both parties, but Party 1 cares most about Problem A and Party 2 cares most about Problem B, then a solution that solves both problems can provide each party with a happy resolution. "You get this and I get that." If there are multiple issues, it may take some trial and error to find what packages will satisfy each party. In our example, if the husband really wants to stay in an informal rustic mountain cabin, and the wife really wants to stay in a fancy hotel at the beach, then another resolution is for them to go to the mountains but stay in a fancy hotel (or an informal beach house at the shore).

- *Offer nonspecific compensation.* Another method is for one party to *pay off* the other for giving in on an issue. The payoff may not be monetary, and it may not even be related to the negotiation. The party paying off needs to know what it will take to keep the other party so happy that they won't care about the outcome of this negotiation. In a house-sale negotiation, for example, the seller might include all window coverings (curtains, drapes, and blinds) as part of the deal. The buyer may be so delighted that he or she decides not to ask for any other price break. In our vacation example, the wife might buy the husband a set of golf clubs, which will make him so happy that he will go anywhere she wants to go (since there are golf courses everywhere).

- *Cut costs.* In this method, one party accomplishes specific objectives and the other's costs are minimized by going along with the agreement. This differs from nonspecific compensation because in this method the other party can minimize costs and suffering, whereas in the other method, the costs and suffering do not go away, but the party is somehow compensated for them. This method requires a clear understanding of the other party's needs and preferences, along with their costs. In our vacation example, the wife says to the husband, "What can I do to make going to the beach as painless as possible for you?" He tells her that he wants to stay in a beach house away from the big hotels to get some rest, and be near a golf course and several places where he can go fishing. They both go down to their favorite travel agent and find a location that offers all these things.

- *Bridge.* In bridging, the parties invent new options that meet each other's needs. Again, both parties must be very familiar with the other party's interests and needs. When two business partners bring in a third partner who can offer resources neither of them wanted to contribute, this is an effective example of bridging. In our vacation example, the husband and wife go to a travel agent and find a place that offers hiking, fishing, beaches, swimming, golf, privacy, and night life. They book a two-week vacation for Hawaii and have a wonderful time.

All these tactics for generating solutions focus on redefinitions of the original problem. That's a powerful strategy, but is not always necessary. The second approach to inventing solutions is to take the problem as defined and try to generate a lengthy list of possible solutions. Sometimes there is a solution nobody had thought of beforehand that works quite well once you uncover it.

The key to finding answers in this approach is to generate as many solutions as possible *without evaluating them.* The solutions should be general rather than party-specific—they should not favor one party over the other. At a later stage, each solution can be evaluated to determine whether it adequately meets the needs and interests of both parties.

What is interesting in this process is that both parties engage in trying to solve the other party's problem as much as they do their own.[9] It is a cooperative endeavor. And, as you have probably heard many times before, two heads are better than one.

 If you get to this stage, but the issues still seem murky, you may need to go back to the problem definition and rework that step. It should be easy to generate solutions if the problem is clearly stated in a way that does not bias solutions toward one party or the other. Otherwise, if you are comfortable with the definition of the problem, forge ahead.

KEY CONCEPT There are a number of ways to generate ideas for solutions. Remember that you are only *generating* solutions in this step, not evaluating them or deciding whether to use them—yet. That will happen in the next step.

- *Brainstorming.* This common method for generating ideas usually works best in several small groups rather than one large one, depending on the number of people involved. Write down as many ideas as possible, without judging them. It is best to write or post the ideas on a flip chart, chalkboard, or similar display device, so that everyone can see them and keep track of what has been done. The key ground rule is that *ideas must not be evaluated as they are suggested.* Don't let anyone say, "Oh, that's a dumb idea!" or "That won't work!" Keep ideas flowing, stay focused on the problem and how to solve it, without associating people with the problem or the solutions.

  It often happens that people quickly think of a few possibilities, and then run out of ideas. At this point, it is easy to think you are done because you have a few solutions. Don't stop here—stick at it for a while longer. Otherwise, you may miss some really good ideas, particularly creative ones that no one has considered before. Ask outsiders for ideas, too. Sometimes they bring a fresh approach to the problem.

- *Piggybacking.* Piggybacking can be used in conjunction with brainstorming.[10] This technique is simply to build on someone else's idea to produce yet another idea. It's often done by working in a sequence order—one person starts with a brainstormed idea, then the next person has to "piggyback" until possible variations on the idea are exhausted.

- *Breakout groups.* In this method, each negotiator works with a small group—perhaps their constituency—and makes a list of possible solutions. These are discussed within the breakout group, then considered, one at a time, by the larger group. They can be ranked in terms of preferences or likely effectiveness. The drawback of this method is that anyone not present at the session will miss out on offering input or helping to shape the solution.

- *Surveys.* Another useful method is to distribute a questionnaire stating the problem and asking respondents to list possible solutions. In this case, each person works alone on the survey, so people miss out on the synergy of working together. However, the advantage is that a number of people who have good ideas but are normally reticent about getting into a group's conversation, can offer their thoughts and ideas without being attacked or critiqued. Another advantage is that this draws in the ideas of people who may not be able to attend the negotiation or formally participate in it.

Prioritize the Options and Reduce the List

Once you have a list of possible solutions, you can reduce it by rating the ideas, much as we prioritized the issues in previous chapters. In communicating your priorities and preferences to the other party, it's important to maintain an attitude of *firm flexibility*.[11] Be firm about achieving your interests, while remaining flexible about how those interests might be achieved. There are a number of tactics to keep the discussion collaborative while being clear and consistent about your preferences:

- Remember that you are only *prioritizing* the list, not yet deciding on the actual solution.

- Be assertive in defending and establishing your basic interests, but do not demand a particular solution.

- Signal to the other party your flexibility and willingness to hear their interests by practicing your listening skills. For instance, use *active listening* by trying to repeat what they said back to them in order to see if you understood their point.

- Indicate your willingness to modify a position or have your interests met in an alternative way. Perhaps you will be able to trade one point for another. This will demonstrate your openness to suggestions and willingness to work together.

- Show ability and willingness to solve problems. Skill in problem solving is valuable here, especially if you get stuck on a particular point and need to find some way to resolve it to everyone's satisfaction. If you can settle this issue, it will help when you get to the next step and are actually deciding on the solution. You will have set the stage for collaboration.

- Keep lines of communication open. If tempers flare, take a break, and talk about it if need be. Also talk with the other party about how you can continue to work on the problem without getting angry or losing control. Make sure both parties feel that they are being heard. Steer discussion away from personalities, and concentrate on the issues: "Separate the people from the problem."[12]

- Underscore what is most important to you by saying, "This is what I need to accomplish," or "As long as I can accomplish ____, I'll be very happy." Resist the temptation to give in just to get a resolution. Giving in is an Accommodating strategy that will not result in the best outcome for both parties.

- Reevaluate any points on which you disagree. Be sure that both sides agree on the adjusted prioritized list so that you will both feel comfortable as you move to the final step.

- Eliminate competitive tactics by identifying them and either confronting them or renegotiating the process. If the discussion becomes competitive, point out that this is happening. Then try to resolve the problem *before* the entire negotiation becomes competitive.

Step 4: Select a Solution

Using your prioritized list of potential solutions from the previous step, narrow the range of possibilities by focusing on the positive suggestions that people seemed to favor most.[13] For example, one way to prioritize is to logroll by packaging each person's first choice together. If parties have the same first choice, but very different preferences for it, try to invent a way for both sides to win on this issue.

Try to change any negative ideas into positive ones, or else eliminate them from the list.[14] Stating alternatives as positives keeps the negotiation upbeat and on a positive note. Avoid attributing negative ideas to any particular person or side.

 Evaluate the solutions on the basis of quality and acceptability. Consider the opinions of both parties. Do not require people to justify their preferences. People often do not know why they have a preference, they just do.

 If you foresee any potential problems with the solution selection process, you may want to establish objective criteria for evaluation before you start the selection process.[15] In other words, before you move toward picking among prioritized options, work against a set of objective facts, figures, data, and criteria that were developed independently of the options.

If a car owner and a garage mechanic are having a dispute about how much it should cost to repair a starter motor, there are books available that indicate the *standard* cost for parts and labor for this repair. Similarly, if a group of people are trying to pick a job candidate from among a group who applied for the job, their work will be considerably facilitated if they spend time developing criteria by which to evaluate the applicants before they actually look at resumes and interview people.

Consider Fairness and Other Intangibles

Intangibles are often operating in the selection of a solution. For example, gaining recognition or looking strong to a constituency may be important factors in someone's selection decision. Acknowledge the importance of intangibles by *building them into the decisions*.

For example, if the other party needs to maintain esteem with a constituency, they may be willing to settle on a lesser point that still allows them to appear in a favorable light. In fact, it will help them greatly if you work with them to determine how to make them look strong and capable to their constituency.

How Do You Know It's Fair?

Fairness is usually one of the most important intangibles. In a win–win negotiation, both parties want to achieve a fair outcome. There are a number of ways to decide what is fair, but three common criteria often apply:[16]

- An outcome that gives each side *equal* outcomes. Thus, it is not surprising that one of the most common ways to solve negotiation problems—particularly win–lose, competitive ones—is for the parties to agree to divide it down the middle.

- An outcome that gives each side more or less based on *equity* (what it has earned or deserves, based on the time or energy committed). In this case, the side that puts more in should get more out. Equity is usually based on the ratio of outcome to input, so that the person who works harder, suffers more, and so on, deserves a proportionately larger share of the results.

- An outcome that gives each side more or less, depending on what it *needs*. In this case, if one side can create a legitimate claim that it needs or deserves a better outcome, there may be a good case to be made for dividing up the resources so that those with greater needs actually gain more.

Emotions Escalating?

If emotions surface, or if people get angry, take a break. Give people an opportunity to discuss the reasons for their dissatisfaction. Be sure everyone has cooled off before you start again, and try to keep personalities out of the deliberations. If taking a break does not work, seek out a third party to help you. Anyone with a modicum of interpersonal and problem-solving skills can be of help, provided they don't have a personal stake in the outcome. And if you wish, you can bring in a trained mediator, facilitator, or problem solver.

Take Your Time

It is very important not to rush the process of selecting solutions, appealing as it may be to do so. If you get to the bottom line too quickly, you may miss some good potential options, and you may fail to assure that both sides participate equally.[17] Collaborative efforts require the participation of both sides; they may also require time to mull over alternatives and think through all the consequences. Good Collaborative negotiation requires time and cannot be rushed.

You Can Always Change Your Mind

Remember that *everything is tentative until the very end.* During the solution-generating phase, some people may even object to writing anything down, as this may make them nervous. They may feel they are being rail-roaded into commitments they have not agreed to. Other than the working documents that you may create as you define the problem and invent options, you may want to begin to record decisions only when the group is close to consensus. That way, nothing is set in stone until the very end. This open, fluid approach makes it possible to share creative ideas and suggestions. The minute one party says, "But you said yesterday you'd be willing to ____," the collaboration starts to unravel as participants begin to worry about being held ac-countable for "positions." This difficult and critical rule is violated too often as people revert instinctively to a Competitive style without realizing the impact on idea generation and sharing.

Tactic #12: Write It Down

After the parties have agreed on solutions and prepared a document to out-line the agreement, it should be passed around for everyone to read. Some people have suggested that this may even be an excellent way to manage the entire prioritization and decision-making process. Start with a tentative draft of what people agree to, then continue to pass it around, sharpening language, clarifying words, and writing out agreements so that all agree with it and pledge to live by it.

SECRETS OF SUCCESSFUL COLLABORATION

Researchers have identified several keys to successful collaboration.[18] They are useful as a checklist for the strategic negotiator in planning and implementing a collaboration.

❏ *Create common goals or objectives.* There may be three different ways the goals will be played out: (1) all parties will share in the results equally, (2) the parties will share a common end but will receive different benefits, or (3) the parties will have different goals, but will share in a collective effort to accomplish them. In any of these cases, both parties believe they can benefit by working together as opposed to working separately, and that the results will be better than they would be if each party worked separately.

❏ *Maintain confidence in your own ability to solve problems.* This is more or less a matter of "If you think you can, you can." As mentioned earlier, it helps to have a strong knowledge of the problem area, but lack of knowledge can be overcome if the desire is there. Probably the most important element is to develop skills in negotiating collaboratively, since it is a less common form of negotiation. The more you do it, the better you will become at doing it.

❏ *Value the other party's opinion.* Valuing the other party's point of view is difficult if you have been accustomed in the past to focusing only on your own position and maintaining it. In collaboration, you value the other party's position equally with your own.[19] You need good listening skills and openness to hear the other party's point of view.

❏ *Share the motivation and commitment to working together.* In collaboration, you are not only committed to the idea of working together with the other party, you take actions to do so. You pursue both your own needs and those of the other party. This means that each party must be explicit about their needs.

In Collaborative negotiation, the parties strive to identify their similarities to each other and to downplay their differences. The differences are not ignored, they are simply recognized and accepted for what they are.

The parties are aware that they share a common fate, particularly if they expect to work together after this negotiation has been completed. They know they can gain more if they work jointly than if they work separately. To do this, they focus on outputs and results.[20]

Motivated, committed parties will control their behavior in a number of ways. Individuals will avoid being competitive, combative, evasive, defensive, or stubborn. They will work at being open and trusting, flexible, and willing to share information and not to hoard it for their own use.

DON'T GO *TOO* FAR

Believe it or not, there is such a thing as too much collaboration. The two parties must not be so committed to each other that they do not look out for their own needs. If they begin to subordinate their needs to the other party, they will be moving toward an Accommodating (or lose–win) style and will lose out on the benefits of collaboration.

 **HOW AND WHY TO BUILD TRUST**

Because trust creates more trust—which is necessary to begin and sustain cooperation—it is important to make the opening moves in Collaborative negotiation in a way that engenders trust.[21] Opening conversations may occur even before the formal negotiations begin, when the parties are just becoming acquainted. If one party finds a reason to mistrust the other party at this time, this may stifle any future efforts at collaboration.

If the parties are new to each other, or if they have been combative or competitive in the past, they will have to build trust. Each party will approach the negotiation with expectations based on the research they did on each other or on history. Generally, we trust others if they appear to be similar to us, if they have a positive attitude toward us, or if they appear to be cooperative and trusting. We also tend to trust them if they are dependent on us. Likewise, making concessions appears to be a trusting gesture, so we are likely to respond in kind.

In contrast, it is easy to engender mistrust. Suspicion is seeded either with a competitive, hostile action, or with an indication that one player does not trust the other. Once mistrust gets started, it is very easy to build and escalate, and very difficult to change over to collaboration.

Trust escalation and deescalation have often been compared with the children's game Chutes and Ladders. In this analogy, it is easy to move down the chute of mistrust, rapidly sliding to the bottom, but much more difficult to climb back up the ladder that will restore and sustain good trust between parties.[22]

OBSTACLES TO ACHIEVING GOOD COLLABORATION

Collaborative negotiation is a lot of work. But the rewards can be great. Sometimes, however, no matter how much you want to succeed, obstacles may prevent you from moving ahead with collaboration. You'll certainly get stuck if one (or both) of the parties do any of the following, so be sure to avoid these mistakes—and try to weed them out of your collaborations, even when the other party plants them by mistake.

Problems arise when one or both parties:

- May not be able to do the required work
- May have a win–lose attitude
- May not be able to see the potential for collaboration
- May be motivated to only achieve their own goals
- May not be capable of establishing or maintaining productive working relationships
- May be inhibited by biases
- May have a constituency that is pressing for competitive behavior or quick outcomes

Further, the situation may contain elements that require a mix of strategies. Then you need to separate the issues into the component parts and deal with each separately.

Sometimes, you may feel that you do not have the time or energy to push forward with collaboration, especially if you encounter one or more of the preceding situations.

WHAT IF THERE'S A BREAKDOWN?

If there is a conflict, try to move the discussion to a neutral point, and summarize where you are.[23] If there is a total breakdown in communication, and you just cannot get the negotiation back on track, you may need to resort to conflict-resolution strategies or to third-party intervention.

And also note that you and the other party can, at any point, reach a mutual agreement to abandon your collaboration and adopt another negotiating style. For instance, you might try collaborating, decide you don't like working together, and decide that you will agree to disagree and revert to a conventional competitive strategy—or toward a more expedient and simple outcome through compromising. Remember, however, that you will give up the relationship benefits, so do not advocate competition unless you decide that your initial estimation of relationship importance was too high.

Since you will have shared much information through your collaboration attempt, it can now be used against you in a competitive negotiation. Therefore, the slide from collaboration to competition is not generally a happy or profitable one because some of the actions you undertook under the assumption that you could trust the other party and work with them may now be used against you as weapons.

COLLABORATIVE NEGOTIATION WITH YOUR BOSS

Since everyone has had some sort of experience dealing with a boss at one time or another, we will take a moment here to look at ways to negotiate collaboratively with a manager.[24] Although performance review, salary, and benefits are usually the major areas for discussion and possible conflict with one's manager, there are others that arise more often.

For example, what if you are asked by your boss to do a project that you realize you cannot possibly complete without working overtime? If you do not mind staying late, go ahead. But if you find yourself doing this frequently and resenting it, maybe you need to consider negotiating about it the next time.

 Negotiating with the boss is often viewed as a competitive, win–lose, or fixed-pie situation. It can also be viewed as a lose–win situation, in which it is better to accommodate and let the boss win all the time, rather than try to argue for a preferred outcome and have the boss be angry at your assertiveness. But if you think about it, both parties might be able to gain something from collaborative negotiation.

Think about the steps in collaboration covered earlier in the chapter. Look at your own needs, as well as those of your boss. Remember that the key to collaborative bargaining is to find a way to solve the other person's problem.

So, in our hypothetical situation, your boss may have been asked by her boss to drop everything and get this project out, at any cost. (Your boss may have some bargaining of her own to do.) At any rate, your boss has to have this project done and there is no way for you to complete it during normal hours, given the other work you have to do and the deadlines for those projects. Your boss could ask someone else to do it, but perhaps she knows you can do the job better and more quickly.

First, clarify the situation. Find out the circumstances from your boss. Be sure you understand the details of the project. Gather information you may need about what you are working on at the present time.

When it is time to discuss the project again, you will be prepared. Be sure your boss knows and understands the situation from your side. List what you are currently working on, and make sure she is willing for you to put those things aside to work on this rush proj-

Negotiating a Strategic Alliance

A business example of the use of negotiation is in the area of strategic alliances, which are gaining in importance worldwide, particularly in Europe. Global competition has intensified the scramble for access to markets, products, and technologies. Strategic alliances are one strategy that companies are using to survive or to keep up with the new developments in industry.

Negotiating a strategic alliance presents a challenge. "A bad negotiation tactic may do lasting damage; good negotiation tactics must be repeated a number of times before the partner accepts this as a pattern."[25] In a strategic alliance, the relationship concerns will be very important.

In 1985, Corning and Ciba-Geigy formed Ciba Corning Diagnostics, an alliance based in the United States, designed to enhance Corning's medical diagnostics business. Ciba-Geigy is a global pharmaceutical and chemical company based in Switzerland. Corning, based in New York, is a world leader in glass and ceramics technology. The alliance combines the strengths of the two partners to develop innovative medical diagnostic tests.

There was synergy in what each partner could offer to the alliance. Negotiation went smoothly, as Ciba was willing to have Corning manage more extensively in the beginning. Corning's managers were willing to concede on points of strong interest to Ciba, and thus they were able to agree on a time line for their work. Each partner appointed its director of research and development to the board of the new alliance, which signaled to the other party a willingness to share technology, while garnering internal support for the alliance as well.

Each side had representatives to build consensus, improve communication, and obtain support for the parent organization. Ciba and Corning actively looked into ways for each partner to gain by opening up possibilities for broadening the product line, marketing, technology, and growth. They were able to negotiate any issues that arose because, as mutual trust grew, they were willing to discuss such problems clearly and openly.

A strategic alliance will not succeed if the two potential partners have conflicting underlying motives. If they are both leaders in their field, it may be difficult for them to collaborate. Likewise, if they have strongly differing views of which activities should take priority or what the time lines should be, the success of such an alliance would be questionable.

To create a successful alliance, each organization must be willing to support the efforts to create an alliance agreement. This means that political support must be generated within the organizations of the potential partners. Building support may take time. For example, the Japanese take a long time to complete this process (at least from the American point of view). Conversely, the Japanese see American firms as being too pushy.

ect. Or does she prefer to have you give it only part of your attention? We knew one person who, when her boss piled new work on her desk, made a list of all the projects she was currently managing. Then she handed the list to her boss, and asked him to number the list in the order that he wanted things done. It made him decide what his priorities were.

You can make a number of suggestions for how to complete the project, given the circumstances. (This means you will have brainstormed for ideas before you meet with her.) One option might be for the boss (perhaps with your help) to find more resources. Two people could perhaps help with the project, thus halving the time it will take to complete.

Another option would be for your boss to get an extension of the time allotted for the project. To do this, she would have to negotiate with her boss.

A third option might be to change the *specs* of the project (e.g., to make it less detailed or more streamlined), which would allow you to complete it in less time.

You also could suggest, "If I stay late several nights to do this project, I would like to take compensating time off," or "If I do this project, then I need help to complete my other projects on time, or else an extension." These are compromising strategies, which are taken up further in the next chapter.

This example illustrates that even an apparently simple negotiation can be more complex than we realize. In this case, it involves not just you and your boss, but her boss as well (and who knows who else?). In any situation, it helps to break down a problem into its component parts and try to get at the underlying needs.

END POINT

This chapter has outlined the Collaborative negotiating game. When playing this game, your objective is both to maximize your outcome on the substantive issues and to sustain or enhance the quality of the relationship between you and the other side. To do so, you need to meet your outcome needs as well as the needs of the other party in a manner that strengthens the trust, mutuality, and productive problem solving in the relationship.

Good collaboration is a wonderful thing to be able to create and sustain. But it is not an all-purpose panacea, and making it work well often requires a large commitment of time and energy. There are times when the parties might be just as well off to Compromise, Accommodate, or even Avoid negotiations. The following chapters will take a look at these alternative negotiating strategies.

The Compromise Game

Compromises are simple, obviously fair ways of settling differences. If you and a coworker each want to take early lunches, but one of you needs to stay on duty, it's easy to compromise by alternating days. You get the desired early period every other day.

Perhaps there are more elegant solutions. Maybe you would prefer to take early lunch two days in a row next week when you have a scheduling problem, but other times you'd be willing to skip lunch hour all week if you could leave a little early in exchange. To explore more sophisticated alternatives such as these you'd need to roll up your sleeves and engage in a more involved negotiation. Competition or (even better) collaboration would do the trick. But to achieve a simple, equitable solution in a hurry, compromising will do.

KEY CONCEPT

Compromising may be thought of as an "adequate for most occasions" approach to negotiation. In this strategy, each side will have to modify their priorities for the relationship and for the preferred outcomes. In both cases, the parties are making a decision that compromising is preferred because, on the one hand, *both* parties gain something (an advantage over Accommodation), both parties gain *something* (as opposed to nothing—an advantage over Avoiding), and yet Compromising does not require all the intentional effort required for Competition or Collaboration.

TIP

While negotiators usually don't start off planning a compromise (particularly if a competitive or collaborative negotiation is possible), compromising is often seen as an acceptable second choice. You should keep compromise up your sleeve for situations in which more involved negotiations don't seem worth the trouble—but you still want to take care of outcome and relationship concerns.

WHEN TO COMPROMISE

There are three major reasons to choose a Compromising strategy (particularly as a default alternative to other strategies):

- A true collaboration does not seem to be possible, but the relationship is important. One or both parties don't believe that true win–win can be achieved because it is simply too complex or too difficult. Or, the relationship may already be too strained for the parties to work together in a manner that fosters and supports good collaboration.

- The parties are short of time or other critical resources necessary to get to collaboration. Compromising is usually quick and efficient. While it may be suboptimal on the quality of the outcomes achieved, the trade-off between achieving a great outcome and the time required to do it may force one to pick time over quality.

- Both parties gain something (or don't lose anything) on both dimensions. As opposed to pursuing a Competitive strategy (and maximizing outcomes at the expense of the relationship) or an Accommodating strategy (and sacrificing outcomes for the relationship), Compromising assures some gain on *both* the outcome and relationship dimensions.

COMPROMISES ARE ALSO A COMPROMISE OF STYLES

Compromise is at the center of the diagram of negotiating strategies in Chapter 6 (Figure 6.2). When implemented, the Compromise style of negotiating is most likely a blend of the other styles. The approach in compromising is to gain something on the outcome dimension, but not push for completely meeting one's objectives and needs. This often translates into *splitting the difference* in some way between or among the parties; by not pressing for the maximum, everyone gets something equitable.[1]

 A compromise may not be an even split, but because it is some kind of *symmetrical* or *logical* split, it is easier to obtain agreement with the other party than it is through competition or collaboration. Moreover, the outcome is likely to be more beneficial than one obtained through avoiding or accommodation.

With compromising, you show some concern for the *relationship* because you do not insist on a complete win (as in the Competitive strategy) and you demonstrate empathy by assuring that the other party gets *something* on the outcome dimension as well. You are also showing that you care, to some degree, whether the other party achieves their outcomes in the negotiation, demonstrating empathy for the others' concerns.

By showing that you care enough to seek an equitable compromise, you may well enhance your image with the other party as someone who is reasonable, fair, and willing to help both sides gain something—key intangibles that often make a difference both to outcome and to relationship.

YOU GET WHAT YOU PAY FOR

The low negotiating costs of an agreement through compromise are beneficial, but they are balanced by the higher *opportunity* costs of the strategy. The compromise may result in satisfying some of each party's objectives, but it does not optimize the situation in the way that collaboration can.

Basically, compromise often means *trading equivalent concessions.* Although both sides end up with less than they wanted ("50 percent of something is better than 100 percent of nothing"), they also don't maximize. The objective is for the deal to benefit both parties to some degree, so that both are invested in making the agreement work.[2]

Tactic #13: After You!

"Let's compromise." How many times has someone said those famous words as an invitation to strike a quick, simple deal when a conflict bogs things down? By saying, "Let's compromise," you immediately signal your willingness to expedite the resolution of the problem.

But don't stop there. In the "after you" tactic, you say, "Let's compromise. What do you think's fair?" This invites the other party to make the first concession. And it sets the bottom limit on what you'll have to give up. It also gives you the opportunity to simply say no—if their offer is clearly more than twice as low as your target. If so, politely say something like "Maybe compromising isn't such a good idea after all." Postpone the compromise, treating the first round as a trial balloon. Then try to initiate a

(Continued)

(Continued)

compromise later on with a more favorable opening (using the same *after you* tactic).

But most likely, the other party's opening offer will be reasonable, and you can start bargaining from there. If they want a compromise, too, they will make a reasonable or even generous opening offer. By letting them go first, you often get a more favorable outcome than if you had made the first offer.

COMPROMISING COMPARED TO COMPETITION

In a Compromising strategy you make a moderate effort to pursue your own outcomes, and make a moderate attempt to help the other party achieve their outcomes. Such a strategy may appear to be a watered-down version of collaboration. In many ways, that is correct—some actually see it as a "lazy" or yielding approach to negotiation.[3]

But a compromise is better than out-and-out competition in situations characterized by the following circumstances:

1. The resources are limited, and can't be expanded or creatively shared. Rather than engage in a big argument in which both sides try to compete to win the resources, or try to collaborate but can't find an inventive way to satisfy either objectives or interests, compromise may be a satisfactory solution.

2. Time is limited. Effective competition and collaboration may both take a lot of time to pursue effectively—the Competitive strategy because it may take a long time to wear the other side down, and the Collaborative strategy because it takes an equally long time to find a good solution and preserve the relationship. Compromise is quick and dirty, with, for now, an emphasis on the *quick*.

3. The relationship is maintained and preserved to some degree. This strategy may be used by a party whose position is weaker than that of the other side. It may also be used by a party that wants to show some degree of concern for the other, and sees the other as weaker—but also does not give the other everything. It can help avoid prolonged conflict.

4. If there are good options available on each side, one party might propose a compromise to obtain a concession on one of their more important objectives.[4]

This works well, for example, if you know that the other party wants a particular concession badly and you are in a position to trade off for something that you want. When the parties have multiple issues on the table, Compromising often employs a quick and expedient logrolling process in which first one side, then the other, offers straightforward concessions to achieve a deal with ease.

WINNING COMPROMISE TACTICS

The following are some suggestions for how to compromise successfully.[5] We consider success in compromising to be a personally satisfying outcome that also leaves the other party reasonably satisfied. Here are the tactics:

- *Do your homework.* Know what you want. Be sure you have clear goals and objectives. You need to know what you want to fight for and what you are willing to give up. You need to be strongly committed to your objectives, or you may be forced into a position of "giving away the farm"—giving away everything, or at least those things that you wanted most.

- *Prioritize your goals.* If you are going to compromise, you need to know what you must have, as opposed to what would be nice to have. The nice-to-haves may be given up to obtain the must-haves.

- *Know your walkaway and alternatives.* This can give you power in the negotiations, because at some point, you may be better off pursuing your alternative than settling for a suboptimal agreement. Know your walkaway point, so that if you need to, you can abandon the negotiation. This, too, can give you power.

- *Know which person will make the decision.* If the person you are negotiating with does not have the authority to make an agreement, you may be spending a lot of time waiting while he or she consults with the one who does. It may be better and more efficient for you to present the benefits of your proposal to the decision maker.

- *Show that you want to negotiate.* Say and do what is necessary to overcome the other party's reticence or distrust. Look at the other party's problems and try to make sure that your proposal effectively resolves some of their key issues. This will give you an image of empathy and fairness, which is necessary for effective compromises.

- *Try not to be the first side to make a major concession.* Because making concessions may be inter-

preted as a sign of weakness, the other party may
take advantage of this and become aggressive, pushing you farther than you wish to go. This will escalate the proceedings so that the more you give in, the
more they will ask for. You will find yourself moved
into an Accommodating strategy, not a Compromising one.

- *Do not wait until the deadline to offer a compromise.* Compromises should be offered from a position of strength, not as a last-ditch gesture, which
  would suggest to the other party that you are in a
  weaker position. If the deadline is close and you
  want to offer a compromise, offer it early enough
  that the other side can truly consider it. If you wait
  too long, the other party's deadline may have
  passed; either they will be very upset, or they will
  have lost all possibility of advantage and now may
  simply want to sabotage the negotiation process.

- *Start with small compromises.* A gradual or staged
  approach can help you to move toward more compromise. If you work in small steps, each party can
  move toward a reasonable solution. Moving too fast
  may escalate the demands.

- *Use your concessions to your advantage.* When
  you make a concession, be sure that the other party
  gets the message that you are interested in a positive
  outcome and want to deal with them. Ask for a reci-
  procal concession in return.

- *Use your offers to communicate where you stand.*
  As you approach the end of your offers, they should
  be smaller and fewer, to signal the other party that
  you are near the end. If the other party is alert, they
  will understand that they cannot push you to make
  further offers. The same is true for your side. Watch
  the other party's offers, and be alert for signs of dis-
  tress. When they have reached their limit, you
  should not push for more concessions. You risk
  breaking off negotiations entirely.

- *Do not push too hard.* Try to avoid the classic assumption of negotiation, that you have to win everything you can. Pushing may result in negotiations
  coming to an abrupt halt, because it sends the message that you are competing instead of collaborating.

- *Remember that the split does not have to be even.*
  In compromising, it may not be possible, or even desirable, to split it down the middle, although that is
  the most frequent way it is done. A compromise is
  often based on where the two parties currently
  stand, but that does not mean that they have made
  equal concessions to get to that point. If one party

has moved $2,000 from their starting point and the other party has moved $5,000, and they are still $4,000 apart, a split down the middle is a compromise, but it yields a deal that means one party only had to concede $4,000 while the other conceded $7,000.

- *Seek win–win compromises.* Consider the well-known story of two girls arguing over an orange. They had one orange to divide between them. The girls could have divided the orange in half to be "fair." But each really wanted something different (underlying interests)—one girl wanted the rind, and the other wanted the pulp. A fairer way to divide the orange was to give each what she wanted—a win–win solution.

 To seek win–win compromises, start with a little problem solving. Ask the other party about their underlying interests and concerns.

- *Try not to close too quickly.* Although a scarcity of time is one of the primary motivators of the Compromise strategy, it does not mean you have to do it with lightning speed. You may be eager to complete the transaction, but if a deal occurs *too* fast, people frequently wonder whether they could have done better. If you are selling, make at least one counteroffer so the buyer will be confident of having obtained the best price. If you are buying, offer low at first, and then move up. People like to feel that they have earned what they've won. Resist going for the "1-2-3" deal (offer—counteroffer—split it down the middle).

- *Promote the long-term benefits.* Point out that there can be an ongoing relationship between the parties (if this is true). One benefit of a successful compromise is that at best, the future is not put in jeopardy, and the possibility of future business together remains viable. In fact, a compromise now might lay the groundwork for future collaboration. Looking at it from another angle, a negotiation that does not go well presents the potential of lost future business.

- *Stay focused on the issues.* The other side may use dirty tactics in trying to push for more concessions. Try to ignore these, if possible, and stay with your established bottom line. In other words, be firm, particularly if the other party switches to a competitive style.

- *Be polite.* Avoid the hardball tactics of competition. Compromises should be civilized deals, marked by respect and good manners.

Everybody wants other people to be polite to them, but they want the freedom of not having to be polite to others.

—Miss Manners[6]

 FIXING A STALLED COMPROMISE

CONCEPT If a session in which you are trying to compromise is faltering, you can sometimes apply a *staged* or incremental process that moves beyond compromise into a true collaborative deal.

Step 1. In the first stage or step, the parties come to a temporary or interim agreement (which may include a compromise). Having established this compromise, both parties agree that this establishes a *floor* for further negotiation—that while they may be able to improve on the deal, they will each do no worse than their current agreement.

Step 2. They then begin to explore some of the processes outlined in Chapter 8, on collaborative negotiation. As a result, the agreement may be enriched, broadened, strengthened, or improved for both sides.

 When seeking collaborative resolutions for stalled compromises, you need to take care to avoid falling into compliance.[7] *Compliance* is agreeing to go along with something that you would really prefer not to do or agreeing to something you really do not want to agree to.

Sometimes people comply with requests when they really prefer not to. Why they do this is something that even *they* may not know. For example, in spite of numerous private and public pledges to the contrary, people buy product offers (books, computer software, and investments) or make gifts and contributions to telephone marketers and door-to-door solicitors. They just can't say no, even to someone they don't really care about and for a product that they don't care much for, either.

For example, a solicitor for a charity will call **CONCEPT** and request a gift of $50. Rather than say no, people often give a gift of $25, just to "compromise" and get the solicitor to go away. This is *not* compromise—it is *compliance*. You need to be aware of this possibility and take time to evaluate what you really want out of the situation. If you have done the careful thinking and evaluation we recommend, this should not be difficult. But because salespeople and marketers often catch you unaware, you have not had a chance to do any of your planning; hence, you comply with at least part of their request.

THE RECIPROCITY TRAP

Compromises are based on fairness, and so it is easy to be drawn into compromising in the name of fairness when you really didn't want to make a deal at all. Reciprocity is the theme in compromising: give and take, tit for tat, I give you something and you give me something.

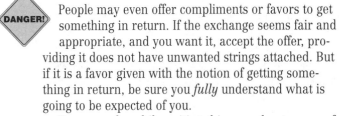

People may even offer compliments or favors to get something in return. If the exchange seems fair and appropriate, and you want it, accept the offer, providing it does not have unwanted strings attached. But if it is a favor given with the notion of getting something in return, be sure you *fully* understand what is going to be expected of you.

For example, while writing this very chapter, one of the authors was called by a marketing firm. The firm offered a choice of "free" videos; the author selected the free video he wanted, and was then told that it was indeed a free gift, but he was required to consider other videos to purchase, 1 per month, for 12 months. The implication—without ever saying so—was that because the marketing firm had started off by doing something for the respondent, it was his "obligation" to reciprocate and do something for them. This is a very popular sales tactic. So what did the author do? What would you do?

THE COMMITMENT TRAP

If you are heavily committed to obtaining something that looks unbelievably attractive (on the surface), you may find yourself the object of a *bait-and-switch* tactic.

A classic example of this is a store advertisement for a product, such as a CD player, that looks like a real bargain. When you arrive at the store to buy the CD player, a salesperson tells you that it is sold out, but that they have another product "of equivalent quality"—of course, it is not on sale, and actually retails for $20 more. If you really need a CD player, you may fall for the bait-and-switch tactic. You may end up with a good product but wind up paying $20 more for it than you expected. Or, even worse, you may end up paying more for an inferior product. There is also the possibility that it is inferior to the one advertised.

Getting Good at Saying No

Our lives are full of attractive-sounding offers from salespeople, business associates, and friends—but many of these deals turn out to be undesirable later on. You should feel free to reject even the most attractive-sounding offer if you don't like the smell of it or even if you simply haven't the time and energy to research it at the moment. But if you decide to refuse an offer, be careful how you do it.

A person making a genuine offer, with "no strings attached," may be insulted if you attack or impugn the offer (or the person's motives in offering it to you). Also, in some cultures gift giving may be much more acceptable than in others. For example, in the American public sector, gift giving is frowned on, but in Japan, presents are part of the early relationship-building process.

You can refuse any gift or other offer, of course, but do so politely and with an *explanation* of why it's impossible for you to accept it. For example, you could say "My company's policy forbids me to accept gifts," or (to that pesky marketer) "I make a practice of never deciding about deals on the phone. You'll have to write me if you want me to consider it." If they object that *they* never do deals by mail, then you'll know something's fishy and you won't mind offending them by hanging up.

The bait-and-switch tactic can be used in negotiation if one party promises to do something, then suddenly switches to a different commitment, saying it is "just the same." To avoid this problem, write down what has been offered. This may increase and lock in their commitment to the initial offer, and prevent switching tactics.

It is also wise to watch out for becoming overcommitted, which puts you in a position where you may not be able to change your mind without losing face.

For example, suppose a salesperson has got you to agree that you will "buy today" if he can get you the sporty new convertible car you want at the right price. You sign the deal and he says that he will have the car prepared for pickup while you go home to get your family. When you come back, the salesperson tells you that the red car you expected to pick up "has already been sold," but he has one "just like it" in an ugly shade of green. Do you walk out, even with your kids crying about not getting a ride in the new car—or do you take the car you don't want?

Never hesitate to indicate that you have changed your mind, or that the other party has not exactly matched your specifications. A little loss of face in front of others is often worth the trade-off, compared to living with a deal you absolutely don't like.

HOW SOCIAL PROOF LEADS TO COMMITMENT

Endorsements and statements of support from others, especially people whom we see as being "experts," tend to help us commit to something. If a person with some perceived expertise on the subject says it is true (e.g., the ancient cigarette advertisement that promised, "Out of 100 doctors, 73 percent prefer X cigarettes"), then we think it must be true. Beware of this tactic. It is important to evaluate such claims for yourself—even though it requires time, effort, and often some research.

 Do not let yourself be railroaded by what looks like strong "expert" proof. Even among specialists, people do not always agree. Any body of knowledge is open to interpretation. If you are concerned about a source's qualifications or education, ask for substantiation of the person's background and credentials or get a second opinion. Request more time to consider what has been presented. Ask an objective person whom you know, respect, and trust, and who will give you a reality check.

WHEN LIKING COLORS JUDGMENT

We also tend to be more easily influenced by someone we like, or find personally attractive. Based on that fact, a negotiating team may be selected for its *likable* qualities—friendliness, congeniality, and personableness.

In many negotiations, the parties spend some time getting to know each other before getting down to business, and in this phase of the process, likability can be critical to warming the other party up. This can also be seen as a variation on the *good guy/bad guy* technique discussed in Chapter 7. It is important to be aware of your personal feelings about the other party, and to be able to separate personalities from the negotiation.

WHEN AUTHORITY LEADS TO COMPLIANCE

From the time we first go to school, we tend to respect people who have formal authority over us—teachers, principals, police officers, the clergy. Other authorities in our lives include those who make and enforce rules, and people with titles (such as Doctor, Attorney, Vice President, CEO, and Judge). We are expected to respect these authorities. However, we need to watch out for overbelieving and overrespecting, particularly when they have an agenda to persuade us.

DANGER! Although some parties have authority by virtue of their title, formal position, or expertise, we tend to *overgeneralize* about their expertise, and those with that authority may tend to *overextend* its application.

For example, in our culture, we tend to view attorneys as smart people who know the law and its applications. Often, lawyers are hired into jobs that have little or nothing to do with their legal training, but they tend to act in those jobs as though they have considerable authority and expertise. For example, lawyers who specialize in real estate may not be as good in criminal law as those who specialize in that area—and they may not know much about business, although they may be willing to provide advice on the subject.

WHEN SCARCITY COLORS JUDGMENT

Scarcity of resources affects our attitude toward them. If you want something, and you learn that the supply is running short, or that only one item remains, or that the merchandise is an "exclusive," are you more tempted to acquire it? Are you more pleased when you manage to get it? Is your curiosity piqued when you are told that something was censored? Some people are willing to pay a lot for one-of-a-kind or limited-offering articles.

To guard against this scarcity-based compliance, consider your underlying reasons for wanting an item or option. Be aware of the temptation associated with scarcity.

COMPROMISING WITH THE BOSS

Negotiating with the boss is not always easy or pleasant, but most of us have to do it occasionally. Although salary is a common topic for competitive negotiation, that usually occurs only once a year, at most. A more frequent issue for negotiation is a situation where you are asked to do work above and beyond the call of duty—in other words, more than your job description or time will permit. Such requests often lead to a compromise since it is important to the employee to avoid a negative style of negotiating.

From the employee's perspective a Collaborative style would be preferable, because this style is most likely to satisfy the employee's needs. While employees would like to use a Collaborative style with their bosses, it is not always feasible. More frequently, employees find themselves entertaining Accommodating, Avoidance, and Compromising deals. There are two primary reasons for this:

- First, employees tend to believe that resources are fixed (that is, they cannot be expanded). Money may already be budgeted, the number of employees is limited by a hiring freeze, the machines can only operate a certain number of hours a day, and so forth. Thus, there must be trade-offs.

- Second, employees do not want to make bosses angry or upset by actively pursuing a competitive or collaborative negotiating style that is high on the outcome dimension (to maximize employees' own outcomes). Because bosses have great control over employees, employees want to keep them happy, and so they pursue the other three strategies.

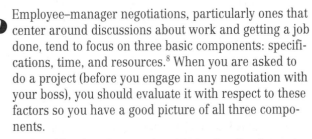 Employee–manager negotiations, particularly ones that center around discussions about work and getting a job done, tend to focus on three basic components: specifications, time, and resources.[8] When you are asked to do a project (before you engage in any negotiation with your boss), you should evaluate it with respect to these factors so you have a good picture of all three components.

- *Specifications* have to do with the details of a project; in other words, what the actual task is, such as making a product, providing a service, or writing a report. In evaluating a project and whether you can do it, you need to know and understand the exact nature of the project. All your estimates and planning will depend on specifying the job correctly. If you are not sure, ask for more details.

- *Time* is also of major importance in evaluating a task. Your estimate should include not only the time involved in actually completing the task, but also any administrative time, such as writing a report on completion of a project, or overseeing the production or printing of a report. Estimate as accurately as possible how long the project will take. Your estimate should include enough time to do a good job— not a slapdash one. Also be sure you build in a *contingency* plan, or time buffer in case of problems. Remember Murphy's law: "If something can go wrong, it will." If your time frame is too tight, you may suddenly have to renegotiate the project when you are in the middle of it.

- *Resources* are the third component of a project or task. Resources are the materials that go into the project, such as human labor, physical materials (such as paper for a report), computer time, or raw materials for the production of a product. It is important to take account of all the resources that you may need for the project, and whether you can make trade-offs among them. For example, if the schedule suddenly becomes tighter, can you hire a consultant or temporary help to complete the project on schedule? Part of your own strategy should be to assure that you will have adequate resources to complete the job.

Once you account for these three factors, they may be traded off, one for another, if necessary. Thus, if your boss wants a project done in 5 days instead of 10, you will need to increase resources to offset the diminished time. You may also need to make clear what jobs are not getting done so that you can devote full attention to this one, and secure additional resources to make sure your other commitments are met. Likewise, if the specifications change on a project, you may need more time to complete the job according to the new specs. Or you may need different labor with different skills.

You will need to know if any of the factors are fixed and therefore unchangeable. This will have considerable effect on the project, especially if another factor changes. Think about what substitutions and trade-offs you can and cannot make. Often a careful examination reveals hidden opportunities—in which case you can go back to the boss with a creative compromise that trades off something that is not so limited—thus securing you a better outcome than you at first expected was possible.

RESPONDING TO A BOSS'S IMPOSSIBLE REQUEST

When you are asked by your boss to do a nearly impossible task, it is tempting to say no immediately. However, it is wise to avoid responding with an immediate no. This may give the impression that you are lazy, disloyal, or uncooperative.[9]

TIP Buy some time by saying that you would like to think about it (use the Avoidance strategy to temporarily withdraw from the boss's invitation to negotiate, because you know that you have no good response to his or her opening position). It is possible that the whole problem will go away, the storm will pass, and you will not have to consider the situation again.

However, the request may well come again, in which case it is a good idea to be prepared. Asking for time gives you an opportunity to look into the situation and evaluate what you want to do. It allows you to try to redefine the problem and initiate collaboration, or—more likely with directive bosses—to keep exploring the situation and discussing the problem until a compromise can be achieved.

When you have evaluated the situation and can no longer avoid responding to your boss, we recommend that you initiate a compromise with a response that is carefully worded to prevent accidental competitive negotiation and conflict.

TIP Use the phrase "Yes, and" rather than "Yes, but," which sounds more like "no." Another good phrase to use if you are going to offer a compromise is "if ____, then ____." For example, "If I do this, then I need to have you do that for me." An even more polite variant is, "If I do this, then can you help me____?"

THE POWER OF THE "YES, AND" RESPONSE

"Yes, and ____" tells the boss you are willing to help with the task. It also adds what you will need—the missing resources—if you are going to be able to do what you are being asked. You are agreeing to do the task, but setting limits on what is possible. For example, "Yes, I will do it, and I will need an assistant for five days." Or, "Yes I can do it, and it will cost $1,000 more than previously budgeted." Or, "Yes, and I'll need to clear my desk of other work for the week in order to get it done. Can you reassign my other projects so I can do this for you?"

This approach maximizes the chances of your boss responding in this same spirit, in which case you will be able to implement a compromise. You and the boss will have to trade one thing for another. And even if the attempt fails and your boss responds rudely that you "better do it or else" without offering supporting resources, you are at least no worse off than when you started.

 With any special request from a boss, be sure you understand exactly what the boss wants, what the time frame is, what resources are available, which aspects are fixed, and which are flexible. The trade-offs you make can result in something close to a win–win situation if you plan carefully.

END POINT

Compromises are an important form of deal making, and mastering the style is well worth your effort. There are many cases in which its ease of use makes compromising the best approach. And in other situations—as when your boss makes impossible requests—it is a great ploy to turn the situation into an opportunity for compromise. And once you get used to compromising, you will find it an easy style to master.

The appeal to reasonable and fair concessions is at the heart of every compromise. With practice, you can learn to take a creative approach. Think about alternative ways of splitting the difference until you come up with a creative but fair-sounding approach that is a little more in your favor. As with all forms of negotiation, compromises benefit from creativity.

The Accommodating and Avoiding Games

Sometimes it's just not worth the trouble. A negotiation, that is. When your reaction is, "Why bother?" then perhaps you should not! There are two distinct ways to handle situations where the outcome does not seem worthwhile.

First, you can cave in, allowing the other party to have what they want. Accommodating makes most sense when you care more about the relationship than the outcome—and where losing won't hurt you too badly.

Or, second, you can sidestep the conflict and avoid the negotiation entirely. Don't give in, but don't pursue a win either. Avoiding makes most sense when you anticipate negatives. If the negotiation would be unpleasant because the other player is angry, for example, then avoiding makes good sense. And if neither the outcome nor the relationship are too important, then you might want to avoid the negotiation so as to be able to devote your energy to more important issues.

Accommodating and Avoiding. Neither game gets you a big win, but each is nonetheless an extremely important approach—and one you should master in order to be well prepared for all circumstances. This chapter will teach you the essence of both games, starting with accommodation.

ACCOMMODATING: LET'S LOSE TO WIN!

Accommodation is used when the relationship is more important than the outcome of the negotiation. The person using this strategy prefers to concentrate on building or strengthening the relationship.

Since other people are usually happy when we give them what they want, we may simply choose to avoid focusing on the outcome and give it to the other side, thus making them happy. And since accommodating someone generally pleases them, it is often wise to make some accommodations as an investment in good will.

The time to repair a roof is when the sun is shining.

—John F. Kennedy

Another reason to accommodate is that we may want the other party to accommodate *us* in the future. Since many social relationships are built on informal expectations and rules of exchange, giving something away now may create the expectation that they need to give us what we want later on.[1] So we give them their preferences now, to obtain a better future outcome. A short-term loss is exchanged for a long-term gain.

For example, in a manager–employee relationship, the employee may want to establish a good relationship with the boss now to have a good evaluation, a raise, or a better position in the future.

Tactic #14: Accommodation with a Request for Future Reciprocation

Employees often choose an Accommodating strategy with their supervisors. For instance, you might decide not push for a salary increase now, at your three-month review, if you expect that this will put you in a better position for a raise at the six-month review. If you use this approach, make sure your boss knows it! Many employees assume that their supervisor knows they feel they are mak-

(Continued)

(Continued)

ing accommodations—but the supervisor never reciprocates. Saying something like, "Of course, I'm happy to accommodate you on this, even though it isn't what I expected (or what my job requires, or what you said earlier). I know you're keeping track and will make it up to me later, right?" If you say things like this with a friendly smile, your boss will probably accept them without rancor. And you've made your point, so the boss knows you expect a future benefit.

Accommodation may be used to encourage a more interdependent relationship, to increase support and assistance from the other party, or even to cool off hostile feelings if there is tension in the relationship. If the relationship is ongoing, then it may be particularly appropriate to back down now, to keep communication lines open and not pressure the opponent to give in on something that they do not want to discuss. In most cases, this strategy is *short term*—it is expected that accommodation now will create a better opportunity to achieve outcome goals in the future.

For example, a manager might not urge an employee to take on an extra task right now if the employee is overloaded with projects and the manager can find another person to complete the task, especially if the manager knows that a big project is coming next week, and everyone is going to have to put in overtime.

In a long-term negotiation or over a series of negotiations, it may happen that one side constantly gives in. This precedent may be noted by the other side and be seen as accommodating behavior (which it is). It should not be construed as an invitation to the other party to be competitive. But sometimes it is. If this happens to you, the other party will begin to compete and take advantage of your guard being down. You will need to learn how to do damage control by switching to a competitive style. And you may also need to reconnect by communicating the relationship costs of the other party's constant push for accommodations.

Tactic #15: Buying Time with Accommodation

Will Rogers once said that "Diplomacy is the art of saying 'Nice doggie' until you can find a rock." Sometimes you feel very strongly about the outcome,

(Continued)

(Continued)

but haven't the strength to press for a satisfactory settlement through a Competitive, Compromising or Collaborative negotiating style at the moment. Maybe you lack support because you haven't been able to get in touch with your management or some other powerful constituency. Perhaps you are waiting for information, funding, or other resources to arrive. Whatever the problem, your hands are tied behind your back.

In which case, you can use an accommodating-for-now approach to delay the negotiation. The way to use this tactic is to make it clear that, while you don't agree, you will go along with the other party for now—and discuss it again later on. Use wording like "for now" and "until I have time to look into it" or "it's okay for now, but I'm not satisfied with it and we will have to go into it later."

Such phrasing makes it clear that you are using the *accommodating-for-now* tactic, and have reserved the right to negotiate later on. When you can find a rock.

We call accommodation a *lose to win* strategy because you sacrifice the outcome for the sake of the relationship. You do so because the primary purpose of the strategy is to *keep the other party happy,* or to build or strengthen the relationship. A lose–win strategy is usually a passive one, employed by a party that does not want to dominate.

 WHEN TO ACCOMMODATE

In general, you should accommodate to build or strengthen personal factors. Use accommodation for the following purposes:

- Build *trust* between the parties, or not destroy trust by pressing for one's own outcome concerns.

- Enhance a show of *respect* for the other's skills, contributions, and assets.

- Affect the *scope* of the relationship—the number of different ways you interact with key people. If you have other negotiations going on in other aspects of your relationship where you *strongly* care about the outcome (for example, two spouses "negotiating" dinner and a movie), you may want to accommodate in this negotiation.

- Make the other party *feel good* because you want to please the person, make the person happy, show empathy, or celebrate an accomplishment. If today is the other person's birthday, you might accommodate to requests that you won't accept tomorrow.

- Bank some *good will*. In complex relationships where there are multiple ongoing negotiations, the parties tend to "keep score." Over the course of time, people generally expect that there is a balance of winning and losing for each side—this time you win and I lose, the next time it will go the other way. Thus, if you have won in the past or want to win in the future, it may be best to use accommodation now.

- Pursue a *hidden agenda*. Accommodation may be used when a party has a hidden agenda. An example of this might be an employee who is planning to ask the boss for a raise in six months. In the meantime, the employee does rush jobs or other tasks beyond the call of duty, without making a big issue of them, in the expectation that the raise will be able to be negotiated in the future. Accommodation is a good strategy when you want to build up a supply of *credits* with the other party that you can cash in at some point.

- Keep the *peace*. If you want to keep conflict to a minimum and keep the other party in a good mood, trying to pursue a trivial outcome is not worth the effort, and accommodating is a better choice.

NOW FOR THE BAD NEWS

The major drawback to accommodation is that the party using it may appear to be condescending toward the other party, or the other party may feel uncomfortable with an "easy win."

You may want to consider putting up a symbolic fight before accommodating, just so the other player doesn't feel like something is wrong.

In addition, it is important to be careful about the extent of use of this strategy. It is not generally appropriate to establish a pattern of *always* giving in. The party that always accommodates to others may open itself to being taken advantage of. Particularly if the other party is not monitoring the give and take in the relationship, they may take winning for granted. If this becomes a problem in an important relationship, the party that is disadvantaged should actively talk about the problem with the other person.

END POINT

In sum, accommodation is sometimes the best game to play. Just let the other player win, and you save yourself a lot of trouble. A forfeit has its place in sports, and in deal making. If you are teaching a child to play a game, you will often go easy, permitting the child to score. Similarly, you often need to permit the people that you have long-term negotiating relationships with to win. Knowing which battles to fight and which to lose is part of the fine art of negotiation.

Now let's look at another game that is also appropriate when you don't want to pursue the outcome actively—avoidance.

AVOIDING: WHEN A LOSE–LOSE IS BEST

Negotiations can be costly, and there are many cases where negotiators would have been better off to drop the matter entirely. In general, it makes sense to avoid the negotiation when neither outcome nor relationship concerns are important to you.

Another way to think about the avoidance option is to ask yourself if the likely costs of the negotiation outweigh the likely relationship and outcome returns. This return-on-investment perspective rules out a number of negotiations that have big potential outcomes, but are likely to be messy and costly.

Tactic #16: The Withdrawal Threat

Use this tactic to encourage a difficult player to begin to move.

Sometimes you try to negotiate, but the other party acts as if they don't care. If your analysis of their position suggests that they ought to care (for instance, your business ought to be important to them because you are a big customer), then make it clear that:

1. You have very good alternatives and aren't locked into working with them.

2. You are considering withdrawing.

(Make these points unemotionally—don't act angry or disappointed.)

Then wait a bit. Give them enough time to make it clear that you are waiting for a response. If they value the outcome and/or relationship at all, they should signal their desire to keep you at the table. They'll do so by offering a concession, or at least by telling you that the deal matters to them. (In which case, you *ask* for a concession.)

Or, in the worst case, they say *they* don't care either. But that's okay, since you were at that point before using the tactic, so at least it didn't hurt your position. Either way, it's often worthwhile to test their commitment by making them question yours.

Avoiding is used infrequently, but it has merit in certain situations—in fact, we feel it ought to be used more often. It is termed *lose–lose* because it often results in both parties sacrificing whatever gains they could have achieved from the negotiation. Unless they compete, neither can win. And unless they collaborate, they can't both win.

However, an active choice to avoid is not necessarily a *loss* on either the relationship or the outcome. Sometimes the costs (in time, stress, and lost opportunities) outweigh the possible gains of a deal, in which case you win in the bigger sense by withdrawing from the game. Lose a battle to win the war, as the old saying goes.

Let's Not Make a Deal

A chronic borrower begged an old friend to lend him a hundred dollars. "I'll pay it back the minute I return from Chicago," he promised. "Exactly what day are you returning?" the friend asked. The man shrugged. "Who's going?"

—Myron Cohen

Avoid when you see negotiation as a waste of time, not worth pursuing. You may feel that your needs can be met without negotiating. Or you may decide that the outcome has very low value and that the relationship is not important enough to develop through the negotiation. Sometimes it's more personal, too—as when you simply don't want to do business with someone because you think they are unethical or you don't like their style.

Whatever your reasons, you feel that the relationship and the outcome are not sufficiently important (at least compared with the costs), and so you take no action or simply refuse to negotiate.

END-RUNNING THE RISKS OF AVOIDANCE

Sometimes it's hard to avoid—particularly when the other players are eager to negotiate with you.

If the avoider refuses to negotiate when the other party wants to, this may have a negative effect on the relationship. Even when the outcome is unimportant, many people will prefer to avoid angering the other party. And so a more moderate method of avoidance may be desirable.

For example, participate minimally without raising any objections to the proceedings. Or just don't show up. If the other party insists on negotiations, and it is important to preserve the relationship, then you might switch to accommodation.

KEY CONCEPT — OPTIONS MAKE AVOIDANCE MORE APPEALING

Avoiding is an especially viable game when you can pursue a very strong alternative outcome. If a strong alternative is available, you may choose not to negotiate.

For example, if you are looking at two different houses to buy, and both meet your needs, you may choose not to negotiate with one seller because you feel the price is too high and the person is inflexible. So you simply select your alternative and employ avoidance in the first negotiation.

PICK YOUR BATTLES

If you get good at avoiding undesirable or suboptimal negotiating situations, you will be better equipped to win in the long run. The idea is that those who pick the time and place for battles generally win the war. Apply this thinking to a difficult business associate or boss, and you will see a big difference over a several-month period.

STUDENT: I don't think I deserve a zero on this paper.

TEACHER: I don't think so either, but it's the lowest mark I can give.

Sun Tzu was the first, and perhaps is still the most important, military strategist, hailing from China around 500 B.C. He advised that "When the strike of a hawk breaks the body of its prey, it is because of timing."[2] The point is important, even where a collaborative situation makes the predatory analogy completely inappropriate. Winning is often a matter of timing.

KEY CONCEPT

If you lack the power and position to obtain a desirable relationship or outcome result right

Avoiding an Undesirable Customer

A builder specializing in country homes in New England was approached by an aggressively eager buyer. The property was a new "spec house" the builder had designed and was currently framing on a pretty piece of land in a quiet town. The buyer was from the big city and wanted a weekend house where he and his friends could pursue their favorite outdoor sports—principally target practice in the back yard. He was so eager to buy he offered to purchase before the house was completed, at an above-market price, and entirely in cash. But he was vague about his profession and where the cash had come from.

The builder didn't feel good about this offer. He had hoped to sell the house to some young family that would fit into the neighborhood better. He also wondered about that cash and wanted to avoid being part of any suspicious money-laundering activities. Finally, he didn't usually set a price on a house before he was far enough along to be sure of his costs. What to do?

Although his Realtor urged him to close the deal, he decided to try an avoidance strategy instead. He sent word that he would need another month to consider the offer because he had decided not to sell the house to anyone until then. A week later he learned that the eager cash buyer had purchased another property in a different town. And in another week, he was approached by a nice young family eager to move into the spec house.

By refusing to act prematurely, this contractor ended up getting just what he wanted and avoiding a deal that didn't feel right. It took some courage to wait it out, but evidently his design and location were right for the market—which meant that more options were likely to arise over time. It is often that way in deal making. If you are in the right place, and have the fortitude to wait out unappealing options, you should eventually find the deal that's right for you.

now, temporary withdrawal is the best alternative. Negotiators rarely have such overwhelming strength of position that they can take the risks of negotiation for granted.

SON: Dad, what's the best way to prevent itching due to biting insects?

FATHER: Don't bite any.

The strategist's approach to battles also applies to any and all of our personal conflict situations. And by picking our battles (and avoiding some of them) we become strategists as well as negotiators. Another metaphor—one we find very helpful—comes from the world of investments. You can think of yourself as managing a portfolio of investments in negotiations. To have a winning portfolio, you need to pick the ones you want in the portfolio. Pick winners, reject losers. Then it's easy to win at negotiations.

In managing your portfolio of negotiations, you may want to prioritize negotiations based on their *likelihood of success*. And where success is unlikely at the moment, a temporary withdrawal is the best alternative. At worst, "temporary" will turn into "permanent," and you will have lost the outcome or relationship result that you did not think you could achieve anyway. But in many cases, the other party will still view the negotiation as of potential value, and will permit you to reinstate the negotiation—when *you* decide the time is right to strike.

If weaker numerically, be capable of withdrawing.

—Sun Tzu, *The Art of War*[3]

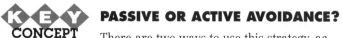 **PASSIVE OR ACTIVE AVOIDANCE?**

There are two ways to use this strategy, active avoidance and passive avoidance. In *active avoidance,* the party refuses to negotiate at all. In *passive*

avoidance, the party simply does not show up for the negotiation, or shows up but voices no objections during the negotiation. The other party and the conflict can thus be put off until some future time, or permanently ended. Often, passive avoidance is easier to get away with. You can delay and delay without actually saying you refuse to make a deal, and if you are lucky the other party will get distracted or find an alternative, and you will never have to actively refuse.

DANGER! However, even with passive avoidance, the other party may be frustrated because efforts to initiate a serious negotiation are stopped or delayed. That is why avoidance is most appropriate where the relationship is not important. If the relationship is important in the long term, then use avoidance only as a *short-term* strategy. And remember, you will have to put effort into overcoming the other party's frustration and rebuilding the relationship before reopening the negotiation in another style (Accommodation, Compromise, or Collaboration).

WAYS TO BENEFIT FROM AVOIDANCE

Avoidance can benefit you in the following ways:

- You may be able to have your needs met *without* negotiation. If you really do not need to negotiate, it makes sense not to spend the time doing so. This would be the case if you have some other way of meeting your needs.

- You have strong alternatives or BATNAs that you can pursue. If you have strong BATNAs, then you may not need to negotiate. For example, if you can do just as well by switching to one of your alternatives, then the present negotiation is not necessary. Thus, a strong alternative is like a trump card that you can play to maintain power and control in the negotiation.

- You have no interest in negotiating on the outcome and you are concerned that if you try to negotiate, you will damage the relationship.

- A final reason not to negotiate yourself is that someone else in your party needs the experience. If this is the case, you may choose not to negotiate so the other person can have the learning experience. You may, however, assist the person in negotiating. Not negotiating with an opponent that you want to help to develop may not be a good choice, because your refusal to engage may not be the best approach for helping them learn how to be more effective.

Tactic #17:   Never Negotiate with Cats

There are some people who don't play by the rules of negotiation—or any rules, for that matter. If you have the opportunity to negotiate with someone like that, we strongly recommend against it. Even competitive negotiation games are open to abuse, and obviously collaboration is out when you don't trust the other players.

Alex used to work with Silicon Valley startups fairly often, and he recalls that once a client was approached by a potentially major investor who was eager to bankroll a new project. But there was something a little off about this investor. He was inordinately into security, lived in a fortified mansion far from the beaten track, and didn't seem to have any prior record of involvement in high-tech companies. In the long run, the client took the prudent course and avoided a deal.

If you suspect someone of being an unpredictable "cat," someone who doesn't play by the conventional rules of personal or professional relationships, follow the simple, commonsense rule that Peter Rabbit does—avoid them! In case you don't recall the children's story to which we refer, it concerns a young rabbit trying to find his way out of a fenced-in garden before Mr. McGregor, the farmer, catches him:

Then he tried to find his way straight across the garden, but he became more and more puzzled. Presently, he came to a pond where Mr. McGregor filled his water-cans. A white cat was staring at some gold-fish. She sat very, very still, but now and then the tip of her tail twitched as if it were alive. Peter thought it better to go away without speaking to her; he had heard about cats from his cousin, little Benjamin Bunny.

—Beatrix Potter, *The Tale of Peter Rabbit*[4]

END POINT

As with accommodation, avoidance sidelines you, keeping you out of a game you don't want to play. But avoidance keeps the other party from playing too, so avoidance is likely to meet with more resistance than accommodation. That's okay if it is important to you to avoid entanglements with the other party. Sometimes the wisest way to negotiate is not to negotiate at all.

Avoiding Legal and Ethical Pitfalls

You don't want to get sued. To avoid possible legal trouble arising from negotiations, you need to have a general understanding of relevant U.S. law. And if you are negotiating with employees, you should also make sure you comply with your company's policies and with employment law in general.

However, legal compliance alone does not insure appropriate and successful negotiations. Many negotiations are legal, but still unsatisfactory because one or both parties feels that something improper or wrong has been done. In these cases, the problems are ethical rather than legal.

KEY CONCEPT Figure 11.1 illustrates the four options that arise when legal and ethical criteria are considered in evaluating negotiation strategy and tactics. Your best option is to be in the upper right-hand quadrant of this graph, where your negotiating behavior is both legal and ethical.

Both law and ethics define and constrain what can be done in negotiation, but in somewhat different ways. The issues are often similar, but the constraints are different. This chapter will show you how to stay out of legal trouble first, and then will go on to the ethical dimension of negotiations.

As you study these topics, think not only about how to avoid legal and ethical missteps of your own, but also how to spot them in others. If someone tries to pull a fast one on you, it is important to know that's what is happening so you can respond appropriately. (See Tac-

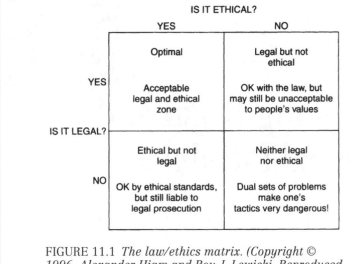

FIGURE 11.1 *The law/ethics matrix. (Copyright ©*
1996, Alexander Hiam and Roy J. Lewicki. Reproduced
by permission.)

Who Can You Trust?

It is a sin to believe evil of others, but it is seldom a mistake.

—H. L. Mencken

tic #18, on responding to illegal or unethical negotiating, page 216.)

KEY CONCEPT — LEGAL CONSTRAINTS ON NEGOTIATION

Is it illegal to lie in negotiations? Not necessarily—although collaborative, trust-building negotiations are
certainly incompatible with deception. However, many
types of lies *are* illegal, so you need to exercise caution.

One expert on negotiation writes that "commercial
negotiations seem to require a talent for deception. In
simple competitive bargaining, when someone asks,
'What is your bottom line?' few negotiators tell the
truth." In this book, and in actual negotiations, you
have encountered many tactics that are based either on
the withholding of some information or on the dissemi-
nation of misinformation. Are these legal? Could you
end up in a court of law from such practices? Legally,
where should you draw the line?

Laws related to fraud, misrepresentation, and the nature of contracts are relevant to the question of when a lie is a "white lie" versus an illegal deception.

 Contract law concerns the establishment of legal obligations; so if you enter into a legal contract and then fail to perform, you are exposing yourself to legal problems. Similarly, if you can create a contractual obligation on the part of another party, it doesn't matter whether they intended to perform or not—now you have them over a legal barrel.

 Fraud law concerns *intentional* misrepresentation— the lies that cross over the line from good negotiation tactics into illegal untruths. If another player could claim that you intentionally misled them and they were injured as a result, then you may have committed fraud. You had better appreciate this boundary before you negotiate!

 And simple misrepresentation, even where a clear intent to lie is not proven, can *also* be illegal in negotiations. The boundaries between negotiation tactics and fraud or misrepresentation are not always clear. We need to explore them in some depth in order to understand their implications for the negotiator.

 **IS IT FRAUD?**

The first point to understand is that there is no general prohibition against the use of deception and posturing in negotiation. The parties do not *have* to tell the truth—legal precedent recognizes that negotiation is a strange sort of dance with its own rules, and that if you do not like the way another party negotiates, your first legal recourse is to walk away from the negotiation rather than sue.

However, the law also recognizes that *some* negotiating behavior is illegal because it is clearly fraudulent. Here is a three-point acid test.

A statement is fraudulent when:

1. A negotiator *knows it is untrue.*
2. The other party *relies on it in a reasonable manner.*
3. The other party *suffers damage* as a result.[1]

What do we mean when we say "the negotiator knows it is untrue"? Exactly that. Let's say you go shopping for a car, but are determined to negotiate hard so as to avoid being fleeced by the salesperson. If you tell him you are not really interested in buying a car today, but are just curious as to what the dealer is selling it for, you are stating something you know to be untrue. Similarly, if the dealer's mechanics fiddle with the odometer to reduce the mileage on a used car, then the business is stating something they know to be untrue (the accurate mileage). You both lied in the opening moments of your negotiation. But are either examples of fraud?

Let's check the rest of the definition. In your opening lie—saying you are not interested when you know you are—will the dealer believe that you are not interested, and hence reveal his true BATNA price to you when he would not have otherwise? Not if he acts *reasonably*, particularly by the standards of competitive negotiation. He is unlikely to rely on your statement because it is a conventional bit of posturing that he understands you used to avoid exposing yourself to a hard-core sales pitch right now. On the other hand, the dealer's resetting of the odometer is not something you assume as a prelude to a negotiation over the price of the car. It *would* be reasonable for you to rely on the displayed mileage. This lie now has two strikes against it.

Let's look at the third element of the definition. Will either lie cause damage? Yours won't, because we already decided the salesperson will not reasonably rely on it. Should he claim later that you lied in the negotiation, and that he therefore gave you too low a price (damaging himself by cutting his commission), the average judge would just laugh at him for being too naive. However, the reset odometer could indeed cause you some damage if you go ahead and buy the car and pay fair market value for a car with that level of mileage. Should you discover the fraud later on and take the dealer to court, the judge would most likely award you the difference in price between a typical car of that model at the estimated real mileage versus the faked mileage.[2]

THE LAW MAY *ASSUME* YOU KNOW THE TRUTH

You might think that the requirement of *knowing* you are stating an untruth creates an obvious legal loophole. Can the other party *prove* you knew you were lying about an important fact? If you avoided communicating with anyone in writing about this behavior, then there will be no direct proof about what you knew or should have known.

Not so fast! The courts often assume you *should* know some facts. A senior manager should know what financial condition the business is in. A salesperson at a car company should know what condition a car is in; witness the "lemon laws" emerging in many states, which hold salespeople responsible for the condition of the cars they sell, even if they really could claim that they didn't know much about who owned them before and what might be wrong with them.

IS IT MISREPRESENTATION?

Another legal minefield lies in the concept of misrepresentation, a close relative of fraud.

 Unlike fraud, misrepresentation does not necessarily entail knowing that a statement is untrue. When a used car salesperson chooses not to mention the condition of the engine as a way to avoid having to disclose information about the engine that is in the car's file in the dealership office, then we are dealing with misrepresentation.

If you misrepresent by not saying anything about a topic as a way to avoid having to lie about it, you are on *somewhat* better ground than with fraud, because it is harder to prove legally. In general, courts punish misrepresentation only in two cases—when superior information is withheld or when partial disclosure is truly misleading.

Superior information might be, for example, the knowledge that your company is about to file for bankruptcy protection. If you did not mention this to a vendor when you negotiated 30-day terms for a large purchase of supplies—and the vendor was then unable to collect because your firm filed for protection from creditors under bankruptcy laws—the vendor could make a credible legal claim of misrepresentation. And you, as a negotiator, should have known that you had gone beyond standard negotiating tactics and breached the legal boundaries of truth in negotiation.

Similarly, you ought to know better than to make a partial disclosure that is obviously misleading. Let's say the vendor actually asked you about your company's financial condition, and you answered, "Well, the company posted record profits last year." Even if that is true, it is a misleading answer if the company is about to fail *this* year, and the vendor could claim misrepresentation in this case, too.

How can you avoid misrepresentation? Many negotiators believe *silence* is the secret (but note that the problems of partial disclosure and superior information are *not* fully addressed by this traditional rule of thumb). When representing a business or other organization or group, it is not difficult for you to claim ignorance or say you are not authorized to discuss certain topics. The topics in question will involve information you do not want the other party to know about, and therefore information that could materially affect the outcome of the negotiation.

While silence is helpful in avoiding fraud, it is still possible that the other party can make some legal claim. For example, they may claim you withheld superior information.

 As a general rule of thumb, a negotiator ought to avoid overly tricky strategies and try to negotiate in a fair manner. Disclose as much as you can without giving away key vulnerabilities or your bottom line. A level playing field is probably a legal one. What you want, however, is to tip the playing field just a little bit toward you—but not so steeply that the other party perceives that a grave injustice has occurred and decides to pursue a legal remedy under either fraud or misrepresentation laws.

If the other party threatens legal action and you have to hire a lawyer, you have probably lost the negotiation, because the extra hassles and costs are doubtless going to negate any advantage won through overly tricky negotiation. Therefore, when in doubt, *it is far cheaper to hire a lawyer up front,* to give you a one-hour hearing and a quick opinion, and thereby avoid stepping over the boundaries of the law.

DOES CONTRACT LAW APPLY?

Contracts often result from negotiations, so you must also consider what negotiation boundaries may be set by contract law.

 The basic goal of a contract negotiation should be to create a contract that is legally binding on both parties, so let's look at what is required for a contract to be enforceable in a court of law.[3] First, there must be *agreement.* That means one party must make an offer, and the other must accept it. An offer has to meet three criteria: (1) It has to be *serious* (an offhand or humorous offer is no good), (2) it has to include *specific terms* (a vague promise to take care of some problem is not an offer), and (3) it must be *communicated* to the other party in a clear manner.

A landlord might tell a month-to-month tenant (or *tenant at will*) that she has to sign a five-year lease, and the tenant might agree in principle to do so. Now suppose the landlord sends the tenant a lease that includes a clause stipulating that the tenant is responsible for 50 percent of the cost of repairs to the building. The tenant signs the lease quickly, but then reads the small print and sets the lease aside on her desk because she is uncomfortable with it. She forgets to follow up and talk with the landlord about it. In the interim, the landlord replaces the roof, and invoices the tenant for half the cost of the work. The tenant argues that the landlord doesn't have a signed lease—but the landlord produces it. He has used his passkey to go into the tenant's apartment and take the lease off her desk. Does the landlord have a legally binding contract? No—the offer was not *communicated* to the landlord, because the tenant had not yet chosen to give him the executed contract.

CONCEPT

For a contract to be valid, there must also be:

Consideration.   Consideration means parties need to get something for what they give up. An *exchange* has to take place. This is rarely an issue in negotiation, but it arises when one party has great power over the other and attempts to force the other to make concessions or agree to perform in exchange for little or nothing. The problem of consideration could also arise if tricky language is used that traps one party into agreeing to do something extra that they did not anticipate when the negotiation was taking place—and for which they did not request proper consideration.

Contractual Capacity.   Contractual capacity means the parties must be competent. Negotiating a favorable purchase with the teenaged son of your deceased business partner is not going to produce an enforceable contract because he will not be recognized as a competent party. Nor can you negotiate with people who are drunk or ill, and expect the results to be legally binding on them, or on an organization or person they represent.

Legality.   The purpose of the contract must be a legal goal that does not run counter to public policy. A contract requiring someone to break the law is not enforceable, for example. This constrains negotiators in terms of the kind of objectives they can pursue. It also constrains employers in the kinds of negotiations they can require their employees to engage in.

For instance, imagine that you are a salesperson whose employer tells you to misrepresent the service record of a product to sell more of the product and more service contracts. You refuse; so she pulls out a copy of your employment contract and reads you a clause that states you must use the sales pitch the company has specified. Hold your ground; your employment contract cannot be used to make you do something illegal.

Genuineness of Assent.   For example, your signature, forged on a contract, does not bind you to the terms of the contract. Similarly, if a low-level employee of your firm signs a highly unfavorable sales agreement with a supplier, you can legitimately claim that the employee was not authorized or prepared to represent the company in such deliberations.

Form. A clear, written contract is generally required. In some situations, the law stipulates what kind of contract is required, and even what language it must be in; but in general, all that is required is a detailed, clear, written document containing the preceding points, and signed by both parties. Contracts also take the form of a renewable agreement, or one that terminates after some length of time.

Despite the requirement of form, many negotiations end in an informal verbal agreement or a short memo from one party to the other confirming their recollection of the outcome. If you want to make a negotiated agreement legally binding, you must take it beyond the level of an informal negotiation process and add one more step: Write and review a formal contract. If it is a complex or important agreement for you, then you need to obtain appropriate legal advice to make sure your contract is complete and binding, and accurately represents the agreement and the parties' interests.

EMPLOYEE NEGOTIATION TRAPS

When negotiating with customers or employees, you must navigate the legal waters of fraud, misrepresentation, and contract law, plus any special laws protecting the interests of the other party.

For example, imagine you are negotiating with a top job prospect to fill an opening—a professional who has asked for a higher salary than you intended to pay. You tell him honestly that he is your first choice, but that you are not sure you can meet his requirements. Then you ask some questions to explore his requirements in more detail, including some questions about his family, age, and health status that you think are relevant to calculating the cost of employing him. While these may seem like reasonable questions to you, they are illegal to ask in a job interview.

The applicant has many legal protections designed to prevent discrimination against prospective employees based on factors such as age and family status. You need to check with your company's human resources department, a law firm, or a text on human resource management before you negotiate in this context.

Similarly, your existing employees have a wide variety of legal protections, and you must avoid crossing legal boundaries in negotiating with them. Sexual harassment, discrimination in promotion, right-to-know issues, and many other legal concerns constrain the employer. The body of law concerning employee–employer relations is large, and you need to check with an expert before trying anything novel in negotiations with an employee.

CUSTOMER NEGOTIATION TRAPS

There are a wide range of laws designed to protect consumer interests. In general, they prevent sellers from misrepresenting their products or services, and from engaging in practices that reduce competition and inflate prices. The law also protects consumers from products or services that significantly underperform versus general expectations—even if there is no written warranty. And a large body of law also protects consumers against damages resulting from the use of products or services. While consumer-oriented law is complex, you will get the spirit of it if you keep in mind these four areas of consumer rights.

In sum, consumers have and cannot negotiate away the rights to the following:

- Honest information
- Competitively low prices
- Reasonable product or service performance
- Safety

Consumer protection laws concerning *warranties* are relevant to product performance and need to be considered by negotiators.

For example, if a business customer complains that a product your company sold her company is defective and should be replaced at no cost, your position might be to point out that the customer decided not to pay for your extended warranty package, and thus your firm has no obligation to right the problem. Note, however, that the law recognizes an *implied warranty,* defined as the expectation that products are fit for normal use.

If the customer is able to show that your product is not "fit for normal use," the law will be on her side in the dispute. (Good sense might dictate that you retain the customer by avoiding competitive negotiations in this context, anyway. To quote the old adage, "Even when the customer is wrong, the customer is always right!")

The law has a great deal to say about price fixing, unfair or predatory pricing designed to drive a smaller rival out of business, and any other business practices that obviously reduce competition and its downward influence on prices. Should you find yourself in a negotiating situation with a competitor in which pricing comes up, do not bother researching the law—just head for the nearest door!

Any negotiation or discussion of prices with competitors is highly likely to be illegal. Don't mention or even listen to talk about prices with your competitors.

ETHICS IN NEGOTIATION

Some people think that *negotiation ethics* is an oxymoron. We don't. At least, we don't think the two words *should* be incompatible. If you wish to build trust so that collaborative, win–win solutions are feasible, you need to take an ethical approach to negotiations. To get "above the line," as we put it in Chapter 1, you need to foster open, honest, caring communications between the players in your negotiation games.

But many negotiators overlook this point. They mistakenly think that negotiations are opportunities to suspend normal rules of conduct and engage in unethical tricks. One reason for this widespread misconception is that there are no standards, no codes of ethics, for negotiators to follow.

The ethics of a negotiator will depend on such personal qualities as their philosophical and religious training, experience, background, and attitude. But even *expected* standards of right and wrong will vary from person to person.

The White Lie in Competitive Negotiating

Some of the deceptive tactics mentioned earlier in this book are thought to be acceptable to use when trying to negotiate the best settlement possible, particularly in competitive situations.

For example, in using competition, it is generally a mistake to be completely open with the other party. After all, the argument goes, if you give away all the information about your bargaining points—particularly your walkaway point, or the least you will take—then you will not have anything left to bargain with. You will be setting yourself up for the other party to take advantage of you. So to be effective in negotiation, particularly in competitive situations, it is to your advantage to be less than fully honest with the other party. On the

Is It Legal? A Test Case

Let's test your newfound knowledge of the legal issues in negotiation with a quick case. Imagine you are a landlord, and you have what you feel is a valuable storefront property. The current tenant has a very favorable lease, which is up for renewal next month. You propose a doubling of the rent to what you think is a fair market price, but she refuses and suggests that a 10 percent increase is more in line with what other retail rents are doing in the community. The difference between the rate you requested and what she proposed is worth many thousands of dollars a year in income for you, so you decide to play hardball and pursue an aggressive competitive negotiating strategy. You ask a real estate agent to publicly list and advertise the space at the higher price, hoping you will receive inquiries from prospective tenants eager to pay it.

The listing process takes longer than it should, and when the time comes to sit down with your tenant again, you still have no alternative tenants lined up. Not to worry—you decide to make the negotiating claim that you have another tenant in the wings who is eager to pay the higher price, and that you intend to evict the current tenant unless she agrees to pay this price too. (Sure, it is an exaggeration, but you still think you *could* find someone if you had the time.) She buckles under the pressure of this strong opening position, signs a five-year lease, and you laugh all the way to the bank.

But next year, your tenant runs into the real estate agent at a party and learns that you made up the whole story. Furious, she threatens to take you to court unless you settle by agreeing to cut her rent back to the previous level and extend it at that rate for another five years.

Does she have a strong legal case or not? Let's apply the most rigorous test: the three questions used to define fraud.

- Yes, you did knowingly misrepresent the situation.
- Yes, the tenant can argue she reasonably relied on the information you gave her.
- And yes, there are damages—the extra rent she has had to pay as a result, and the impact that this higher rent may have had on her business.

Solution: You had better settle with her right away, because the courts may not look favorably on your negotiating technique. And you had better be more honest next time you negotiate! There is a fine line between clever negotiating tactics and illegality, and this case clearly crosses that line.

other hand, if the parties are completely deceptive all the time, it may be impossible to strike any kind of meaningful agreement.

Some people feel that it is okay to engage in tactics that emphasize the positive aspects of the negotiation, and downplay the negative. For example, if you're selling a used car, it's okay to emphasize the good points about the car, and not tell the potential buyer that the car needs major engine work. Is this truthful and ethical behavior? Some white lies may be rationalized, if they are for a particular purpose. Again, this depends on your point of view and your personal ethical code. Because the level of truth telling and ethics differs from person to person, it is hard to predict what the other party will do in negotiation. There is a further difference between what people *believe* is ethical, and what they *say* is ethical.

Three Major Views of Ethical Conduct

People tend to confront an ethical decision in three ways:[4]

1. *The ends justify the means.* You have probably heard this expression many times. In negotiation, this belief allows the person to engage in questionable behavior because it results in a preferred resolution, which, after all, is the objective of the negotiation. As you can see, the bigger the stakes or potential outcome for a negotiation, the easier it will be to rationalize using marginally ethical tactics to get it.

2. *Absolute truth versus relative truth.* If you believe in *absolute* truth, then you think that rules must be followed with no exceptions. You must go by the book. If you believe in *relative* truth, you think that everything is relative, and therefore each person must make his or her own value judgments. Your choice of beliefs, whether absolute black and white or relative gray, will affect how ethically you behave in each situation.

   So, for example, if you are an *absolutist,* you believe that it is important to tell the truth, even if telling the truth gets you in trouble. If you've made a big mistake, and your boss asks you what happened, telling the truth might mean you will get fired for making the mistake. An absolutist would tell the truth and take the risk, believing that being ethical is more important than the consequences. A *relativist,* on the other hand, might try to avoid saying anything, be evasive, or—at the extreme— deny any responsibility or blame somebody else, simply to avoid the possibility of being fired.

3. *There is no such thing as "truth."* You may believe that telling the truth is of utmost importance. The difficulty here is in defining *truth*. What exactly *is* "telling the truth"? Where is the line between "truth" and "falsehood"? Some people may believe that bluffing, exaggerating, or concealing are okay if used in the service of the higher good. They may feel that these are within the boundaries of truth, and therefore are acceptable. Are white lies a form of lie or just a stretching of the truth?

EXAMPLES OF UNETHICAL TACTICS

Before we describe some of the questionable tactics that might be used in negotiation, let us repeat that we do *not* advocate using any of these tactics, unless you feel comfortable doing so and understand the possible consequences. Negotiators sometimes use these tactics just to experiment, or they think that the other party will not be smart enough to discover what has happened. This is usually not the case. Negotiators should not use unethical tactics if:[5]

- They will be dealing with the other party again in the future, and want to have a positive, long-term relationship.

- There is some likelihood that the other party can discover that the tactics are being used.

- The other party has enough power to get revenge or punish the perpetrators of unfair tactics.

- They can't be effective in using them, or their conscience will bother them or give them away.

 We primarily offer and describe these tactics here so that you can be aware of possible unethical tactics that may be used against you. Some negotiators will find some of these moves acceptable under certain circumstances; others will not. The more *moderate* tactics are often seen as more acceptable than the extreme ones.

Moderate Tactics

These first few tactics, though violations of the truth, are used by negotiators fairly often. It is important to note again that these tactics are more often used in a Competitive negotiation situation than in a Collaborative one.

Selective Disclosure and Exaggeration

There are a number of ways to be selective in what you disclose to the other party, or to exaggerate the information you share. For one, a party might selectively omit important information—not disclose a defect, problem, or weakness in their argument. For another, the information might be "stretched" to make a point seem more or less important, such as exaggerating the benefits of going through with a particular deal.

Further, a negotiator might neglect to report the whole story to his or her constituencies, so as to manipulate their impression of the progress and content of the negotiation. The other party may be completely unwilling to move on an issue, but the negotiator chooses not to tell the constituency that, believing that over time, the opponent will soften up and begin to move.

Another related type of exaggeration is to start with an opening point that is a lot greater (or less) than you really want. For example, a union might start out by asking for a 15 percent raise when they really will be satisfied with 7 percent. Starting high is frequently used as a tactic to show strength, create tension, and expand the bargaining range so that when concessions are made, we will actually achieve what we want. In general, more exaggerated opening offers tend to lead to better settlements, unless the opening is so extreme as to defeat credibility with the other party.

Hiding the Real Bottom Line

In this tactic, you try to prevent the other party from knowing exactly what you want so you can get there more or less without their knowing. This might involve hiding your starting points and bottom line, or misleading the other party about this information.

More Troublesome Tactics

This group of tactics has even stronger ethical implications than those we have just discussed, because they involve more outright falsehoods or distortions of the truth.

Exaggerating or Disguising Facts

A party might manipulate the facts to make their position appear more favorable. Or, they might try to make the other party's position appear less favorable. A common tactic is to disguise information about your position, key facts, or what is likely to happen if the deal goes through. For example, in selling a piece of real estate, you may know that the land is not buildable because of the soil conditions, but tell the potential buyer, "We don't know whether the land will support a large office building or not."

Another type of misrepresentation involves a deadline—to act as though you are unhurried and have all the time in the world, when in fact you are anxious to settle. Often you do this when you know that the other has a major deadline, and that if you stall, you can pressure them into giving in first. For example, if you know that the seller of a house is desperate to get out as soon as possible (and you are really anxious to get into the house yourself), you can nevertheless negotiate as though you have all the time in the world, and hope that they will make a major concession if you agree to close the deal quickly.

Manipulating Power

In this type of falsification, the party makes its reputation seem better than it is, or claims more expertise than it has, the object being to appear to have a more legitimate and stronger position than the other party. Misrepresenting one's credentials or status to fool the other party can backfire if the other party finds out. It can have repercussions in future negotiations if reputations are at stake.

Extremely Troublesome Tactics

The next group of tactics is considered by most people to be totally unethical; but even so, such moves are sometimes used in negotiation. Note that many of these are controlled by laws preventing their use. These tactics are usually discovered (although the user tends to believe that they will not be), with the result that the negotiator loses face and credibility and, when a formal contract or business is at stake, may be taken to court.

Outright Lying

In this instance, the party gives totally false information to intentionally mislead the other party. Contrast this with a "white lie," in which stretching the truth is dismissed as "necessary under the circumstances." As stated earlier, what *you* define as a white lie may be different from what *I* define as a white lie. But usually, there is no argument about whether an outright lie is a lie.

Giving Gifts or Bribes

Giving the other negotiator presents, favors, patronage, or other distractions is often thought to be a way to soften them up so that you can get more concessions and a better bargaining outcome. The question is, when is a gift appropriate and when is it just a bribe? Giving gifts, benefits, and "perks" used to be an extremely popular practice in the sales business, particularly with a company's good customers. In many cases, the ethical rules governing these practices have tightened considerably, and many companies now have rules that prohibit giving or receiving any gifts at all, or any "large" gift (over $25 in value).

Manipulating the Other Party's Constituency

Sometimes one party will "romance" or coerce the other party's constituency to turn the constituency against its own party. The thinking is, "If the other party's constituency is on my side, I have a better chance for a good outcome." An alternative is that if you don't like your opponent and think you can get him or her fired, you might talk to the other party's constituency and try to undermine your opponent's credibility and effectiveness.

Making False Threats or Promises

A party may signal its intentions with threats or promises that are actually bluffs. For example, a threat might be, "If you will not go down on your price a little, I am going to stop negotiating with you" (when, in fact, you were planning to stick it out a little longer). Or a party might make a false promise, such as, "If you buy this car, I will pay for a complete cleaning and detailing for you" (when you have no intention of doing so). The bluffer may or may not be called on this tactic, but will eventually be discovered. In the long run, this negotiator's reputation and credibility will suffer. In addition, the other party may resort to revenge or even take the issue to court.

Demeaning the Other Party

Another ploy is directly insulting or slandering the other party to undermine his or her confidence. Public accusations may increase one party's power relative to the other, but again may backfire if the other party retaliates.

Deliberately Underpricing

This tactic is used to steal a job or deal from the other party.

Spying

Spying on the other party by going through their trash, bugging their phone, or burglarizing their files or offices to get information on them may result in loss of reputation, ending of the negotiations, and litigation (because it is often illegal as well as unethical).

Stealing

As with spying and bugs, stealing information is a very risky tactic with similarly dire consequences.

As you can see, there are a broad variety of tactics with varying degrees of acceptability. The range of what is considered appropriate varies from person to person. There seem to be some tacit rules, however.[6] Consider your reactions to each of the preceding tactics as you were reading about them.

If you reacted strongly—saying "Now, I *know* that's not the right thing to do"—it's likely to be unethical.

There are some ploys that are just unacceptable by most standards. However, when you are in the situation, and under pressure to get what you want, it's surprisingly easy to rationalize these feelings and use one of these tactics. Remember that the party using such tactics runs the risk of the other party retaliating and thus escalating the emotional climate and ending the negotiation.

HOW PEOPLE JUSTIFY UNETHICAL TACTICS

If a negotiator has used unethical methods, then they are usually adept at *rationalizing* their behavior. To defend the use of a particular tactic, the party might say:[7]

- "It was unavoidable. It could not be helped. I had to do it in order to win."

- "It was harmless. No one got hurt. We all got more or less what we wanted."

- "It helped avoid negative results. Look what would have happened if I hadn't done this. . . ."

- "It helped accomplish good results. Look at the good things that resulted because I did this. . . ."

- "The other party deserved it" [the revenge motive at work].

- "Everybody's doing it. Why shouldn't I do it too?" [the social context factor].

- "It was fair, under the circumstances" [the justice motive].

While all these arguments are flawed, they may be sufficient to justify unethical behavior in a negotiator's mind. With such justification, unethical tactics that accomplish desired results will probably be used again in the future. But continued unethical behavior will eventually damage the reputation of the party using it. Over time, the party will lose power, trust, and credibility. The party will be viewed as exploitative. Word travels. Reputations get around. *Bad reputations are easy to get and hard to get rid of.*

Tactic #18: Defusing Improper Behavior

What can you do if you detect unethical or illegal behavior in a negotiation? Try the following sequence of responses, escalating only as far as needed to put the brakes on the other player.[8]

1. *Ignore it.* Sometimes if you simply ignore unethical or illegal behavior, it will subside. If not:

2. *Identify it.* Say what they're doing and why you think it is wrong. Don't make it sound like a personal attack—try to be objective. Often people will stop doing something wrong when it is brought into view. If not:

3. *Warn them.* Say they are endangering the negotiation by continuing their improper behavior and that you'll walk out of the negotiation if it continues. If that doesn't do it:

4. *Set ground rules.* Take time out to talk about how the negotiation is progressing, and try to negotiate new ground rules. If you don't get significant concessions, though, you should either walk away or, if you feel you can't avoid this negotiation:

5. *Tell them the consequences.* Tell them how you will respond if they repeat the improper behavior. Be clear in your own mind on how you will respond, so that this threat is realistic and actionable. In general, threats should be about breaking off the negotiation, about using some kind of hardball tactic, or about appealing to a third party (like a boss) who has some power over the person you are threatening.

6. *Act.* If you decide to retaliate, you might try a very strong scolding, anger, or even a competitive or unethical tactic of your own. Sometimes a tit-for-tat approach brings the other party into line—but not always, so this is a high-risk approach. Besides, it often leads you to use unethical tactics that you don't like, so in a sense you lose even if you win.

You should also consider two other actions that are easier to control: withdrawing from the negotiation, and bringing in a third party with authority to stop the offending behavior.

END POINT

Ethics is an important aspect of negotiation. Because negotiation is often part of a Competitive process, where parties are competing for scarce resources or for getting the best possible deal, parties are often prone to move from the realm of honest behavior into dishonest behavior.

In addition, as pointed out in earlier chapters, good negotiating—particularly in a Competitive context—requires a *little bit* of dishonesty. We ask for more than we really think we can get. We don't tell the other party "the truth, the whole truth and nothing but the truth," because it would give away our bargaining position. We exaggerate a bit about the advantages of what we want, and play down the deal we don't want.

While these are not completely and absolutely honest, they are a regular part of negotiation. In contrast, if we completely distort the facts, make up information, outright lie, or steal or sabotage our opponent, we have strayed over the line into highly unethical behavior.

The challenge is to make sure that both parties fully understand *where the line is* and to maintain that understanding even when the proceedings get a little hot and heavy.

Good negotiations are conducted when both parties respect the same ethical rules—they agree on their definitions of appropriate and inappropriate behavior. To make the line very clear, some people have called for a negotiator's code of ethics, perhaps written rules and regulations for negotiation. To establish these standards, however, would be a monumental task, given the variations among people's views of ethics. In addition, because we negotiate every day, usually in an informal manner, it is not clear that the code could be extended to apply beyond the more formal negotiations that go on within a particular industry, such as labor relations, real estate, and sales.

To a great degree, negotiators—those who negotiate on a regular basis, anyway—tend to police themselves. This is because they know that a bad reputation can be worse for business than the payoff from any single negotiated outcome. In addition, most of us negotiate with the same people on a regular basis—spouses, suppliers, customers, coworkers, and partners—where our tactics will catch up with us quickly. A bad reputation, loss of credibility, and an unwillingness for others to deal with us are far more serious than anything we can gain by taking short-term advantage of our opponent.

Deals in a Lifetime

This chapter will give you an opportunity to reflect on and use the many points about negotiation that we have tried to raise in this book. We have selected eight of the most common negotiation situations that people find themselves in during their adult lives, and show you how you can use the principles of negotiation that we have outlined in the previous chapters. While you will probably encounter many other negotiation situations, we are confident that they will have much in common with the ones that we address here.

We have ordered the eight common negotiating situations in the sequence one might encounter them in one's life: from buying one's first car (usually a used one) to making other major purchases (new car and house), getting married (a major multiparty negotiation), getting a job, negotiating for a salary increase in a job, and having the house repaired.

We hope that our advice is helpful to you, and that it allows you to achieve your objectives while still maintaining a strong, positive relationship with those you love, live with, and have to work with on a regular basis.

DEAL 1: BUYING A USED CAR

One of the first big deals in a lifetime is buying your first car. Some people get to relive this joy when helping a child or relative buy their first used car. Here's a checklist of things you should remember when you go out to buy that car:

1. Figure out your *requirements* for the car. How are you going to use it? Getting back and forth to work or school? Transporting just you, or several other people as well? Putting on lots of miles or just a few? Maybe hauling tools or equipment? Thinking this out should let you define:

   - The appropriate mileage level
   - The size (compact, midsize, or pickup truck)
   - Sporty models versus more conventional sedans
   - Other distinctive features required (e.g., four-wheel drive, trunk size, luggage rack)

   These are your *interests*.

   Define these interests clearly and don't waiver from them. When you get out looking at cars, it is very easy to get distracted by models and types that don't meet these interests. Define what you want and don't change from it unless you have a really good reason to do so.

2. Figure out how much you can afford to spend. If cash, can you pay it all now, or do you need to pay it in several payments? If you are thinking of borrowing money for a car loan, visit a bank *before you start looking for a car* and specifically find out how much they will lend you and what the monthly payments will be. Have them help you think about what your budget should be and how much you can afford. These become your financial *targets* and *limits* (*walkaways*).

3. Locate several cars that meet your specifications. Places to look for cars include:

   - Your local newspaper, either in the classified ads for used cars or in the used car ads placed by dealerships
   - "Auto trader" or other newspapers specializing in buying and selling used cars
   - Car lots (new and used)
   - Word of mouth, friends, bulletin boards at work, school, and so on
   - "Drive-bys"—cars sitting in yards or empty lots that individuals are trying to sell

   Car dealers make their money by buying cars at a low price and reselling them at a higher price. So when you deal with a dealer, you are paying more for the car than the dealer did. Sometimes this is good because dealers may *warranty* a car for 90 days against defects, mechanical work, and so on. Private sales from individuals may be cheaper to you, but you probably can't get any guarantee and don't have anyone to complain to when you discover problems (see the Tactic #19 box on inspection, following).

Objective: Find several cars that meet your interests. Your job now is to find out how to get the best deal on that make, model and year of car. For example, if you find a 1994 Ford Escort that you like, start looking for other 1994 Ford Escorts so you can really compare mileage, wear and tear, quality of other features like the radio, tires, cleanliness, and so on.

4. Research the *book value* of the car. There are many books on the market that tell you what any car of a specific make, model and year should be selling for. These books often list the *average* book value, what a car in *very good* condition might be worth, or what a car in *poor* condition might be worth. All banks have these books, and all good bookstores have them as well.

Many of these organizations now have Internet sites as well. We particularly like www.edmunds.com.

5. Contact current owners. Go to the used car lots or set aside a Saturday morning and call some of the newspaper ads.

- Find out the initial price

- Look over the car. Take a friend with you who is not emotionally invested in the car to help you spot defects, damage, wear and tear, and so on.

- Ask about the car's history. Particularly if it is being sold by a private owner, ask how long they have had it, whether they kept the service records, how and where it was driven, and so on.

- Test drive it. Get a feel for how it starts, runs, and so on.

Tactic #19: Independent Inspection

While you can get an outside opinion on almost any deal, it is particularly useful when technical issues make it hard to assess the situation—as when buying a car. Many cities have gas stations or garages that will perform an independent mechanical inspection of the car without pressuring you into buying their repair work (e.g., new tires, brakes, etc.). If you have doubts about mechanical condition, paying $50 to have the car fully inspected is well worth the time and the satisfaction. And it gives you that vital information edge that often makes the difference between a winning and losing negotiation game.

6. Begin the negotiation. Assuming you have decided to try to buy this car, here's where all your planning and preparation come into play:

- Make sure you have set your target price (based on what you can afford and what the industry standard says for the value of the car).

- Also know your walkaway point (the most you will pay) and a BATNA (what a similar car might be available for in the neighborhood, etc.).

- Ask them to set the price. Even if you are in a dealership and there is a big price sticker in the window, ask whether that is the best price they can give you today.

- How you negotiate depends on who you are dealing with. If this is a private sale from a stranger, or a dealership, you are most likely in a *Competitive* negotiation. On the other hand, if you are buying the car from a friend or relative, you will not want to bargain hard and make them angry. You might pay a little more but you must also worry about preserving your relationship with them. Chances are, *they* are going to be as worried about this as you are.

7. Counteroffer:

- You might want to start the bidding by making them an offer. If you do, offer them about 85 percent of what they are asking, or a price that is 5 percent below the blue book value of the car. Some people suggest you should counteroffer even less, just to find out how serious they were about their first offer.

- Be ready to justify your counteroffer with a list of arguments about why the car is not worth what they want for it—or at least not worth it to you. This might include:

    High mileage

    Wear and tear on paint, nicks and dents, upholstery, smells, and so on

    The cost of immediate work you have to do to get the car in good condition (even if you never intend to actually spend that money)

8. Bargain hard until you get to your target:

- Be prepared to spend a lot of time. The longer you stay at it, the more likely they may be to make big concessions, just to get it over with

- If it is a private sale, ask how quickly they have to sell. The longer they have had it or the more quickly they need the cash, the more willing they may be to come down quickly.

Take the Haggling Out of Used Car Buying

New used car *superstores* are opening across the country that take the haggle and the uncertainty out of used car buying. Companies like AutoNation and CarMax are selling reconditioned rental and leased cars at "fixed, no-haggle prices" (usually about $500 over book value).

These stores offer a great BATNA for those who want less stress and hassle and are willing to pay more for it. You won't get an outstanding deal, but you will get a good, clean reconditioned car at a reasonable price.

If you want to haggle, visit the superstore to determine their price and then see if a private sale will beat it. However, make sure the two cars are of the same quality and condition.[1]

- Make very small concessions. Try to get them to give more and give more often.

- Be prepared to walk away if their counteroffers do not make significant movement toward your target.

In many communities, a mechanic will provide an independent examination of a used car for you, tell you what shape it is in, whether it has been in an accident, and so on. You might pay $50 for the evaluation, but you will know much better what you are getting into.

DANGER! Watch out for emotional decision making. Don't fall in love with the car or the seller unless you are willing to pay several hundred dollars more for that love affair. The more you fall in love with this car, this seller, or having to "drive it today," the more likely you are to pay too much. Love affairs are never cost-free!

DEAL 2: BUYING A NEW CAR

Many of the principles for buying a new car are the same as those for buying a used car (see the previous section). You are encouraged to read that section over before proceeding here. We will repeat some of these major points for your benefit:

1. Figure out your *requirements* for the car you want to buy. How are you going to use it? Getting back and forth to work or school? Transporting just you, or several other people as well? Putting on lots of miles or just a few? Maybe hauling tools or equipment? Thinking this out should let you define:

   - Size (compact, midsize, or pickup truck)
   - Sporty models versus more conventional sedans

- Other distinctive features (e.g., four-wheel drive, trunk size, luggage rack)

These are your *interests*.

Define these interests clearly and don't waiver from them. When you get out looking at cars, it is very easy to get distracted by models and types that don't meet these interests. Define what you want and don't change from it unless you have a really good reason to do so.

Make sure you also specify *all* of the options and features you want on the car (e.g., quality of radio, special brakes, sun roof, leather interior, etc.). When you begin to get prices, you will want to find a car loaded with all the features you want, and then compare prices on that *identical* car.

2. Figure out how much you can afford to spend. If cash, can you pay it all now or do you need to pay it in several payments? If you are thinking of borrowing money for a car loan, visit a bank *before you start looking for a car* and specifically find out how much they will lend you and what the monthly payments will be. Have them help you think about what your budget should be and how much you can afford. These become your financial *targets* and *limits* (*walkaways*).

Know your target payment (total dollars or monthly payment) and your walkaway (most you will pay) *before* you begin any discussions with car dealers. Walkaways can also be determined by understanding the dealer's costs (see following).

It is also helpful to know your BATNA. What will you do if you do not buy a new car at all (for example, can you drive your existing car for another year)?

3. Do research on new cars. Places to look for information include:

- Books and magazines that describe all the new makes and models
- Consumer guides that rate new cars on appearance, safety, performance, reliability, and so on
- Websites for the car manufacturers or for consumer guides (again, we like www.edmunds.com)
- Annual auto shows (in large cities)
- Car dealerships

We do *not* recommend visiting car dealerships until you have decided on a few specific makes and models, unless you have a lot of time to kill. Otherwise, you will have high-pressure salespeople trying to talk you into something you may not need or want.

If you do, insist that you are just looking, and take home their literature on the cars you are evaluating.

4. Determine if the timing is right, and how much time you have. While dealers sell all year, many have end-of-year specials in late summer when the models change. However, the more that they discount the selling price automatically to get rid of the car, the less negotiating room you may have.

Take time to shop. Don't be pressured by a dealer to make a quick decision.

5. Locate several car dealerships that meet your specifications. Places to look for cars include:

- Yellow pages for car dealerships
- Your local newspaper, either in the classified ads or in car ads placed by dealerships
- Car lots

Find several cars that meet your interests. Your job now is to find out how to get the best deal on that specific make, model, and collection of options.

6. If you are trading in an old car:

- Check the *blue book* value of that car—that is, what that particular make and model, in good or average condition, is now worth (see the preceding section).
- Decide whether you want to trade in or sell the car separately.
- Selling separately is more of hassle but you may get a few more dollars by doing it.

Always negotiate for the price of the new car *separately* from the value given on the trade-in. Many dealers will try to confuse you by giving some discount on the car combined with an offer on your car, and will not clearly break it out separately.

7. Go back to your information sources (books, articles, or websites). Check out the dealer cost on your specific targeted cars (including all of the options and add-ons). This is what the dealer pays the manufacturer for the car (sometimes even this number is discounted because dealers get rebates on volume discounts or promotions from the manufacturers).

Hint: You probably should set your *opening bid* at dealer cost (or below, if there is reason to do so). The dealer will not be happy, but it is a fair opening. Try to set your *walkaway* at about $500 above dealer cost.

8. Consult at least *two* dealers and ask them to give you a price on the outfitted car. Use one price as the BATNA and ask another dealer to beat it. Seesaw

them back and forth until they both have stopped at the same number (see Tactic #20, page 228).

Take your time! Don't make a deal until the third or fourth visit. Get the salesperson to invest a lot of time in you—they will be more willing to try to help you get a good price. Make concessions *slowly*.

Decide whether you want to take a spouse or friend with you. If you and your friend don't agree, or one is more impatient than the other, you may expose weakness that the dealer will exploit. In general, it is best to let the most experienced bargainer negotiate alone. Don't let yourself be distracted by others who need to leave early, go somewhere else, or are getting bored and pressuring *you* to give in quickly.

9. Ask lots of questions. Find out how they determine price, dealer markup, cost of extras, and so on. In some dealerships, the money issues are handled by a person separate from the car sales staff. You may want to talk to this person about financing packages, warranties, and so on.

10. Nibble at the end for *extras,* such as undercoating, special molding or trip packages, running boards, and so on.

Watch out for *their* attempts at nibbling by adding lots of charges, costs and options (paint sealer, undercoating, etc.) at the end. Get *all* of this included in the price. If it is not clear whether something is included, *ask lots of questions.*

We have found that when we negotiate great deals on cars, the dealer often tries to change the price, value of the trade-in, and so on, on the day we show up to take delivery. Don't hesitate to *walk out* of the negotiation if you sense they are trying to change the price or the deal. Any reasonably sized city has *several* dealerships that sell the same car.

DEAL 3: PLANNING A WEDDING

Planning a wedding is one of the most stressful and complex negotiations most of us ever do. There are several reasons for this:

● It is a very emotional time. Everyone wants everything to go "just perfectly" (but they all have different ideas of what *perfectly* means). People's choices and preferences are often based on very sentimental reasons and logic. Hence, it is hard to negotiate with those who feel most strongly about the way things should go.

● There are many people who have to be pleased. While the event is for the bride and groom, both sets of parents and relatives also have high expectations—and are also paying the bill.

 Planning a wedding successfully is often a task worthy of Nelson Mandela, Jimmy Carter, or some other international peacekeeper. It requires great diplomatic skill and coordination to assure that everyone gets what they want and are still talking to each other after the marriage is consummated.

1. Issues: What kinds of things get negotiated in weddings? You probably should buy a bridal book or magazine that has a number of special checklists for all of the planning events.

   Phase 1 (early planning):

   - Date and time of wedding
   - Location (near parents or near where marital couple are now?)
   - Number of guests (is this a *big, moderate* or *little* wedding?)
   - Location (wedding and reception)
   - Religion (what kind of prewedding coordination and indoctrination is required?)
   - Responsibilities of ushers, bridesmaids, best man, and so on
   - Finances—(in general, how much is available to pay for everything?)

   Phase 2 (within 60 to 90 days of the actual event):

   - Guest list (who is invited?)
   - Honeymoon location and arrangements
   - Bridal party (how many and who on each side?)
   - Rehearsal dinner and reception (alcohol, meal served, band or other music, seating, etc.)
   - Picking out gifts (china pattern, silver pattern, etc., and registration)

   Phase 3 (within 30 days):

   - Menu (dinner versus cocktails)
   - Band versus disk jockey
   - Groom's attire
   - Wedding rings

2. Planning and early discussion:

   - Meet with the spouse and with each set of parents to determine their primary interests.
   - Figure out what is most important for them in the wedding planning (e.g., location, church, reception, food, guest list).

CONCEPT Let the other spouse decide on those issues that are key to him or her—divide up the most important issues for each side.

- Pick your battles.
- Let each side decide those issues that are most important to them, and *drop* all further discussion of them.
- Delegate decisions to other people. Let the bridesmaids coordinate and agree on their dress colors.

CONCEPT Decide whether it is *your* day (i.e., you and your spouse-to-be make the decisions) or your *parents'* day (they get to make the big decisions—if they are paying the bill, it should be their day).

3. Let parents make decisions that are unimportant to either spouse, and vice versa.

Everyone should feel that they have had real input into planning. Involve them and invite people to take responsibility for making certain things happen. Share the responsibility and the decision-making power.

4. Do not hesitate to negotiate with the major service providers. Particularly if it is a large wedding, here are some of the key negotiables:

- Wedding ring: Look at several different rings based on amount of gold, size of stone, and so on. Visit several shops. Make a counteroffer.
- Brides' and bridesmaid's dresses: Since you are buying several dresses, see if you can get a bulk price, or make sure all alterations are included in the price.
- Rental of tuxedos, limousines, other equipment.
- Price for flower arrangements (table decorations, bouquets, etc.).
- Reception: Negotiables include the prices of dinners and drinks, special arrangements for dancing and music, table decorations, and so on. Once again, if you can specify what you want, get several bids on the entire package.

Tactic #20: Seesawing Candidates

Whenever you negotiate a deal in which you have a choice of vendors, partners, or other sorts of players, try to find a way to play them off against each other in order to find out who will give you the absolutely best deal.

(Continued)

> **(Continued)**
>
> The bidding process for caterers, florists, bands, and locations when planning a wedding is a particularly good opportunity to seesaw the parties back and forth. Get a good offer from one, go back to the other and ask them to beat the offer, go back to the first and ask them to beat the second, and so on. They shouldn't take offense—after all, these are their competitors, and you have every right to shop around.

DEAL 4: NEGOTIATING A NEW JOB WITH A LARGE COMPANY

After buying a car, the next major life negotiation is to get hired by a company and negotiate your new salary. Many people do not even try to negotiate starting salary (they are just happy to have a job offer), and others assume that starting salary packages *cannot* be negotiated. This is definitely not true. Negotiables in this process may include:

- Salary
- Starting date
- Vacation time (and length)
- Incentive or signing bonus
- Moving/relocation expenses
- Work schedule and job duties
- Location where you get assigned

We have found that negotiating with the bigger companies is somewhat different than trying to negotiate with a small business. So we will cover them separately. This section focuses on getting hired by a large company.

 Unlike buying a car, which suggests a very short-term focus and limited discussion with the car dealer, negotiating a salary and job has long-term consequences for you and the relationship with the company. Therefore, a *Collaborative* strategy is most desirable.

1. Do your homework on the company and the job you want. There is much that we could say here, but space limits the discussion. We are assuming that you know what kind of job and position you want, and that you have interviewed several companies and received a formal offer for one or more or those jobs.

 If at all possible, generate more than one offer from more than one company. The power of a good BATNA is again obvious. It will be much harder to negotiate with only one company than if you have a BATNA offer.

2. Determine your target, walkaway and opening:

- *Target.* What you think you should be paid. You may decide this on the basis of studying the pay and pay grades for certain jobs, gaining information from a career counselor, reading the want ads, and so on. Gather information that will help you determine what a person with your current skills, education, experience should be paid. Be fair and reasonable, but try to benchmark yourself against similar people in the job market at this time.

- *Walkaway.* What is the least you are willing to be paid for this job? You may decide this based on the same information gathered about the target, or your current needs and expenses, and so on.

- *Opening.* Set this number at least 10 percent above your target.

Although companies usually make an opening offer when they want to hire you, many ask in the interview "What are your salary requirements?" or "What are you expecting?" State your *opening* number, not your *target*.

3. Convey to your employer the need to weigh other options. Indicate that until the discussions are completed, you may continue to pursue other job interviews and options.

4. Question their opening offer!

- Ask if the offer is consistent with recent market offers

- Ask if the offer is consistent with offers given to others who have the same portfolio of skills, background, experience, and so on.

- Ask (nicely) "How did you get that number?" (their opening offer). Try to discover the thinking and logic they used to put together that offer.

"How did you get that number?" is always a great question for uncovering the logic, thinking, analysis, and information of the opponent. The more you understand their thinking and information, the more you will learn how to present counterinformation and logic to challenge their view and support your own.

Don't Be Ridiculous

Here's a true story that illustrates the danger of outrageous demands.

Reaching the end of a job interview, a recruiter asked the enthusiastic MBA, "And what starting salary were you looking for?"

The MBA candidate said, "In the neighborhood of $125,000 a year, depending on the benefits package."

The recruiter said, "Well, what would you say to a package of 5 weeks vacation, 14 paid holidays, full medical and dental, company matching retirement fund to 50 percent of salary, and a company car leased every 2 years—say, a red Corvette?"

The MBA sat up straight and said, "*Wow!* Are you kidding?"

And the recruiter said, "Certainly—but you started it."

5. Negotiate for base salary rate first. Try to get an agreement on the base salary, and then negotiate the rest of the package later.

Tip

Many large companies fix their starting salaries based on internal salary grading systems (tying specific salary levels and ranges to specific entry level jobs). Therefore, you may *not* be able to negotiate starting salary, but you can often negotiate the add-ons.

6. Think about what *add-ons* are desirable to you, and try to negotiate these separately. These might include:

- A signing bonus
- Moving costs
- Reimbursement for extra trips to visit the company or look for housing
- An automatic cost of living increase
- Location of assignment (where you go to work)
- Benefit packages, including various health care options (HMO, dental plans, etc) and payment into retirement plans and 401(k)s
- Assistance in paying college tuitions
- Insurance packages
- When you start the job
- A vacation (when you get it, how long it is)
- A bonus or profit-sharing plan based on excellent individual or company performance
- A company car, uniform allowance or other extras necessary to do the job
- Level of clerical or administrative help and assistance

7. Package and repackage until you get the deal you want. Combine and tradeoff these add-on elements to get the best deal you can.

Do not let this negotiation get competitive. Be honest, fair, and reasonable at all times, and treat the other party kindly. But do not allow yourself to be talked into a salary or job requirements that you will only come to dislike in a few weeks. It is unreasonable to go back to your boss and complain about the compensation package a month or two after starting. You'll need to make some significant contributions before you can justify a better deal.

DEAL 5: NEGOTIATING A NEW JOB WITH A SMALL COMPANY

There are several differences between negotiating with a big corporation or government organization and a small company:

- Small companies may have less of an idea of what you are *worth* in the market, and you may have to take greater initiative to educate them.

- Small companies may offer you less money but more opportunity to get good experience in a variety of jobs and situations.

- Small companies usually don't have fixed salary grades for starting positions, particularly entry-level management positions. So you have more freedom to actually negotiate salary as well as add-ons.

Again, plan to use a Collaborative approach. Your reputation and relationship with key company officials is the most important thing. Don't push hard for money if it will make them angry or make you look greedy.

1. Research the company and the job. Again, much could be said here. Ask lots of questions about the job, your duties and responsibilities, people you will work with, and so on.

   - Find out what the company's interests are—ask questions about why they are hiring, what they are looking for, and what potential they might see in you.

   - Meet lots of people. Get a sense of who they are, what they are like, how you feel about them, and whether you like to work with them. Learn how they see the company and its future.

2. Define your interests and goals:

   - Realize that your contribution is much more visible in a small firm than a large one.

- Decide why a small company might be better for you.
- Find out your market value.
- Find out the average starting salary for your region given the industry, your level of work experience, and so on.

3. Be ready to identify and discuss your strengths:
   - Education, including graduate degrees.
   - Previous job experience.
   - Things you have learned in past jobs.
   - Your interests and career plans.
   - Particular skills you could apply to this job to get up to speed fast.
   - Tell them how you would add value to the company immediately.
   - Bring examples of your previous work to show what you can do (reports, studies, projects, testimonials, and so on).

4. Have your walkaway, target and opening salary numbers clearly identified (see the preceding section on negotiating a job with a large company).

5. Create a BATNA if possible. Have more than one offer on the table if possible.

It is tempting to "invent" or make up a BATNA, even if you don't have one. Be careful about being dishonest (see Chapter 11). While some negotiators say it is okay to do this, be aware that the other party can always double check and then you will be caught telling a lie even before you are hired. Oops!

If you don't have a BATNA, work hard to determine industry norms and standards for the specific kind of job you are being offered.

6. Try to build a relationship with the person who will be determining your salary:
   - Find out *their* interests and needs. What are they looking for? Why do they want to hire someone like you? Be ready to talk about how your skills and qualifications match their interests.
   - Get to know them. He or she is likely to be your boss or a coworker. Find out if you can work together successfully.

7. Don't hesitate to negotiate *add-ons* (see the preceding section). You want to achieve the best *package,* not necessarily the best starting salary.

If they will not negotiate salary now or increase their offer, ask whether you can obtain an early performance review. In most companies, performance is reviewed once a year, and salaries are determined by the performance review. If you think you can make a quick and visible contribution, ask for a performance review after six or eight months.

 Have a target for all negotiable elements of the deal. Rank them in order of importance:

1. Salary

2. Stock options

3. Vacation

and so on.

Know where you can make trade-offs (e.g., is one less week of vacation equivalent to getting a full time secretary?).

8. Always have a walkaway point! Don't be pressured into accepting a job offer that you will dislike in a month and which will send you back into the job market, starting over.

DEAL 6: NEGOTIATING A RAISE

Suppose you have reached the point where you feel that you want to try to negotiate a raise, promotion, or change of responsibilities. You are not unhappy enough (yet) to leave the company, but you are certainly not feeling completely satisfied or highly well treated. So you decide to go to your boss and try to negotiate a pro-motion, a raise or a change of responsibilities. Here are the things you need to do to maintain control and focus in those negotiations.

 This is another negotiation that must be kept at a professional level. Work toward Collaboration or Compromise at all times. Be clear about what you would like, but do not press too hard or use any Competitive tactics. (Really! Trust us on this one! It's best not to burn your professional bridges!)

1. Do research:

   ● Learn what the industry norms might be for a person of your current duties, job level, past education and experience, and so on.

   ● Try to benchmark yourself against comparable salaries for your kind of work in your region, territory, type of industry, and so on. The Department of Labor has these statistics, as do most major metropolitan areas. Get your local reference librarian to help you.

2. Make a complete list of your accomplishments. Have it typed and organized into a clear outline with bullet points.

- Be clear about what you have *personally* accomplished.

- Be clear about what improvements or changes have occurred during your tenure.

- Quantify the value, worth, and cost savings of these contributions

- Focus on those things that were unique, hard to do, ways you overcame major obstacles, and so on.

3. Ask around the company about raises. Find out if others have successfully negotiated a raise, and, if so, how it was done.

- Talk to people who have negotiated with your boss

- Find out how salary budgets are structured, and how much discretion there is in them.

4. Know your walkaway and BATNA:

- Determine whether you will stay with the job or the company if you do not get what you want.

- If you have decided to move, begin your job search *now,* because if the salary discussion turns ugly, you may wish you had a choice to move quickly.

Know your BATNA. You may wish to interview with another company to determine:

- How interested they are in you
- What they would offer to pay you

Do not use your BATNA as a threat in your negotiations. No one likes to be threatened. You may want to make it clear that if you do not get a raise or promotion, you may have to look at the market, but do not threaten to walk if your demands are not met. You may find yourself on the street sooner than you wanted to be.

Think about where you want to conduct this negotiation. Some negotiators suggest that you get the boss to a table where you can maintain level eye contact and fairly close distance.[2] Do not negotiate while the boss sits in the high leather chair behind the big desk—this is the power seat where he or she makes most of the *no* decisions! Taking the boss to lunch might also be a good idea.

5. Make a clear strong request:

   - Quote your opening number.

   - Tell the boss how you decided on your opening number—that is, tie your request to research you have done on job grades and levels, profitability of the work you have done, and so on.

   - Justify it with the list of accomplishments you have prepared.

   - Be able to point to the value of those contributions as a reward for your hard work.

Keep your emotions in check. Do not get upset or afraid. If you are reading this, chances are you are not in a minimum-wage job. Do not talk about how you need a raise to pay your bills—your spending habits are *your* problem, not your company's.

6. Listen clearly to the boss' response:

   - Find out what his or her interests and concerns are.

   - Find out how he or she evaluates your performance and accomplishments.

7. If you are refused, ask questions in order to learn how you might qualify for a raise in the future.

If you can do no more, negotiate a plan for how you *can* qualify for a raise, or when it might happen, or how you can improve your work in order to get a raise.

8. Close the deal. Ask your boss if it would help to write a memo summarizing what you have agreed to. This will allow you to put it in writing, and will ensure that the facts are remembered if your boss is transferred tomorrow or too much time passes.

DEAL 7: BUYING A HOUSE THROUGH AN AGENT

Another major negotiation that we face in our lives is buying (and selling) one or more houses. Particularly if we are not familiar with an area or neighborhood, or don't have the time to do all the legwork on our own, most of us use professional real estate agents as intermediaries.

As noted in Chapter 2, negotiating through an agent is significantly different from doing the deal yourself. So the first thing we ask you to do is to review pages 36 to 39. Understand that you will be negotiating with someone who is doing the negotiating for you, but you can maintain an active role by giving instructions and directions, coaching, and calling the strategic shots.

1. Once again, everything starts with research. Find the neighborhood, type of housing, square footage of house and lot, location, and so on that meets your needs.

   - Talk with your spouse and decide on the most important elements for a house. These might include location of schools, availability of public transportation, configuration of house, size of lot, and so on. Rank order these and make sure you stick with them as you look at possible properties.

   - If you are very unfamiliar with the area, contact a brokerage agency that has contacts throughout the city·and ask to be given a general tour of neighborhoods, price ranges, quality of schools, and so on.

   - Find a broker or agent who you like and who understands what you are looking for. Don't hesitate to talk to several brokerages or agencies to find a person who is willing to work with you and understands your needs.

   - Decide whether you need your own agent. Agents usually represent only the seller. But you can hire a buyer's agent if you think that person has a unique set of skills, or you want someone loyal to you in the negotiations, or you will be out of the area and want someone local to handle it for you.

   - You want to try to negotiate the agent's commission. A commission is normally 6 percent for the seller, 3 percent for the buyer. If there are unique circumstances, try to negotiate the commission.

2. Get a general idea of the amount you can afford to pay monthly on a mortgage, and the amount of cash down. This is your general starting number. Also

know what you can afford to put down as cash toward the purchase, because the rest will be mortgaged. Both banks and brokerages will have books that translate loan amounts into monthly payments on 15- and 30-year notes.

3. Apply for a loan *now*. This will allow you to know whether you qualify for the requested loan amount *before* you find the house of your dreams, and will allow you to move much more quickly if and when you find the place. Ask your agent for banks and mortgage companies offering the best rates, or check the financial page in the local newspaper.

4. Set your walkaway price. This is usually the price for the house *plus* the estimated cost of remodeling to make the house livable or up to your standards.

   The challenge is now to find a house, once repaired and moved into, that will cost you no more per month than you have allocated.

 Make a list of all the things in a house that need to be done—cleaning, repainting, remodeling and repair, new appliances, and so on. Have the agent help you figure out approximate costs. This list will also be helpful to you in arguing why the current asking price should be discounted.

5. Find your BATNA. Figure out comparable houses and prices in the same general neighborhood. Your agent can identify all the properties in the neighborhood that sold in the past year, and the relevant details about those houses. Find another one on the market that you would like to own.

6. Visit the house and tour the property. Try to talk to the owners about the house:

   ● Why are they selling and how quickly do they have to sell?

   ● What are the great things they have loved about the house?

   ● Are there any problems or drawbacks that they know about?

 Try to identify the owner who is more willing to talk. One is usually more conversational than the other. Strike up a rapport. Ask about how long they have lived there, what they like about the house, the neighborhood, and so on.

7. Define the strong and weak features of the house. (e.g., love house, hate kitchen).

 Consult with others who might be able to give you an objective assessment of the house, property, and neighborhood:

- Come back without the agent and talk with the neighbors.
- Ask other agents about the property.
- Find out what the current owners paid for the house, and how long ago.
- If you have doubts about the structural nature of the house, insist that it be inspected by a building inspector, pest control specialist, and so on.

 How long has the house been on the market? How desperate are the sellers to sell? These are critical questions to determine the sellers' willingness to negotiate. If they are moving out next week regardless of whether the house is sold or not, and the house has been on the market for more than a few weeks, chances are you will have much more negotiating leverage.

8. The price will generally already be set. Be ready to make a counteroffer:

- Define whether the price covers any current repairs to the house (painting, yard repair, fixing leaks or breaks, etc.).
- Offer about 90 percent of the asking price if the repairs are included, less if you have to pay for them yourself. Be ready to justify your offer.
- Have your priority list present. Define what you *must* have, what you would *like,* and what is truly *optional,* relative to this house.
- Invent possible options for settlement (no remodeling, remodeling done, some work done, etc.).
- Get their commitment to tell you if someone else is looking at the house.
- Ask them whether they will take some of the mortgage themselves. Then you can pay them directly, perhaps at a lower interest rate than what the bank will charge.
- Don't take the first counteroffer! Make a concession of 1 to 2 percent of the asking price and reoffer. Try packaging and repackaging with throw-ins.

This is often a good place to try *throw-ins* (e.g., we'll pay that price but you have to include the current refrigerator, the deck furniture and the pool table in the basement).

If it is important to you, one great throw-in is the closing date (the date when you actually sign and exchange money and paperwork). If you are preapproved for a loan, you could close quickly if that would help you (and them), or postpone it if necessary.

If you are with your spouse, make sure only one of you does the talking. One spouse is usually more willing to compromise than the other; the "hard" one should do the talking, and you should only talk among yourselves *out of earshot* of the buyer *and* the agents.

DEAL 8: NEGOTIATING A HOME REPAIR CONTRACT

Now that you have bought that new house, it may be several weeks or several years before you will have to have it fixed. Whether this involves a simple paint job, a complex kitchen makeover, or doubling the entire square footage, you will need your negotiation skills as much as you did when you bought the place. Here are a few pointers to get you through.

1. Figure out what changes you want to make. It may be wallpapering, changing some cabinets, redoing a room, or more.

   You can get good ideas from home repair contractors and from decorators who work on a fee basis. House and home magazines also offer lots of ideas.

2. Get at least *two* estimates for anything. Pick the contractors you call on the basis of *personal referrals.* Look for trucks in your neighborhood working on local houses. Ask people in your church or club who they have used. If you recently bought the house, ask the real estate agent for recommendations. If you have to pick a company blind, based only on the phone book, ask each contractor to give you references of work they have done in the area. *Call and check the references.*

3. Most remodeling work is done by small contractors who are often not good businessmen. So you need to monitor and check them more closely than if they were big and established:

   ● Get them to create an itemized estimate for the work you desire.

- Find out when they intend to start and complete the work. Also find out how busy they are and how long it will take.

- Find out whether there will be one person on site to supervise the job, or whether there will be groups of workers there without supervision.

Many contractors do 90 percent of the work quickly and then take forever to finish the job. Meanwhile, you live with the dust and mess. That's why the following tips are helpful:

- Check out their promptness and craftsmanship when you do reference checks.

- Build in a cash incentive for them to start and finish on time.

4. Make sure each contractor submits a detailed written bid of the work to be done, and a time line for when each piece will be completed:

- Agree that no charges will be assessed unless you sign off on them.

- Agree that if either party changes the agreement (i.e., you make changes or they suggest different equipment), *change work order* paperwork will be completed.

- If you have two written estimates for the same work and they are quite different, find out why. There may be times when you care about high quality and craftsmanship, and there are other times when inexpensive plywood will do.

5. Meet and talk with the contractor and workmen regularly. Offering free coffee or donuts in the morning is cheap compared to the cooperation and care you will receive from them.

6. Never pay the contractor in full until you have inspected the job and determined that it meets all of your expectations.

END POINT

These may not be all the negotiations in your life—but they are the majority of them! There will be lots of "little negotiations"—with spouses, neighbors, coworkers, friends, children, and parents. As we have pointed out many times, day-to-day living is a series of ongoing negotiations. We hope this book has prepared you to tackle most of them. Good luck!

CHAPTER 1

1. Based on a briefing to the Polyurethane Manufacturers Association by Alex Hiam, March 1998.

2. Judith Martin, in an interview appearing in *Psychology Today* (March/April 1998), p. 27.

3. Scott Sindelar, "Temper, Temper," *Entrepreneur* (September 1994), p. 176.

4. J. Gordon, "Beating the Price Grinder at His Game," *Folio* (May 15, 1993), pp. 31–32.

5. G. F. Shea, "Learn How to Treasure Differences," *HR Magazine* (December 1992), pp. 34–37.

6. Burke Franklin, *Business Black Belt.* (Business Black Belt Press, 1997), p. 266.

7. R. Bramson, *Coping with Difficult People* (New York: Anchor Books, 1981); R. Bramson, *Coping with Difficult Bosses* (New York: Carol Publishing Group, 1992); J. Bernstein and S. Rosen, *Dinosaur Brains: Dealing with All Those Impossible People at Work* (New York: John Wiley & Sons, 1989); M. Solomon, *Working with Difficult People* (Englewood Cliffs, N.J.: Prentice Hall, 1990).

8. W. Ury, *Getting Past No: Negotiating with Difficult People* (New York: Bantam Books, 1991).

9. R. Bramson, *Coping with Difficult People* (New York: Anchor Books, 1981).

10. M. Freedman, "Dealing Effectively with Difficult People," *Nursing 93* (September 1993), pp. 97–102.

11. T. Gordon, *Leader Effectiveness Training* (New York: Wyden Books, 1977).

12. Shea, "Treasure Differences."

CHAPTER 2

1. For examples, see J. C. Freund, *Smart Negotiating* (New York: Simon & Schuster, 1992); S. Kozicki, *Creative Negotiating* (Holbrook, Mass.: Adams Media, 1998); A. Schoonmaker, *Negotiating to Win* (Englewood Cliffs, N.J.: Prentice Hall, 1989).

2. G. Nierenberg, *The Complete Negotiator* (New York: Nierenberg & Zeif, 1976).

3. C. R. Rogers, *Active Listening* (Chicago: University of Chicago Press, 1957).

4. H. Lancaster, "You Have to Negotiate for Everything in Life, So Get Good at It." *Wall Street Journal* (January 27, 1998), p. B1.

5. W. Zartman and M. Berman, *The Practical Negotiator* (New Haven, Conn.: Yale University Press, 1982).

6. R. J. Lewicki, J. Litterer, J. Minton, and D. Saunders, *Negotiation,* 2nd ed. (Burr Ridge, Ill.: Richard D. Irwin, 1994), p. 4.

7. Consult the Myers Briggs Type Indicator published by Consulting Psychologist's Press. Also see Paul D. Tieger and Barbara Barron-Tieger, *Do What You Are* (Boston: Little Brown, 1995).

8. M. C. Donaldson and M. Donaldson, *Negotiating for Dummies* (Foster City, Calif.: IDG Books, 1996).

9. H. Weisinger, *Emotional Intelligence at Work* (San Francisco: Jossey Bass, 1998), p. xvi.

10. D. Goleman, *Emotional Intelligence* (New York: Bantam Books, 1995); Weisinger, *Emotional Intelligence at Work*.

11. Lewicki, et al., *Negotiation,* 2nd ed., pp. 239–291.

12. If you are responsible for developing or training a negotiation team, there are numerous resources you can consult on this process. We suggest J. R. Katzenbach and D. K. Smith, *The Wisdom of Teams* (Boston: Harvard Business School Press, 1993) and A. Donnellon, *Team Talk* (Boston: Harvard Business School Press, 1996).

13. Barrey, Kausner, and Russ-Eft, *Highly Responsible Teams: The Key to Comnpetitive Advantage* (San Jose, Calif.: Zenger-Miller, 1993).

14. Lewicki, et al., *Negotiation,* 2nd ed., pp. 289–291.

15. G. Nadler and S. Hibinio, *Breakthrough Thinking* (Rocklin, Calif.: Prima Publishing & Communications, 1990).

16. J. W. Salacuse, "Your Draft or Mine?" *Negotiation Journal* 5(4):337–341.

CHAPTER 3

1. Brian Dumaine, "The Trouble with Teams," *Fortune* (September 5, 1994), p. 90.

2. Dumaine, "The Trouble with Teams."

3. R. Fisher and W. Ury, *Getting to Yes* (Boston: Houghton Mifflin, 1981); W. Ury, *Getting Past No* (New York: Bantam Books, 1991).

4. Shaquille O'Neal, *Shaq Attaq!* (New York: Hyperion, 1993), p. 29.

5. R. Fisher and W. Ury, *Getting to Yes;* R. Fisher, W. Ury, and B. Patton, *Getting to Yes: Negotiating Agreement without Giving In,* 2nd ed. (New York: Penguin Books, 1991).

6. D. Lax and J. Sebenius, *The Manager as Negotiator: Bargaining for Cooperation and Competitive Gain* (New York: Free Press, 1986).

7. Fisher, Ury, and Patton, *Getting to Yes,* 2nd ed., p. 40.

8. "Ten Guidelines for Effective Negotiating," in Lewicki, Litterer, Saunders and Minton, *Negotiation: Readings, Exercises and Cases,* 2nd ed. (Burr Ridge, Ill.: Richard D. Irwin, 1993), p. 26–27.

9. Kevin R. Murphy and Jeanette N. Cleveland, *Understanding Performance Appraisal: Social, Organizational, and Goal-Based Perspectives* (Thousand Oaks, Calif.: Sage Publications, 1995).

CHAPTER 4

1. Burke Franklin, *Business Black Belt* (Business Black Belt Press, 1997), p. 13.

2. L. Blessing, *A Walk in the Woods* (New York: New American Library, 1988).

3. Margaret Kaeter, "Buddy, Can You Spare a Million?" *Business Ethics* (May/June 1994), pp. 27, 28.

4. Daniel Goleman, *Emotional Intelligence: Why It Can Matter More Than IQ* (New York: Bantam, 1995), pp. 97, 104.

5. H. Calero and B. Oskam, *Negotiate the Deal You Want* (New York: Dodd, Mead, 1983).

6. *Time* (August 3, 1959), as quoted in "1948–1960," *TIME 75th Anniversary Issue.*

7. W. J. McGuire, "Inducing Resistance to Persuasion: Some Contemporary Approaches," in L. Berkowitz, ed., *Advances in Experimental Social Psychology,* vol. 1 (New York: Academic Press, 1964), pp. 191–229.

8. D. W. Johnson, "Role Reversal: A Summary and Review of the Research," *International Journal of Group Tensions* 1:318–334 (1971); C. Walcott, P. T. Hopmann, and T. D. King, "The Role of Debate in Negotiation," in D. Druckman, ed., *Negotiations: Social Psychological Perspectives* (Beverly Hills, Calif.: Sage, 1977), pp. 193–211.

CHAPTER 5

1. Bruce Pandolfini, *Weapons of Chess: An Omnibus of Chess Strategy* (New York: Simon & Schuster, 1989), p. 240.

2. R. J. Lewicki, "Negotiating Strategically," in A. Cohen, ed., *The Portable MBA in Management* (New York: John Wiley & Sons, 1992), pp. 147–189.

3. Bob Davis, "South Korea Played the Reluctant Patient to IMF's Rescue Team," *Wall Street Journal* (March 2, 1998), pp. A1, A12.

4. A. E. Roth, J. K. Murnighan, and F. Schoumaker, "The Deadline Effect in Bargaining: Some Experimental Evidence," *The American Economic Review* 78:806–823 (1988).

5. J. Kotter, *Power and Influence: Beyond Formal Authority* (New York: Free Press, 1985).

6. A. Teger, *Too Much Invested to Quit* (Beverly Hills, Calif.: Sage, 1980).

7. K. Short, "Watch Where They Sit in Your Class," in P. Jones, ed., *Adult Learning in Your Classroom* (Minneapolis, Minn.: Training Books, 1982), pp. 19–20.

8. Bruce Fortado, "Subordinate Views in Supervisory Conflict Situations: Peering into the Subcultural Chasm," *Human Relations* 45(11):1141–1167 (1992).

9. L. Greenhalgh, D. I. Chapman, and S. Neslin, "The Effect of Working Relationships on the Process and Outcomes of Negotiations," paper presented to the Academy of Management, 1992; M. Tuchinsky, J. Escalas, M. C. Moore, and B. H. Sheppard, "Beyond Name, Rank and Function: Construal of Relationships in Business," paper presented to the Academy of Management, 1993.

10. R. J. Lewicki and B. B. Bunker, "Trust in Relationships: A Model of Trust Development and Decline," in J. Z. Rubin and B. B. Bunker, eds., *Conflict, Cooperation and Justice* (San Francisco: Jossey-Bass, 1995).

11. M. Neale and M. Bazerman, "The Role of Perspective-Taking Ability in Negotiating under Different Forms of Arbitration," *Industrial and Labor Relations Review* 35:378–388 (1983).

12. K. W. Thomas, "Conflict and Conflict Management," in M. D. Dunnette, ed., *Handbook of Industrial*

& Organizational Psychology (Chicago: Rand McNally, 1976), pp. 889–935.

13. M. G. Hermann and N. Kogan, "Effects of Negotiators' Personalities on Negotiating Behavior," in D. Druckman, ed., *Negotiations: Social-Psychological Perspectives* (Beverly Hills, Calif.: Sage, 1977), pp. 247–274.

14. See J. Z. Rubin and B. B. Brown, *The Social Psychology of Bargaining and Negotiation* (New York: Academic Press, 1975); R. J. Lewicki, J. Litterer, J. Minton, and D. Saunders, *Negotiation,* 2nd ed. (Burr Ridge, Ill.: Richard D. Irwin, 1994).

15. Pandolfini, *Weapons of Chess,* p. 42.

16. D. Kolb and G. G. Coolidge, "Her Place at the Table: A Consideration of Gender Issues in Negotiation," in J. Z. Rubin and J. W. Breslin, eds., *Negotiation Theory and Practice* (Cambridge, Mass.: Harvard Program on Negotiation, 1991), pp. 261–277.

17. I. Ayres, "Fair Driving: Gender and Race Discrimination in Retail Car Negotiations," *Harvard Law Review* 104:817–872.

18. B. Gerhart and S. Rynes, "Determinants and Consequences of Salary Negotiations by Male and Female MBA Graduates," *Journal of Applied Psychology* 76:256–262 (1991); G. F. Dreher, T. W. Dougherty, and W. Whitely, "Influence Tactics and Salary Attainment: A Gender Specific Analysis," *Sex Roles* 20:535–550 (1989).

CHAPTER 6

1. G. T. Savage, J. D. Blair, and R. L. Sorenson, "Consider Both Relationships and Substance When Negotiating Strategically," *Academy of Management Executives* 3(1):37–48 (1989).

2. Robert L. Bodine, "How to Find and Keep Good Contract Workers," *Training & Development* (February 1998), pp. 55–57; telephone call to Robert Bodine at Synesis (February 18, 1998).

3. K. Thomas and R. Killman, *The Conflict Mode Inventory* (Tuxedo Park, N.Y.: XICOM, 1974).

CHAPTER 7

1. R. Fisher and W. Ury, *Getting to Yes* (Boston: Houghton Mifflin, 1981); R. Fisher, W. Ury, and B. Patton, *Getting to Yes: Negotiating Agreement without Giving In,* 2nd ed. (New York: Penguin Books, 1991).

2. L. Putnam and T. S. Jones, "Reciprocity in Negotiations: An Analysis of Bargaining Interaction," *Commu-*

nication Monographs 49:171–191 (1982); G. Yukl, "Effects of the Opponent's Initial Offer, Concession Magnitude, and Concession Frequency on Bargaining Behavior," *Journal of Personality and Social Psychology* 30:323–335 (1974).

3. Kathy Aaronson, "Winning at the Sport of Negotiation," in *Selling on the Fast Track* (New York: Putnam).

4. Fisher, Ury, and Patton, *Getting to Yes,* 2nd ed.; W. Ury, *Getting Past No: Negotiating with Difficult People* (New York: Bantam Books, 1991).

CHAPTER 8

1. R. E. Walton and R. B. McKersie, *A Behavioral Theory of Labor Negotiations: An Analysis of a Social Interaction System* (New York: McGraw-Hill, 1965); A. C. Filley, *Interpersonal Conflict Resolution* (Glenview, Ill.: Scott, Foresman, 1975); R. Fisher, W. Ury, and B. Patton, *Getting to Yes: Negotiating Agreement without Giving In,* 2nd ed. (New York: Penguin Books, 1991); D. G. Pruitt, *Negotiation Behavior* (New York: Academic Press, 1981); D. G. Pruitt, "Strategic Choice in Negotiation," *American Behavioral Scientist* 27:167–194 (1983); P. J. D. Carnevale and D. G. Pruitt, "Negotiation and Mediation," *Annual Review of Psychology,* M. Rosenberg and L. Porter, eds., 43:531–582 (Palo Alto, Calif.: Annual Reviews, 1992); D. G. Pruitt and P. J. D. Carnevale, *Negotiation in Social Conflict* (Pacific Grove, Calif.: Brooks-Cole, 1993).

2. Fisher and Ury, *Getting to Yes.*

3. Filley, *Interpersonal Conflict Resolution;* G. F. Shea, *Creative Negotiating* (Boston: CBI Publishing, 1983).

4. A. Williams, "Managing Employee Conflict," *Hotels* (July 1992), p. 23.

5. Fisher and Ury, *Getting to Yes;* Fisher, Ury, and Patton, *Getting to Yes,* 2nd ed.

6. M. Freedman, "Dealing Effectively with Difficult People," *Nursing 93* (September 1993), pp. 97–102.

7. T. Gosselin, "Negotiating with Your Boss," *Training and Development* (May 1993), pp. 37–41.

8. D. G. Pruitt, "Achieving Integrative Agreements," in M. Bazerman and R. Lewicki, eds., *Negotiating in Organizations* (Beverly Hills, Calif.: Sage, 1983); R. J. Lewicki, J. Litterer, J. Minton, and D. A. Saunders, *Negotiation,* 2nd ed. (Burr Ridge, Ill.: Richard D. Irwin, 1994).

9. M. B. Grover, "Letting Both Sides Win," *Forbes* (September 30, 1991), p. 178.

10. G. F. Shea, "Learn How to Treasure Differences," *HR Magazine* (December 1992), pp. 34–37.

11. D. G. Pruitt, "Strategic Choice in Negotiation, pp. 167–194; Fisher, Ury, and Patton, *Getting to Yes,* 2nd ed.

12. Fisher and Ury, *Getting to Yes.*

13. Filley, *Interpersonal Conflict Resolution;* D. G. Pruitt and P. J. D. Carnevale, *Negotiation in Social Conflict* (Pacific Grove, Calif.: Brooks-Cole, 1993); Shea, *Creative Negotiating;* R. Walton and R. McKersie, *A Behavioral Theory of Labor Negotiations* (New York: McGraw–Hill, 1965).

14. Shea, "Learn How to Treasure Differences."

15. Fisher and Ury, *Getting to Yes.*

16. B. H. Sheppard, R. J. Lewicki, and J. Minton, *Organizational Justice* (New York: Free Press, 1992).

17. R. H. Mouritsen, "Client Involvement through Negotiation: A Key to Success," *The American Salesman* (August 1993), pp. 24–27.

18. Pruitt, "Strategic Choice in Negotiation"; D. G. Pruitt, *Negotiation Behavior* (New York: Academic Press, 1981); Filley, *Interpersonal Conflict Resolution.*

19. Fisher, Ury, and Patton, *Getting to Yes,* 2nd ed.

20. Freedman, "Dealing Effectively with Difficult People."

21. C. M. Crumbaugh and G. W. Evans, "Presentation Format, Other Persons' Strategies and Cooperative Behavior in the Prisoner's Dilemma," *Psychological Reports* 20:895–902 (1967); R. L. Michelini, "Effects of Prior Interaction, Contact, Strategy, and Expectation of Meeting on Gain Behavior and Sentiment," *Journal of Conflict Resolution* 15:97–103 (1971); S. Oksamp, "Effects of Programmed Initial Strategies in a Prisoner's Dilemma Game," *Psychometrics* 19:195–196 (1970); V. Sermat and R. P. Gregovich, "The Effect of Experimental Manipulation on Cooperative Behavior in a Checkers Game," *Psychometric Science* 4:435–436 (1966).

22. R. J. Lewicki and B. B. Bunker, "Trust in Relationships: A Model of Trust Development and Decline," in J. Z. Rubin and B. B. Bunker, eds., *Conflict, Cooperation and Justice* (San Francisco: Jossey-Bass, 1995).

23. R. H. Mouritsen, "Client Involvement through Negotiation: A Key to Success," *The American Salesman* (August 1993), pp. 24–27.

24. T. Gosselin, "Negotiating with Your Boss," *Training and Development* (May 1993), pp. 37–41; M. B. Grover, "Letting Both Sides Win," *Forbes* (September 30, 1991), p. 178.

25. Stephen Gates, "Alliance Management Guidelines," *Strategic Alliances: Guidelines for Successful Management.* New York: Conference Board, Report Number 1028, 1993.

CHAPTER 9

1. Material in this section comes from a number of sources, including J. Calano and J. Salzman, "Tough Deals, Tender Tactics," *Working Woman* (July 1988), pp. 74–97; D. G. Pruitt and J. Z. Rubin, *Social Conflict: Escalation, Stalemate and Settlement* (New York: Random House, 1986); F. Greenburger with T. Kiernan, *How to Ask for More and Get It* (Garden City, N.Y.: Doubleday, 1978); R. L. Kuhn, *Dealmaker* (New York: John Wiley & Sons, 1988).

2. Calano and Salzman, "Tough Deals, Tender Tactics," pp. 74–97.

3. Pruitt and Rubin, *Social Conflict.*

4. Greenburger, *How to Ask for More and Get It.*

5. Kuhn, *Dealmaker.*

6. Judith Martin, in an interview appearing in *Psychology Today* (March/April 1998), p. 27.

7. Most of the concepts in this section are fully presented in R. B. Cialdini, *Influence: Science and Practice,* 3rd ed. (New York: HarperCollins, 1993).

8. T. Gosselin, "Negotiating with Your Boss," *Training and Development* (May 1993), pp. 37–41.

9. S. M. Pollan and M. Levine, "Turning Down an Assignment," *Working Woman* (May 1994), p. 69.

CHAPTER 10

1. T. A. Warschaw, *Winning by Negotiation* (New York: McGraw-Hill, 1980).

2. Samuel B. Griffith, *Sun Tzu: The Art of War* (New York: Oxford University Press, 1963), p. 92.

3. Griffith, *Sun Tzu,* p. 80.

4. Beatrix Potter, *The Tale of Peter Rabbit* (New York: F. Warne & Co., undated), p. 46.

CHAPTER 11

1. R. Miller and G. Jentz, *Fundamentals of Business Law* (Minneapolis, Minn.: West, 1993), pp. 112, 163–164.

2. G. Richard Shell, "When Is It Legal to Lie in Negotiations?" *Sloan Management Review* (Spring 1991), pp. 93–101.

3. Miller and Jentz, *Fundamentals.*

4. J. R. Boatright, *Ethics and the Conduct of Business* (Englewood Cliffs, N.J.: Prentice Hall, 1993); T. Donaldson and P. Werhane, *Ethical Issues in Business: A Philosophical Approach,* 4th ed. (Englewood Cliffs, N.J.: Prentice Hall, 1993); J. Rachels, *The Elements of Moral Philosophy* (New York: McGraw-Hill, 1986).

5. R. J. Lewicki, "Lying and Deception: A Behavioral Model," in M. H. Bazerman and R. J. Lewicki, eds., *Negotiating in Organizations* (Beverly Hills, Calif.: Sage, 1983), pp. 68–90.

6. R. J. Lewicki and G. Spencer, "Ethical Relativism and Negotiating Tactics: Factors Affecting Their Perceived Ethicality," paper presented at the meeting of the Academy of Management, Miami, Fla., August 1991; R. J. Anton, "Drawing the Line: An Exploratory Test of Ethical Behavior in Negotiations," *The International Journal of Conflict Management* 1:265–280 (1990).

7. S. Bok, *Lying: Moral Choice in Public and Private Life* (New York: Pantheon, 1978).

8. We've modified and extended an approach first proposed by Fisher, Ury, and Patton in *Getting to Yes.*

CHAPTER 12

1. "Will he own the road? Wayne Huizenga changed the way we rent videos with Blockbuster. Now he wants to do the same for car buying," *US News & World Report* (October 20, 1997), pp. 45–57; "Haggling in Cyberspace Transforms Car Sales," *Wall Street Journal* (December 30, 1997), p. B1.

2. M. C. Donaldson and M. Donaldson, *Negotiating for Dummies* (Foster City, Calif.: IDG Books, 1996).

3. Walter Kiechel III, "Asking for a Raise," *Fortune* (January 9, 1984).